SUCCESSFUL SCRIPTWRITING

SUCCESSFUL
SCRIPTWRITING

Jurgen Wolff

A N D

Kerry Cox

Writer's
Digest
Books

Cincinnati, Ohio

92 91 90 89 88   5 4 3 2 1

Library of Congress Cataloging-in-Publication Data

Cox, Kerry, 1956-
  Successful scriptwriting.

  Bibliography: p.
  Includes index.
    1. Motion picture plays—Technique. 2. Television plays—
Technique. 3. Motion picture authorship. 4. Playwriting.
I. Wolff, Jurgen M. (Jurgen Michael), 1948-   . II. Title.
PN1996.C818   1988   808.2'3   88-10769
ISBN 0-89879-325-4

Design by Christine Aulicino

To the memory of Lester Cole:
screenwriter, teacher, and member of
the Hollywood Ten.

—J. W.

To Leah, Rachel, and the one on the way.

—K. C.

ACKNOWLEDGMENTS

We wish to thank all those who allowed their interviews to be used in this book; Scott Reneau, the former editor of *The Hollywood Scriptwriter* who conducted a number of the interviews and contributed to the format section of the chapter on writing features; Rose Berman of RSB Enterprises for her public relations services; Jim Heacock of Heacock Literary Agency for his support and professional efforts; and Kirk Sullivan for his administrative support.

CONTENTS

I. LEARNING THE CRAFT

II. APPLYING THE CRAFT

III. TURNING THE CRAFT INTO A BUSINESS

I

LEARNING THE CRAFT

CHAPTER 1

Introduction

WHAT IS THE APPEAL of writing scripts? Certainly there's money to be made, there's glamour in having your words spoken by famous actors, and there is at least a measure of fame associated with writing a successful screenplay. But there's more to it than that.

Writing a script gives you a wonderful opportunity to play God. In the case of a feature film, you start with 120 blank pages and, if you do your job well, when you are done a new world will exist. People will have come into existence who can make the reader (and ultimately the viewer) laugh, or cry, or think about things he or she has never thought about. What happens to these people is up to you. You can have them get married, send them to Jupiter, take a life to save a life, do foul deeds that make the flesh crawl or brave and noble ones that inspire. It's all up to you.

When you are writing the script, it's a private world you are creating. But if the script sells and the picture is made, your new world will be shared by millions—maybe hundreds of millions—of people around the world. What you have created will be admired or criticized by professional critics and by as many amateur critics as there are people who have gone to see your movie. If it's truly a special film, which will require that the actors and director and everyone else associated with the production do a brilliant job too, then the world you have created may take its place along with the spy-infested landscape of *Casablanca*, the dangerous territory where men looked for the *Treasure of the Sierra Madre*, and the distant time and land where the Empire battled rebellion in *Star Wars*. Most movies don't reach those lofty heights, of course, but we're allowed to dream. In fact, dreams are what movies are all about.

If you prefer to focus your efforts on television programs, you have equally worthwhile models to emulate. Who wouldn't be proud to come up with (or simply write well for) a character like Archie Bunker, or to write a television movie as brilliant and important as *An Early Frost*, or a miniseries as groundbreaking as "Roots," or a drama series that equals the realism and attraction of "Hill Street Blues"?

Even in the forms that some consider less prestigious there are worthy goals to strive for. Long before Movies-of-the-Week took on social issues, for example, soap operas were using their storylines to make their viewers aware of such things as the importance of breast examinations. Let's not forget, also, the value of sheer fun and entertainment provided by many types of programming; after all, sometimes a show that can just help us forget about our troubles for a half hour or an hour is worth its weight in gold.

Writing for film and television is a craft that at times transcends itself to become art. Art arises from genius and inspiration; you can't learn it. But you can learn the craft, and it's very unlikely that a real work of art will come from someone who hasn't first mastered the craft. Woody Allen is a good example. If you look at his early films, like *Bananas* or *Take the Money and Run*, you'll see a great deal of talent but a certain naivete about the craft. His wonderful sense of humor was already in place, but he was still learning what makes films tick. Script by script he learned more and more about the craft, until ultimately he was able to come up with rich (and some would say inspired) creations like *Annie Hall* and *Hannah and Her Sisters*.

The *craft* of scriptwriting is what this book is all about. Both of the authors have written and are currently writing for television and film, but we have no illusions that we are masters (although we have hopes that we'll get there someday). In the process of developing our craft, however, both of us have learned a great deal—mostly the hard way. We had no reference, no source of information that would detail the nuts and bolts of writing scripts, and give us the "How To's" that would make our efforts ring of professionalism and expertise rather than amateuristic inexperience. In fact, it was this dearth of information that led Jurgen Wolff, newly arrived in Hollywood and searching for a way to open some doors, to found *The Hollywood Scriptwriter*, a newsletter targeted solely at scriptwriters. As editor/publisher he now had credibility, which allowed him to approach and pick the brains of some of the finest and most successful professionals in the field. At about this time Kerry Cox, a fledgling writer of audiovisual scripts and magazine articles, came on board to help out, and together we churned out newsletters and, using the advice of the pros, eventually broke into the business. With this book, we now make the same invaluable advice and guidance available to you.

Now you too can benefit from writers of such films as *Ordinary People* and *Tootsie*, writers who have created television shows such as "M*A*S*H" and "L.A. Law," and who have made important contributions to soap operas, Movies-of-the-Week, variety shows, and animation. To that end, many of the chapters in this book begin with a basic explanation of the topic under consideration, and then go on to an interview with one or more of these experts. The interviewees in this book read like a *Who's Who* of TV and film writing. We haven't followed the usual path of asking them what they eat for breakfast, whether they write with a yellow pencil or a word processor, and what it was like to work with Dustin/Burt/Barbra/Lord Larry. Instead, we asked them nitty-gritty questions about how they structure their scripts, how they make their characters come alive, how they write dialogue that sparkles, how they collaborate, and a hundred other keys to making a script not just good, but great. And, to our delight and gratitude, they took the time to answer these questions thoughtfully and completely, and thereby shared the knowledge that has made them so successful.

This book has three sections. Chapters 1 through 6 make up Part I: a basic course in scriptwriting. In these chapters you'll learn the fundamental skills and essential ingredients of writing a script, working with the most basic form, the feature film. Here we'll cover such things as how to arrive at a good idea, how to create characters, how to structure a plot, how to write an outline and then go from that to a treatment and on to a script. When you have worked through Part I you will be able to tell a story effectively in script form, and this skill will stand you in good stead no matter what form of scriptwriting you decide to make your specialty.

Part II, Chapters 7 through 13, shows you how to apply your newfound skills to the many different types of TV and film scripts. Although the basics of telling a story in script form are much the same, formats vary widely between sitcoms, soap operas, and animated films, for example. When you've worked through Part II, you'll be able to apply your basic scriptwriting skills to just about any type of script.

The third and final part, Chapters 14 through 20, shows you how to handle the business of being a scriptwriter. This often overlooked subject includes detailed coverage of such topics as getting an agent, protecting your work, effectively managing your time, and "pitching" your script ideas. When you are finished, you will know how to be professional in your pursuit of a scriptwriting career.

This is not to say that this book is all you'll need to become a professional scriptwriter. Make no mistake—when you decide on TV or movie writing as a career, you are entering a fiercely competitive, highly selective field where only the very dedicated, talented, and persistent succeed. Nobody is waiting around for you to come along. Instead, you must apply the knowledge gleaned from this book to write the best, most professional script you can, and then go about marketing yourself in exactly the same manner. You must remember that the only people working as scriptwriters are the ones who didn't give up, who didn't take rejection personally but instead translated it into constructive criticism, and tried again. It *is* possible to break in, it's being done all the time. But nobody will do it for you, and simply reading this book isn't enough. It will, however, provide you with the insight and realistic, practical knowledge that will put you head and shoulders above those trying to break in cold.

Throughout this book we have tried to illustrate our points with real-life examples, and in doing this have necessarily made reference to television shows that may no longer be on the air at the time of this reading. Unfortunately, the worlds of TV and publishing move at a radically different pace, and in fact, TV changes so rapidly that very often even the weekly program guides in your local newspapers can't keep up! At each occasion where a program is used as an example, however, we've tried to rely on shows that were very familiar and long-lived. Many will be around in syndication for a long time to come, so you will still be able to refer to them if necessary. At any rate, the guidelines and strategies this book presents are and will remain current, and the procedures outlined will still apply in providing you the knowledge you'll need to break in.

We hope you will find this book to be the comprehensive guide to scriptwriting you've been looking for. We trust that you will enjoy reading it, but it won't have done its job unless it motivates you not only to read, but also to write. If you have a dream, let the information in this book give you the wherewithal to move that dream from your mind onto the page. With luck, it will get from there onto the small or large screen and, with even more luck and your unique talent, may take its place among the wonderful stories that people talk about when the subject turns to their favorite movies or TV shows.

CHAPTER 2

How to Check the Salability of Your Idea

THE TRUTH IS, NO ONE KNOWS exactly what will sell. If anyone did, he would produce nothing but hits. Some producers are more consistent in having hits than others, but nobody has an infallible touch. Even Steven Spielberg had his *1941* and Sylvester Stallone had his *Over the Top*. For one thing, public taste is fickle: one year it may love the redneck approach of *Rambo* and the next it may embrace the more realistic and painful *Platoon*; initially it may flock to teen exploitation pictures but then suddenly it will say "enough, already" and look for more substance.

The one thing most producers have in common, though, is that they *think* they know what will sell. In fact, that belief is absolutely necessary if they are to get on with the business of convincing the money people to back their projects. When they fail, they blame some fluke of the marketplace and get on with the next one, the one that will really be a big box office winner.

On the assumption that you are writing your scripts to sell, it will be helpful for you to know some of the criteria that producers and studios use in evaluating scripts or ideas presented to them. What they are looking for are elements of salability. Remember that the sales process hasn't ended when you sell your script; it has barely begun. Let's say a producer options your script (that is, he pays you a certain amount in exchange for which he receives the sole right to try to get the script financed during a specified period of time, perhaps six months or a year). During that six months he has to sell a studio or other financing entity on his belief that this script is worth the expenditure of millions of dollars. He also has to sell stars and a director on the idea that they should dedicate several months of their lives to working on this picture. If he succeeds and the picture is made, the studio then has to convince distributors that this picture is worth exhibiting. The studio and distributors have to sell the public the notion that the picture is worth seeing—more so than the other twenty or fifty that are playing that same night. This is why all along the line people are trying to evaluate the salability of this project.

Please don't misunderstand. We are not suggesting that commercial appeal be the only criterion you use when deciding what to write or present. Don't start off your career by copying the trend of the moment or turning out some piece of schlock that you personally wouldn't pay to see but that you guess might appeal to The Great Unwashed. But at the same time don't forget that if a story comes off as completely uncommercial you are going to have a very difficult time selling it. Ideally you will find a story that really means something to you *and* that has some market appeal.

Let's look at some of the elements that generally are considered to add to a project's salability.

• DOES IT HAVE A HOOK?

A "hook" is an aspect of a story that allows it to be quickly and interestingly summarized in a line or two. Such stories are also often referred to in the industry as being "high concept." *Back to the Future* had a strong hook: a young man travels back in time, where his mother falls in love with him. *Tootsie* had a strong hook: an unsuccessful actor suddenly becomes a huge success—when he's pretending to be a woman. There was a strong hook for *E.T.*, too: a young boy has to save a friendly alien from the humans who hunt him. In his time, Shakespeare had a great facility for coming up with stories with hooks: the two young lovers who have to overcome the objections of their feuding families; the Prince who suspects that his father was murdered by his mother and her lover and has to figure out how to confirm his suspicions and take revenge; the old King who divides his kingdom between his toadying daughters, and then finds that the only one who truly cares for him is the one he excluded. Clearly, having a strong hook and being of high quality are not mutually exclusive.

Why the stress on stories with a strong hook? Mostly because if you can get people interested in the film with one or two sentences you have the makings of a terrific ad campaign. In the movie ads that appear in newspapers there's only room for a picture and a line or two. Similarly a fifteen- or thirty-second TV ad only gives you time for a couple of clips and a few lines from the announcer. If you can use these ads to lure people into the theater they will in turn spread the word (for better or worse). Some people carefully read reviews and use them to make up their minds about what they'll see, but a far greater number simply leaf through the newspaper ads "to see what looks good."

However, there are also wonderful projects that have no real hook. *The Trip to Bountiful* is a good example. It's about an old woman who wants to go back once more before she dies to the small town where she grew up. What got this picture made was not the story hook, but Horton Foote's fine writing and Geraldine Page's agreement to star in it. Typically a nonhook picture makes up for it with star casting or particularly fine writing, but these projects are harder to get off the ground initially.

There are various types of hooks. One is the main character. The story may be about a historical character in whom people are interested, such as *Gandhi*. Or it may be a fictional character who is already well established in some other medium as was the case with the James Bond books. Or it may be a new fictional character who is fresh and appealing (like Crocodile Dundee). Naturally all movies ultimately are about characters, but if the character is to serve as a hook, there has to be something outstanding about him or her, something that can be summed up in a phrase: the world's top spy who has a license to kill, or a genial innocent from the outback of Australia who ends up in Manhattan, to give two examples.

Another hook is the situation that may dominate a story. Examples would be a man who decides to get vigilante revenge when his family is killed (*Death Wish*—one, two, three, and so on, ad infinitum and, some would say, ad nauseam), or people stuck in a sinking ship (*Poseidon Adventure*), or a CIA officer who has to figure out who killed everyone in his section before the killer finds him and kills him as well (*Three Days of the Condor*).

Another hook is a social issue such as wife battering (*The Burning Bed*), the rights of the father in a divorce case (*Kramer vs. Kramer*), or AIDS (*An Early Frost*). These types of stories are particularly popular as subjects of television films, and indeed two of the cited examples were Movies-of-the-Week. Even *Kramer vs. Kramer* might have ended up as a television film, had it not been for the powerhouse casting of Meryl Streep and Dustin Hoffman.

The final hook is having the story be based on real events. People seem particularly drawn to finding out the behind-the-scenes facts regarding events they've read about or followed in the news. Sometimes feature films result (*All the President's Men*) but more often these stories end up as miniseries or Movies-of-the-Week (*Poor Little Rich Girl* among countless others that are cited as being "based on a true story" or, if the writer has really strayed from the actual events, "inspired by a true story").

Many stories are a combination of the above elements. For example, *Beverly Hills Cop* had a strong central character, a hip young black detective, and a strong situation—namely, this same detective being let loose in snooty Beverly Hills. But often one element will predominate, and that becomes the story's central hook.

• IS THE STORY TOPICAL?

Again, it is not absolutely necessary that a story have this quality, but it helps. By topical we don't necessarily mean that it was ripped from yesterday's headlines (the time factor involved in making movies means that truly topical material usually ends up on the small screen rather than the large one). What we do mean is that the subject is timely in a general way. For example, when *Mr. Mom* came out, people were discussing the way that changing roles were affecting people's lifestyles, and househusbands had appeared on the "The Donahue Show" (it's a pretty safe bet that the issues that you see talked about on "Donahue" or "The Oprah Winfrey Show" are at that very minute the subjects of feature or television movie negotiations). Similarly, *The Money Pit* and *She's Having a Baby* dealt with Yuppie concerns. Currently one of us (Wolff) is working on a rewrite of a picture called *Home Again* which deals with the phenomenon of grown children returning home to live. Naturally what people are looking for in these types of pictures is entertainment, not documentaries about social issues, but if your story can be about something already on people's minds, so much the better.

• IS THE STORY FRESH?

Come on, you may be saying, every other film is a sequel or a remake or an out-and-out rip-off. Why tell people to come up with something fresh? Because you have to keep in mind your position in the industry as a newcomer. If they want a sequel, they'll go to the people who made the first version or, if they are not available or now cost too much, bring in experienced writers. If they want a remake, first they have to buy the rights to the original picture, then they bring in an experienced writer. And if they want to rip off some successful picture, again they'll go to someone who they know can do it quickly and competently. So these are all unpromising arenas for the newer writer—and you should be glad that's so. Presumably you are getting into this business because you have something interesting and fresh to say, as well as the desire to make large amounts of money.

Sometimes you find that your idea is similar to scripts that have been produced recently even though, perhaps, you had your idea long before these films came out. Does that mean you have to throw out your script or put it into a drawer until everybody's forgotten about the similar pictures? Not necessarily. It may be possible to give your material a twist that will make your story more appealing and less obviously similar. One such switch is changing the gender of the lead character. Part of the appeal of *Alien* and *Aliens* was that this was the first real space heroine we'd ever seen. Similarly, a wonderful and underrated picture called *Gloria* cast Gena Rowlands as a woman who takes on the mob to protect the life of a young child.

Another twist is to change the setting of the story. *Outland* basically was *High Noon* on a space station. How would it impact your story if the setting were rural instead of urban, or vice versa? What would happen if you set it in another country? Or a unique part of this country? For the latter, consider *Witness*—a pretty ordinary storyline that was made special by the fact that it took place in an Amish community.

You can also change the time period of your story. One of us (Wolff) recently sold a Movie-of-the-Week to CBS, a story that basically is a Western but is set in Los Angeles in 1919, when Bat Masterson and Wyatt Earp are old men. Sometimes a topical story is more palatable when set in another time. Such was the case when Arthur Miller wrote about the Salem witch trials in *The Crucible*, but was also making points about the McCarthy political witch-hunts of the 1950s.

Finally, you can play with the basic motivation of the protagonist. To go back to *Gloria* again, her motivation in taking on the mob was protecting the life of a small child, a situation that was especially delicious because she was a decidedly unmaternal woman. This made it much more interesting than if she'd simply been after money or revenge.

Naturally you can't change these elements at random. You must be sure that changing them will not damage the integrity of your story, but often that is possible and results in a more salable project.

• IS THE STORY ABOUT SOMETHING MEANINGFUL?

The best movies tend to have some sort of underlying message or moral or theme, even when they are basically escapist. *Tootsie*, for example, as well as being one of the funniest pictures of recent times, was about a man learning firsthand how people treat women, and coming to change because of that. *The Trip to Bountiful* was about having roots, and the need to acknowledge them. When a picture is about something meaningful, that gives it a foundation, something upon which the story is built. This theme or moral doesn't have to be obvious. In fact, it shouldn't be obvious, or the film may seem heavy-handed or propagandist. Maybe the majority of filmgoers will never stop to think about it, but it will be there and it will have served you, the writer, as a central if hidden aspect of your story.

• DO YOU HAVE A GOOD CONFLICT?

As we will discuss in some detail in the next chapter, most movies are about someone who wants something and someone or something trying to stop him from getting it. You should be able to identify easily what it is your main character wants. It could be to track down a killer, to go back home before she dies, to lead the Arabs against the Turks in World War I, to help an alien get back home, to steal the crown jewels, to win the woman of his dreams, or whatever.

Next you should be able to state who or what is opposing your main character in his quest. It could be the police, her daughter-in-law, the British military hierarchy and the Turks, scientists, Interpol, or the parents of the woman of his dreams.

The match between your protagonist and antagonist(s) has to be a pretty even one if the story is going to stay interesting. After all, the most exciting sports events are the ones that aren't decided until the final moments. If one team has a huge lead at halftime, we tend to lose interest. Of course in many pictures it's a foregone conclusion that the hero will win; it seems pretty unlikely that James Bond will ever be defeated by the forces of evil, for example. Nonetheless, the writers keep trying to come up with more and more villainous opponents for him, so that we can at least pretend for a while that this may just be the bad guy that does him in. Your protagonist can be an underdog. But if he is, he has to have certain skills or advantages that compensate for the other side's superior strength. This can go from the sublime to the ridiculous as, for example, in *Rambo*, where one man takes on an army and wins—but then Rambo was an American, and one who was not only mad as hell but also muscular, and the others were only skinny foreigners. In its own comic book terms, it worked.

The conflict has to be strong in order to sustain us through two hours of a movie. If it's just a little disagreement, one that could be worked out easily, then the movie is going to sag badly in the middle. You've got to find a conflict that doesn't lend itself to compromise.

• DOES YOUR STORY HAVE A CLEAR-CUT AND POSITIVE ENDING?

For a while in the sixties there was a vogue for films that left everything unresolved at the end. That is no longer the case. Moviegoers seem to feel that if they have paid five or six bucks, they want an ending as well as a beginning and a middle. Furthermore, they seem to want happy endings. And a lot of times what the audience wants—or the studio decides the audience wants—the audience gets. A case in point was *Pretty in Pink*, in which an appealing poor girl is jilted by a caddish rich kid and then finds that true love is available in the form of an appealing goof who's been her friend all along. At least that's the way it started out. Test screenings showed that the audience (heavily skewed toward teenage girls) preferred to see the girl end up with the rich guy, no matter what a cad he'd been. So the cast was recalled and the ending was reshot. Now, it could be argued that the original ending was actually the "happy" ending, but certainly the second version was more conventionally satisfying (and to make sure that the goofy friend also went away happy, the kind of beautiful girl who for the other 90 percent of the movie wouldn't have given him the time of day suddenly seems to develop an intense passion for him at the prom).

Writing in the January/February 1987 issue of *American Film*, Anna McDonnell states, "It is virtually impossible to get a studio to make a movie with an unhappy ending," and as examples of scripts or films that at some point underwent surgery to make their endings happier she cites *After Hours*, *Lucas*, *Crossroads*, and *Jumpin' Jack Flash*. She does backtrack a bit, though, saying: "However, it is not impossible to get movies with unhappy endings made in Hollywood—just incredibly hard." As the possible methods of bucking the trend, she gives the attachment of a major star or director or both, or basing the script on an important novel, or writing a script that is just so spectacularly good that people can't ignore it.

Again, there are some stories that simply will not work with a happy ending. If yours is one, and you believe in it, go ahead and write it. Just be aware that you'll have a more difficult time selling it.

• IS IT EASY TO CAST?

As the writer, you will have no involvement in the casting of your screenplay. However, it's something you should think about ahead of time because the people who are considering producing the picture will be giving it a lot of attention.

Does your script have one or two starring roles? That is, roles that clearly dominate the film? This is the norm, although there are also ensemble pictures, like *Diner* and *The Big Chill*, in which there is no clear star. Those are more difficult to get made unless they are ensemble comedies like *Police Academy*. If your project is inherently an ensemble piece, fine. If not, you may want to consider consolidating several of the minor characters into more major roles.

Secondly, can you think of a number of stars who correspond to the general description of your main characters? In comedies, for example, there's a class of likable ne'er-do-well who can easily be played (and has) by Tom Hanks, Chevy Chase, Dan Aykroyd, or Bill Murray. If they aren't available, there are a lot of second-string versions of them warming up in the wings, so that type of character will be easy to cast. Let's say, however, you write a part that can only be played by Linda Hunt, or some years ago could only have been played by Orson Welles, or some other particularly individualistic actor. If that one actor is not available or doesn't want to do your project, you're in trouble. Yes, there's an "out" to this, too, namely that the producers might be willing to cast an unknown actor (and you can find literally any size, shape, age, and look if you go through the membership of the Screen Actors Guild). But most producers like to be able to cast known performers in the lead. The warning is the same: if this type of casting is essential to a project close to your heart, proceed, but be aware of the hardships down the line.

• DOES THE STORY HAVE VISUAL VALUES?

Producers are interested in luring people away from the small screens at home, to the big screens in the movie theaters. The films that do that most effectively are often the ones that take advantage of the fact that the screen is large and the sound system is good. If your script lacks visual values, you may find that people say they like the story but it's "too small" for a movie, and suggest that you try getting it made as a Movie-of-the-Week. What gives a film interesting visual values? Well, certainly unusual or foreign locations, action sequences, and special effects all contribute. This is not to say that if you have a small story you have to wrack your brains for ways to add explosions and spectacular action sequences set in the Andes. But even if all you want to do in a scene is to have two characters talking, sometimes it helps a lot to get them out of the kitchen or the living room, to a location that adds something to the scene. For example, when the guy is about to dump the girl, maybe he takes her back to the lovers' lane that overlooks the city. (Cruel, isn't he?) Or when the word arrives that her husband has been kidnapped by terrorists, his wife is in the middle of a spectacular society party.

• HAVE YOU DONE A GOOD JOB OF CHARACTERIZATION?

We will dedicate a whole chapter to the elements of successful characterization, but for now let's look at the few key ones that producers seek out. First of all, they want to know whether you have created a character with whom the audience can identify. There's a difference between liking someone and identifying with him, and many protagonists are not necessarily people we'd like to have over for dinner. Going back to Shakespeare, the Macbeths were not exactly a fun couple, but we can see some elements of ourselves in them. While we presumably haven't killed for professional advancement the way Macbeth does, at least we can understand how tempting the grab for power can be, how poor judgment can take over in situations like that, how once you've made a major mistake it's impossible to go back and undo it so you go on making more and more mistakes. In more recent times, the characters in the *Godfather* movies have been a pretty unsavory bunch, but they have just enough humanity that we can identify with them on some level. More typically, the protagonist is someone we do like and perhaps someone we'd like to be. Most of us would enjoy going back in time, for example, and we'd probably be just as bewildered by the experience as the Michael J. Fox character was in *Back to the Future*. Similarly, whether or not we've actually been in combat we can vicariously experience the confusion and moral dilemmas encountered by the Charlie Sheen character in *Platoon*. The more your script allows the audience to live the movie rather than just watch it, the more successful it will be. You can probably remember some films that grabbed you and held you so well that you forgot that you were in a movie theater at all—that's what you're going for, and one way to achieve it is to create a central character with whom we can all identify.

On the other hand, much of the audience will probably be turned off if you have relied upon stereotypes based on race, occupation, nationality, sex, sexual preference, and so on. Keep in mind that if you have lazy Mexicans, limp-wristed gays, dull accountants, or blonde bimbos populating your script not only will you be insulting part of your audience but also you'll be falling back on unfair and discredited bigotry. Often these stereotypes are used in an attempt at humor; if you're talented, you can find comedy without resorting to them.

There's one element of salability we may not have touched upon yet. That is the special factor that makes you want to spend precious time writing the particular story you've chosen. If there is something about it that really turns you on, maybe that same factor will make others enthusiastic about it, whether or not it happens to be one of the aspects of salability we've mentioned. Think about why this is the story you want to tell—that may be its biggest sales point.

• SALABILITY CHECKLIST

When you are first considering an idea, you may want to take a few minutes to consider its salability, too. To make it easier for you to do that, here are the main questions in this chapter, in checklist form:

1. Does the idea have a strong hook? (See if you can state it in a sentence or two.)
2. Is the idea topical? (If so, how?)
3. Is the idea fresh?
4. If the idea is similar in major ways to pictures produced recently, can you give it a twist that will make it different enough? (If so, how? Possibilities include changing the protagonist's gender, the setting, the time period, and the basic motivation of the protagonist.)
5. Does the story have a basic theme or moral? What is it?
6. Does the protagonist have a strong goal? What is it?
7. Who or what is opposing the protagonist? Why? And is the conflict a strong one that can't easily be settled?
8. Are the protagonist and the antagonist evenly matched? If the protagonist is an underdog, what are the forces that help him match up to the opponent?
9. Is there a clear resolution of the story? A happy ending?
10. Are there one or two starring roles for which you can think of several appropriate actors? (If not, would it make sense to combine some of the smaller roles?)
11. What are the visual values of the story that set it apart from a play or television film?
12. Will the audience be able to identify with the protagonist on some level?
13. Have you avoided the use of offensive stereotypes?
14. Can you state what it is about this story that makes you believe it's worth telling, and that will make people pay five or six dollars to see it?

You can analyze the salability of an idea before you have worked it out in detail. Before you write it, give careful consideration to its structure and the characters. Chapter 3 will help you structure your plot; Chapter 4 will help you write three-dimensional characters.

CHAPTER 3

How to Structure Your Plot

IT'S A LONG WAY FROM AN IDEA to a complete story. The distance between the two is defined by the structure of your plot—the way that you organize the events that comprise the story. There is an age-old pattern that applies to every type of storytelling and that is a valuable tool for the scriptwriter.

• THE THREE-ACT STRUCTURE

The fundamental underpinning of all forms of drama (including comedy) is the three-act structure. This observation may have been stated formally for the first time by Aristotle, but even he derived it by analyzing plays written before his time, and it remains true of today's films, plays, and television scripts. It is that three-act structure that we will be looking at closely in this chapter.

It's very important to note the difference between this basic shape of drama and the *technical* act structure of the various formats available to you as a scriptwriter. For example, sitcoms are divided into two acts, each about thirteen minutes long, with commercials dividing them. Most one-hour television dramas are divided into four acts of about thirteen minutes each, punctuated by commercials. Television movies are divided into seven acts, each about fourteen minutes long, again with commercials dividing them. But these are matters of format and they will be explained in the relevant chapters later in the book; they don't change the fact that each of these forms has an underlying three-act structure, even though that structure may not be visible to the naked eye.

The three-act structure is a way of looking at the unity of the story that is being told. If a story doesn't have unity, if it doesn't progress logically and believably from incident to related incident, then we find it unsatisfying, whether or not we're able to pinpoint exactly why we feel that way. Please don't think, however, that we are presenting some sort of formula that will be a straitjacket that prevents you from telling the story in your own way. All architects learn that in order not to collapse, a building must have a sound foundation, but the need to provide that foundation doesn't constrain them from designing a wide variety of buildings—fanciful or utilitarian, modest or huge. By the same token, learning the nature of dramatic structure will not keep you from writing what you want to write, but will help ensure that your scripts have a solid base.

• THE OVERVIEW

It has frequently been observed that most stories feature a main character who wants something, who has a goal. His quest for this goal becomes the overall thrust of the story. There are people or forces opposing him in his quest, and these are the source of the obstacles he encounters. (If he encounters no obstacles, it'll be a very short picture.) At the end he either reaches his goal or he doesn't.

This progression has also been capsulized this way: Get your character up a tree. Throw rocks at him. Get him down or have one of the rocks hit him and kill him.

These may sound like grotesque oversimplifications, but if you apply them to even the most esteemed works you will see that they fit. Going back to *Hamlet*, our hero has the goal of finding out what really happened to his father and responding appropriately. The obstacles arise from his own doubts and hesitations as well as from the fact that his mother and stepfather are trying to cover up their awful deed and later to get Hamlet out of the way. He does find out and punishes the responsible parties. Of course there's more to the play than that, and most people would agree that it's Shakespeare's brilliant execution of his plots, rather than the plots themselves, that account for the longevity of his works. Nonetheless, the starting point is the basic story, whether it's *Hamlet* or *Rocky*. In the latter case, the beginning of *Rocky* (any of them) is that he decides to take on a top opponent, the middle consists of him overcoming obstacles such as self-doubt, limited resources, dirty tricks by his opponents, and so on, and the end is the fight that he wins (whether literally, or just by hanging in there for the full fifteen rounds).

The basic three-act structure may seem so obvious that you wonder whether it's even worth discussing. It is, if only because so many scripts (even ones that are made into films) stray from it. Typical mistakes include not defining the character's goal very clearly, so that the audience doesn't get a feel for where the picture is going; digressing into a completely different story for a while, usually in the middle of the picture, so that the momentum of the plot is lost; and having the story resolved by something that happens from out of the blue, so that the audience feels cheated. Using the three-act structure will help you avoid such errors.

Having an overview of your entire story is essential if you want to take a professional approach to writing your screenplay. It's true that some novelists begin writing a book with only the vaguest notion of where it's going, but the novel is inherently a much more sprawling form than the screenplay. For one thing, a novel can take 200 pages to get where it's going, or 2,000. A film script usually has to be between 90 and 120 pages. Also, readers of novels often are more flexible in their tolerance of experimental devices, such as passages of free association or a sudden change in who is telling the story. Films, or at least most American films, are far more conservative in their approach to storytelling.

Most film writers compose at least a rough outline before they start writing a script. We have talked to some writers who say they have it all in their heads instead of on paper, and even a few who claim, like some of their novelist colleagues, that they wait for their characters to tell them what should happen. Those who operate this way successfully tend to be veteran writers who will admit that when they were starting out they did rely upon some sort of written summary or outline.

It is our strong suggestion that when you first come up with your basic idea you take some time to think about it in a free-form way. Don't immediately try to jam it into an outline, or you may stunt the creative process. Give yourself some time to stare into space, jot down random thoughts, and in general give the idea an opportunity to germinate.

When you feel that you've mulled enough, make some notes about what you think should happen in each of the acts. Answer for yourself the following questions:

ACT I: Who is my central character and what does he want?

ACT II: What does my central character do to bring about his goal and who or what opposes him? What are the three or four key obstacles my central character overcomes along the way? What is the "moment of truth" in my character's quest, from which there can be no retreat?

ACT III: What are the events that finally bring my character to reaching (or definitely failing to reach) his goal?

Let's go through this with an example. We'll take a simple storyline—one that may not make a brilliant screenplay but that will be easy to follow for purposes of illustration. First, let's assume that we've read a newspaper story about a convict who escaped from prison and was captured outside a church in which a wedding was taking place. In real life, the location was a coincidence—he had nothing to do with the wedding—but this starts our minds going. What if this guy escaped in order to get to the wedding? Why? To see his daughter get married? To stop the wedding for some reason? At this point we don't know, but it seems like it might make an interesting starting point for a film and over the next few weeks we spend some brainstorming sessions on it. Seeing his daughter get married seems pretty sentimental and not likely to lead anywhere, so we drop that. What if the guy getting married was his partner in the major crime that landed him in jail? Let's say our character took the fall for the crime, and the partner got away. Why wouldn't he want the other guy to marry? Well, one thing that changes when you marry is that if you die, your spouse will expect to get most of your assets. What if the partner on the outside has a will saying that half his money (which he got from the job they pulled together) will go to the man in jail? This could have been part of the payoff for our character to do his time quietly. But the partner's wife would question it if the prisoner got the money instead of her, and the whole deal could be blown. Let's try to put the story into three acts.

ACT I: The central character is Bill Randolph, a convict who has another three years to go on his sentence for armed robbery of a Brinks truck. One of his cohorts was killed at the site, another got away with the money ($2 million), which has never been recovered nor has the other man ever been identified. Bill's goal is to break out of jail and get to a wedding he reads about in the newspaper. (Note that at this point we don't need to reveal to the audience why he wants to get to the wedding.)

ACT II: In order to reach his goal, Bill Randolph breaks out of prison on visitors' day and has to travel halfway across the country to get to the wedding. Along the way he teams up with a hooker who is also on the run from the law, for stealing a customer's money. Opposing them are the police and, later, a hit man that his former partner hires to kill him. The major hurdles he has to overcome are (1) the security system at the prison itself (2) the danger that the hooker will turn him in when she realizes who he really is (3) a state trooper roadblock which he and the woman approach in a stolen car (4) an attack by the hit man whom he thinks will help him, but who turns out to have been hired by his ex-partner to kill him. The "moment of truth" comes when Bill corners his former partner in the church, which is surrounded by police.

ACT III: Bill forces his ex-partner to give him the key to the safe deposit box that contains the money from the robbery, but the ex-partner then tries to kill him, and Bill ends up killing the ex-partner. Pursued by the police and the partner's men, he manages to make his way to where the hooker is (he's fallen in love with her in the course of the picture) and he gives her the key before he is shot to death.

Having gotten this far, we'd want to take some time to look at this basic idea in terms of its salability before deciding whether or not to pursue it. We'd probably conclude that while this would make a good episode for a one-hour detective series, there's nothing so inherently wonderful about it that it would make an easy feature sale. However, if we believed in it we might elect to go ahead, on the assumption that the execution could make it special. There are any number of action-adventure films that have been hits even though thin on plot—for example, *Lethal Weapon* and even the top-grossing *Beverly Hills Cop*. The latter had the energy of Eddie Murphy and a lot of good music, but the plot was tissue-thin. Therefore if we chose to go ahead with this story, we'd be looking for some ways to make it fresh, using the approaches described in the last chapter. For example, would it make it more interesting if the convict was a woman, and the person she picked up on the road was a male petty thief? If we don't go so far as to change his gender, can we at least find some interesting aspects of his personality that will give it a fresh feel? Also, can we find an especially interesting setting for at least part of the action? Furthermore, what about the industry's preference for a happy ending? It's possible that if it's clear that the woman would be starting a new life with the money that the ending as described above might have a positive enough aspect to be acceptable, but we'd also have to give more thought to the possibility of having both of them survive, with or without being able to hang on to the money.

If we are able to answer these sorts of questions to our satisfaction, then we can go ahead and fill in some of the gaps in order to come up with a more complete structure for the piece. Because character and plot are inseparable, a good way to proceed is to work out a basic overview of the action, as in the example above, then spend some time fleshing out your characters (using the techniques described in the next chapter) and then return to the plot once more to fill it out, act by act. You will find that thinking about plot leads you to ideas about character, and vice versa, all throughout the writing process.

Let's now take a look, in more detail, at the elements that comprise each act.

• THE BEGINNING: ACT ONE

The first thirty minutes of a two-hour film are crucial for several reasons: they introduce us to the central characters of the story; they establish the overall tone of the picture; they tell us what the central character's goal is; and they set the scene for the complications that will follow in act two. In this first half hour you must capture the audience. Even though they won't be giving their opinions of your film until it's over (unless they go to the extreme of walking out), much of their feeling about the picture will be formed early on. For the writer trying to sell a script there is an even greater importance to the first act, in that a producer or agent who isn't impressed by the first twenty or thirty pages probably won't read beyond that. Having a dynamite ending or a wonderfully funny scene in the middle won't save you if the beginning of the script doesn't work properly.

When the picture starts (or when we turn to page one of your script) we know nothing about your characters or the situation. There-fore you have to decide what it is that we need to know, and when we need to know it. Let's go back to the man who wants to escape from prison. There are all sorts of questions that come to mind as soon as we see we're dealing with a convict: What did he do to land in jail? How long has he been there? Is he guilty? What sort of person is he? What's the specific reason that he wants to escape? What's his plan? The easi-est way to get all this information across would be to open on him in his cell as a new cellmate is ushered in. The new guy sits on our man's bunk, introduces himself, and asks him all the questions we've just listed. This would be a very efficient way of getting the information we need. It would also be very undramatic. Hearing about something is never as exciting as seeing it, and since film is a visual medium you should show rather than tell. Also, remember that you don't have to reveal everything at once. Having the audience wonder for a while what the guy is in for may add some suspense that can work for you. So one of your first steps is to decide how much we need to know right up front, and how much can be delayed. Then, of course, you have to fig-ure out the best way to impart that information. If you want the prison-er to be a normally mild-mannered guy, we might meet him in the pris-on library in the first scene. On the other hand if you want to show that he's a volatile tough man, perhaps we meet him in the prison yard dur-ing the exercise period and see him confront and back down another convict over some small matter. These choices are immensely impor-tant because they give the audience its first impression of the central character, and that first impression (in film, as in life) tends to stick.

In terms of the action that you want to show in the first act, you must include an event that makes the character take the first step to-ward the goal that becomes his major preoccupation for the rest of the picture. In this case, since escaping and reaching his former partner be-fore the wedding is that goal, what starts him on that path? Obviously it is that he finds out in some way that the wedding is going to take place. You have a wide variety of choices as to how that might happen: he might read it in a newspaper, another convict might be aware of it and tell him, he might get a letter from the ex-partner. You also have some choice as to how early in the first act you want to have this take place. That will depend partly upon the type of tone you have in mind for the movie. If you want this to be a character study as well as an ac-tion picture, you might elect to first show Bill in his routine at the prison and let us learn through his actions there what sort of man he is. Then, perhaps halfway through Act I (about fifteen minutes into the picture) he finds out the news and we see what sort of reaction he has to it. On the other hand, if you are interested in a nonstop action picture, Bill might find out almost immediately, and spend the rest of the act planning and then carrying out his escape. In either construction, Act I ends with the main character's solid commitment to his major goal. In this storyline, that would be the moment when Bill has successfully escaped from prison. Now he's on his way.

• THE MIDDLE: ACT TWO

Now we have about sixty minutes in which to cover the middle part of the story. What should go into this section? Well, the best stories are organic; that is, each part of the story logically grows out of the one that came before it. Therefore the events of Act One should smoothly lead to the events in Act Two. In the example we're using, what implications does the first act have for the second act? First, Bill has escaped from prison, so logically the authorities are going to be going after him. This will be a continuing obstacle to him all the way through the rest of the story. Since he is a fugitive, he will be looking for some sort of cover identity as he travels across the country. This makes it logical (although not inevitable) that he would team up with a woman. The fact that he's obviously in some sort of trouble makes it logical that the only stranger that would team up with him is one who is in trouble herself. In Act I we established that Bill wants to get to his partner before the wedding takes place. That gives us a time deadline that he'll be fighting all the way through the second act. Although we didn't reveal in the first act exactly why Bill wants to get there before the wedding, by reading between the lines the audience will be able to tell that it's not so that he can congratulate the happy couple. If it is clear that his arrival will in some way threaten the groom, it will also become logical that the ex-partner, who will hear about the jailbreak, may take some steps to protect himself. As you can see, all of the major story elements that will give us conflict and suspense in the second act are in some way planted in the first act.

The nature of the story you are telling will suggest the complications that will make up the middle part of the picture. The example we've been using is a simple one of good guys vs. bad guys. (Yes, the good guy is actually a bad guy, but if we do our job correctly the audience will root for him—besides, we'll be establishing that the ex-partner is an even worse guy, so by comparison our man is a good guy.) The specifics may be different for a more subtle story, but the pattern will be the same. Let's say we're writing a story about a man whose world is being torn apart by alcoholism. His goal is to overcome it and be reunited with his family. What sorts of complications might he run into? The biggest problem for an alcoholic is his own inner drive to drink, but if we are going to make a movie about this we have to externalize this internal force. For example, we might show him at a social event where everyone else is drinking and trying to get him to join in. We might show him losing his job or experiencing some other crisis that adds so much stress to his life that he goes into a bar. We might show the physical effects of his withdrawal from alcohol. Whatever our choices we would again be showing a series of obstacles to the main character's achievement of his goal.

It is very important that you orchestrate these obstacles so that they grow as the movie proceeds, and so that each one in some way derives from the ones before it.

First let's consider why the obstacles have to keep getting bigger and bigger. If we make a movie about a fighter, and he faces his toughest opponent at the beginning of the second act, we're not going to be very interested in what happens during the rest of the movie, are we? The character has already overcome his biggest hurdle, so the rest of the film will be an anticlimax. But if we see him fight his way up step by step, with an occasional setback that makes us wonder whether he's really going to make it, then we're with him all the way, and our interest keeps growing. It's simple logic that we want the story to keep growing more and more, yet many scripts defy that logic. They have the most suspenseful, biggest challenge to the central character come perhaps halfway through the story, and then move him on to some much less daunting obstacles. The result: the story sags, the audience fidgets, vaguely aware that it is bored.

The other important part of the equation for a successful second act is that each development should be prompted in some way by the ones that preceded it. This doesn't mean that you can't have surprising developments. For example, in the story of the boxer, maybe at some point you want him to get the backing of a millionaire in his quest for the title. If suddenly a check for $100,000 arrives in the boxer's mailbox, that's an out-of-the-blue development that doesn't seem plausible. But as long as you lay the groundwork for it, there's no problem. Maybe the millionaire goes, incognito, to the gym to watch the fighter train. Afterwards he talks to the boxer, and it comes out that the millionaire once wanted to be a boxer. He sees a lot of himself in the fighter and realizes that without financial backing the guy doesn't have a chance. A few days later, a check for $100,000 arrives in the boxer's mailbox. Naturally, if you establish a character who is this important to the boxer's quest, you'd want to keep him active in the rest of the story, and probably to establish him in some way in the first act.

When you've done some brainstorming about the obstacles that your character is going to encounter, play with them. Try them out in different orders, to see which works the best in terms of both logic and escalation. If one of the obstacles logically has to come later but doesn't seem as impactful as earlier ones, try to think of ways of strengthening its impact. Remember that this is not a sheer matter of numbers. If a man has to fight his way through twenty gang members, that's going to be a pretty active "big" scene. If in the next sequence he fights an additional gang member, that will be an anticlimax. But suppose instead that he comes up against one other person—his best friend, who has betrayed him and now challenges him to a fight to the death. Although the opponents have gone down in number, from twenty to one, the second scene actually has more impact because of its emotional content.

In the second act you are leading up to what has often been called "the moment of truth." It is the point at which the character is about to embark upon his final and biggest battle to reach his goal. This battle will determine whether or not he succeeds. The actual battle will come in the third act, but it is set up at the end of the second act. Going back to our example, the escaped convict has overcome all the obstacles and made it to the church where the wedding is about to take place. The scene is set for the final showdown. The simplest version of this "moment of truth" can be found in hundreds of Westerns, both good (*High Noon*) and bad (too many to mention). In *High Noon*, which is worth watching on videocassette as an elegant and simple model of story construction, the end of Act II is the point at which Frank Miller arrives on the noon train and rides into town. Gary Cooper has tried to get help from various sources, but they've all failed him. Now the final conflict is about to take place.

• THE END: ACT THREE

The last thirty minutes of the film will play out the final conflict that is set up at the end of Act Two, and will answer the question of whether or not the central character reaches his goal. In *High Noon*, the main sequence of the third act is the gunfight between Gary Cooper and the outlaws. In our escaped convict example, it would be what happens once he has gotten to the church: cornering his ex-partner, forcing him to give him the key to the safe deposit box, having to kill the partner, and getting away. That finishes the main story we've been concerned with all along. The reunion with the hooker would have to be handled quickly at the end, just as was Gary Cooper's speech to the townspeople after he and his wife have defeated the outlaws. Some movies go on for a while after they are really over, which can damage an otherwise effective picture. As a rule of thumb, remember that as soon as the question "Does my character achieve his goal or doesn't he?" has been answered, the picture is over. If you want to add what in effect is an epilogue, go ahead, but be quick about it.

The most common mistakes writers make in their third act is to abandon the rule that we have discussed in terms of the first two acts: namely, that any new developments must fit the logic of the situation and must have been prepared for in some way. Instead, they find sometimes that they have done such a good job of painting their character into a corner that they have to resort to some far-out and illogical way to rescue him. As we have seen, the major developments of the first and second acts come about due to what the character does and how people react to what he does. If he escapes from jail, the police come after him. If he poses a threat to his ex-partner, the ex-partner tries to have him killed. This pattern must continue in the third act. It just isn't satisfying if the final problem is solved by coincidence, or by the intervention of people or forces that we've never seen before in the film. In the case of *Pretty in Pink*, what makes the rich boy suddenly decide at the end that he will beg the forgiveness of the Molly Ringwald character? As mentioned in the previous chapter, the marketing department found out that the audience would prefer this ending. But nothing in the picture itself led up to it—it came out of the blue, and made the whole picture seem off-kilter. It didn't follow the logic of the rest of the picture, nor was it organic to what had come before.

Generally, the resolution should very clearly result from the actions of your major character. After all, we didn't follow him this far just to see somebody else take over the story at the last minute. Of course others can be involved, and can even be instrumental. If Grace Kelly hadn't been able to overcome her Quaker beliefs, Gary Cooper would have been in deep trouble, but it was his courage and principles that led her to help him, and he still did the bulk of the fighting.

• TWO EXAMPLES

The best way to get a feel for how successful film stories are structured is to analyze movies that work. The fact that videotape recorders and film rentals are within almost everybody's financial reach these days makes this a lot easier than it used to be. Watch the film with a watch at your side and a notepad in front of you. Jot down the basic action of each major scene and keep track of how much time has elapsed. When you are done, divide the story into three acts. As we've said, the first act ends when the character makes a commitment to his goal. The second act ends when the final conflict or moment of truth relating to the goal is about to take place. And of course the third act ends when the picture does. Usually the first act will run about thirty minutes, the second act will run about sixty minutes, and the third act will run about thirty minutes (with proportional adjustments for movies that are longer or shorter than two hours). When you go over your notes, see how each major scene plants the seeds for scenes further on in the picture. Ask yourself whether logic prevails, whether the conflicts escalate throughout the second act, and whether the resolution in the third act is organic. If the structure doesn't work very well, take the time to give some thought to how you could improve it.

To give you an idea of how such a structural breakdown looks, we are including outlines of two very successful films, *E.T.* and *Ordinary People*. The time references indicate at what point in the picture we are at the end of each sequence. Let's start with *E.T.*, written by Melissa Matheson.

OUTLINE: E.T.
ACT I

E.T. and his fellow aliens have landed in the forest. While exploring, E.T. runs into some hunters. E.T. tries to hide, but the hunters soon spot him and give chase. The other aliens are alerted and take off in their space ship before E.T. can get back to them. E.T. is stranded. (1 min.)

Elliot watches his older brother Mike play "Dungeons and Dragons" with his friends. The older boys ignore Elliot until the pizza man arrives, and they send Elliot out to get the pizza.

While retrieving the pizza, Elliot hears some mysterious noises coming from his backyard.

A frightened Elliot claims there is something—a goblin, maybe—hiding in the backyard. The older boys investigate and find nothing. (7 min.)

That night, Elliot hears another mysterious noise outside. He investigates with a flashlight and gets his first look at E.T. Both flee in terror. (12 min.)

The next day, Elliot spreads some candy through the forest to lure E.T. back to the house.

That night, at dinner, Elliot again faces skepticism from his family regarding the experience of E.T. In his frustration, Elliot hurts his mother's feelings by mentioning their father, who has run off to Mexico with another woman.

Later that night, Elliot sits outside and waits for E.T. When E.T. waddles out of the garage, Elliot is speechless. (14 min.)

Elliot leads E.T. through his house and hides him in his room. They begin to communicate with hand gestures, and their fear of one another slowly evaporates.

We see the hunters combing through the woods, hot on E.T.'s trail. (20 min.)

The next morning Elliot is bedridden with a fever. Alone with E.T. for the day, he takes the opportunity to demonstrate the functions of various objects. E.T. takes a keen interest in his earthly education. Boy and alien are getting along famously. (25 min.)

When Mike comes home from school, Elliot allows him to see E.T. Mike is stunned, but his reaction is nothing compared to the squeal of horror when little sister Gertie sees the alien.

When Mom comes home, Elliot makes his brother and sister swear not to tell her about E.T. Elliot declares he's going to keep the little alien for himself. For once, Elliot is in charge—and respected. (30 min.)

ACT II

We get another glimpse of the hunters surveying the area. Their high-tech equipment suggests they are some kind of agents.

The three kids feed E.T. in Elliot's room. Using a picture book drawing of the universe, Elliot tries to get E.T. to say where he's from. E.T. answers by causing a bunch of balls and fruit to rotate above the book—the first indication of E.T.'s magical powers. (36 min.)

Elliot and Mike head off to school. The kids in the neighborhood make fun of Elliot's claim that there was a goblin in the garage.

Back home, E.T. goes exploring through the house. We intercut between Elliot in his biology class and E.T. It becomes clear that some unusual form of communication is going on between E.T. and Elliot. When E.T. drinks a beer, Elliot burps in class. When Elliot prepares to dissect a frog, E.T. communicates to him to set the frog free.

In the midst of exploring the house, E.T. figures out the function of the telephone and gets the idea of using it to communicate with his space ship. (40 min.)

When Mom gets home, she gets a call from school informing her that Elliot has been misbehaving. Little Gertie, meanwhile, teaches E.T. to say a few words.

Once Mom gets Elliot home, he is surprised to find that E.T. can talk. E.T. says for the first time, "E.T. phone home." Elliot realizes he CANNOT keep the alien—that he has to help him communicate with his space ship. (50 min.)

We see more of the federal agents, this time camped out in front of Elliot's home.

Elliot and Mike collect gadgets for E.T. to use to construct a communication device. Mike observes that E.T. is not looking well.

E.T. constructs the device. (55 min.)

It's Halloween, and the kids have a plan to get E.T. past Mom—they've dressed him up as a ghost.

Once past Mom, a costumed Elliot, Mike, and E.T. move through streets packed with trick-or-treating youngsters. (60 min.)

Elliot and Mike are taken on a bicycle ride through the sky as E.T. guides them toward the spot where he can communicate with his spaceship.

Once they land on the site, the three of them set up the communication equipment.

Meanwhile, the federal agents break into Elliot's home and search for signs of E.T.

Back in the woods, E.T. tries to explain to Elliot that he is growing ill. Elliot grieves at the prospect of E.T.'s departure. (64 min.)

The next morning, Elliot wakes up in the woods next to the communication equipment. E.T. is gone.

Elliot, who appears ill, returns home and tells Mike that E.T. has disappeared. Mike sets out in search of E.T. (70 min.)

As Mike rides his bike in search of E.T., he is tailed by federal agents.

Mike finds E.T. in a drain. The alien appears withered and pale.

Mike brings E.T. home and Mom sees him for the first time. Elliot announces, "I think we're dying." (72 min.)

The federal agents, garbed in protective clothing, quickly move in and seal off the house.

Elliot and E.T. are quarantined and attended to by scientists and doctors. Elliot pleads with them to leave E.T. alone and let him go home. It becomes clear that they want to study E.T., not save him.

E.T. loosens his grip on Elliot, and Elliot's health revives. (76 min.)

The next morning, E.T.'s condition deteriorates rapidly. Elliot desperately warns them that they are killing the alien. Unfortunately, he's right—E.T. is declared dead. (83 min.)

ACT III

E.T. is packed in ice by the agents.

Elliot is allowed to have one final moment with E.T.'s remains. In the midst of his heartbreak, Elliot discovers that E.T. is still alive. He decides that he has to get E.T. out of there. (88 min.)

Elliot and Mike plot to hijack the van carrying E.T.'s remains.

The boys hop in the van and take off with E.T. They are pursued by the cops. (94 min.)

Elliot and Mike ditch the van in a playground where they rendezvous with a group of friends on bikes. The kids pedal away, the cops hot on their tail. Just when it looks like they're cornered, E.T. sends the bike riders flying through the air. (98 min.)

That night, the kids land in the woods, where E.T.'s spaceship touches down.

Mom and little Gertie arrive at the site just in time for E.T. to say goodbye to them, and to see him say goodbye to Mike and Elliot.

The spaceship leaves with E.T. (103 min.) Closing credits.

Now let's look at this story in the terms suggested earlier in the chapter. The central character is Elliot, and his goal is to find a friend. Early in the picture we see that his brother and the older boys ignore him, and from his dinner comments we find out that he has no father. In Act I he first only hears his new friend, then he gets a glimpse of him, then he uses candy to attract him. Then he takes him to his room and they learn to communicate. By the end of Act I, it looks like Elliot has made a commitment to his goal—he's got a friend, and he's going to keep him.

Naturally there have to be obstacles. One that is established early in the picture is the presence of the hunters who are looking for E.T. Another obstacle is the close link between Elliot and E.T., which initially seems harmless but eventually imperils Elliot's life. Yet another obstacle to the kind of friendship Elliot wants is E.T.'s desire to get back to his own home. These separate conflicts escalate throughout the second act. If you go through the outline, you'll see exactly how each conflict builds, and how they all are skillfully tied together at the end of that act. The biggest obstacle to Elliot's goal—the "moment of truth"—comes when E.T. is declared dead. This sets up the resolution in the third act, in which Elliot takes action to rescue his pal. Of course E.T. does go home, and although it's a bittersweet moment, it is essentially a happy ending because Elliot has learned that if you love a friend, you want what's best for him, not necessarily what's best for you.

As with any fine film, it is the execution as well as the structure that makes it work, and *E.T.* has many wonderful moments that are not adequately captured by an outline. However, it is the structural soundness of the basic story that paved the way for the script's skillful execution.

Now let's see the structure of a more realistic and serious drama, *Ordinary People*, written by Alvin Sargent based on the novel by Judith Guest.

OUTLINE: ORDINARY PEOPLE
ACT I

Conrad Jarret springs up in bed from a nightmare.

Beth and Calvin Jarret arrive home from a night at the theater. Calvin notices that Conrad is awake and checks on him. He asks Conrad if he's thought about calling the doctor. Conrad says he hasn't.

At breakfast the next morning, Conrad says he isn't hungry and Beth irritably grabs his food and throws it down the disposal. First indication of mother/son estrangement. (4 min.)

While riding with his buddies to school, Conrad says little. He has a flashback to a cemetery.

At school, he appears restless. He doesn't pay attention in class. He decides to call Dr. Berger and set up an appointment.

Later that night, Conrad dreams about his brother Bucky and the boating accident that killed him. (9 min.)

Conrad has his first meeting with Dr. Berger. Conrad acts nervous and defensive. He explains to Dr. Berger that he tried to "off" himself, and that he'd like to have more "control" over his life. Berger asks to meet with him twice a week, and Conrad agrees only after he considers that it will mean giving up swim practice. (16 min.)

Dinner at home: Conrad tells his parents that he's seeing Dr. Berger. Calvin reacts positively, but Beth receives the news coldly.

At swim practice, the coach lectures Conrad about his inattentiveness—and then makes a rude remark about Conrad's psychiatric care. Conrad says nothing; he seems to be holding it all back.

Conrad meets Jeanine Pratt in the school hallway. They have an awkward, shy exchange. There seem to be romantic possibilities.

That night, Beth talks with Calvin about taking a trip for Christmas. Calvin doesn't want to take Conrad away from the doctor, but Beth doesn't seem to think that's an important consideration. (21 min.)

Beth arrives home from shopping. She walks into Bucky's room, reminisces to herself. Conrad shows up and startles her, and the two of them proceed to talk past one another. Again: no communication between mother and son. (25 min.)

Beth and Calvin attend a party full of upper-middle-class socialite phonies. When Beth overhears Calvin telling someone about Conrad's visits to Dr. Berger, she becomes indignant. (29 min.)

Conrad has another meeting with Dr. Berger. He is more comfortable with the doctor than at his first meeting. He confesses he misses the hospital where he had friends who understood his problems. (33 min.)

ACT II

Conrad meets Karen, one of his friends from the hospital, for lunch. They get along well until Conrad starts talking about missing the hospital. This upsets Karen.

Beth joins Conrad in the backyard for a friendly conversation, which quickly deteriorates into an argument.

Later, Conrad attempts to make amends by offering to help his mother set the table. She rudely rejects his offer.

Conrad meets with Dr. Berger, discusses how he doesn't "connect" with his mother. Conrad appears right at home in Berger's office. (41 min.)

Calvin talks with a friend about his familial worries.

On the way home from work, Calvin flashes back to his two sons when they were boys. He then flashes back to the horrifying night he found Conrad with his wrists slit open. (47 min.)

Conrad tells his swim coach he's quitting the team. The coach gets very angry. Conrad is reserved.

In the school hallway, several boys confront Conrad about why he quit the team. In his frustration, Conrad yells at them to mind their own business.

At Berger's office, Conrad is forced to confront his suppressed anger. Berger provokes Conrad in an effort to get him to release his emotions. (50 min.)

Conrad's grandparents are in town for Thanksgiving. When Conrad and Beth are forced to pose together for a picture, Beth becomes nervous and Conrad gets angry.

Beth later confides to her mother she doesn't know how to deal with Conrad anymore. (55 min.)

After choir practice Conrad and Jeanine strike up a friendly conversation. Conrad walks home singing to himself, buoyed by Jeanine's friendliness.

Conrad works up the courage to call Jeanine and ask her for a date. She accepts. (62 min.)

While Conrad and Calvin put up the Christmas tree, Beth angrily confronts Conrad about why he quit the swim team and why he didn't tell her. Conrad becomes angry and the two of them have a shouting match. Calvin tries in vain to be a peacemaker.

Calvin comforts a crying Conrad in his room. Conrad asserts that his mother hates him. (64 min.)

Back with Berger, Conrad discusses the latest family argument and comes to an important self-insight: that he can't forgive his mother for her limitations, and he can't forgive himself. (69 min.)

While jogging and pondering his problems, Calvin becomes disoriented and trips.

Calvin has a meeting with Dr. Berger, wanting to "shed light on things." He later comes to the conclusion that he wants to talk about himself. (73 min.)

Calvin asks Beth about an incident during Bucky's funeral when she fussed over Calvin's shoes. She has no apologies, but she does manage to hug him.

Later, Beth and Calvin meet for lunch and Calvin asks her to go see Dr. Berger. She angrily refuses. She then proposes that they both go away to Houston for a vacation. With little enthusiasm, Calvin agrees—it's dawning on him he doesn't love her anymore. (79 min.)

Conrad and Jeanine at a restaurant: she asks about his suicide, he tentatively begins to tell her about it. Unfortunately, he's interrupted by a group of rowdy kids, and when Jeanine is distracted by them, Conrad is hurt.

Conrad, depressed, takes Jeanine home. She tries futilely to cheer him up. They agree to talk about "it" later, but Conrad has clearly lost his confidence in her.

Beth and Calvin arrive in Houston and play golf. (84 min.)

Conrad watches his former teammates lose a swim meet.

Later Conrad gets in a fight with an obnoxious friend who makes a lewd comment about his relationship with Jeanine. Conrad seems to be losing control, closing himself off from his friends. (91 min.)

A distraught Conrad arrives home and decides to call Karen. He finds out she's committed suicide. Shocked—horrified—Conrad contemplates taking his own life, then runs out of the house. (94 min.)

ACT III

Running aimlessly through the streets, Conrad flashes back to the boating accident. He finally reaches a pay phone and calls Dr. Berger. Berger agrees to meet with him immediately.

At Dr. Berger's office, Conrad lets it all out. He cries, he screams, he throws things on the floor. Berger helps him to realize that what he did wrong was "hang on the boat"—survive—and that's why he hasn't been able to forgive himself. He hugs Berger when Berger tells him he's his friend. (98 min.)

Conrad visits Jeanine and apologizes for his behavior on their date. He seems self-controlled and more confident than we've seen him before.

In Houston, Beth and Calvin argue over Conrad. Calvin confronts Beth for the first time about her selfishness, and she becomes angry and defensive.

Beth and Calvin fly home. Calvin flashes back to better times in his marriage. (106 min.)

At home, Conrad hugs his mother goodnight. She doesn't return the hug—she shrinks away. Calvin watches regretfully.

Late that night, Beth awakens to find Calvin sitting alone in the kitchen. Tearfully, Calvin tells her that he doesn't love her anymore.

Devastated, Beth packs her things. (110 min.)

Conrad awakens the next morning to find his mother driving away in a taxi.

Conrad finds his grieving dad outside—and comforts him. Closing credits. (120 min.)

In this case, Conrad is the central character and his goal is to get well—even though he doesn't necessarily know it early in the picture. Often the first act of a film is given over to the central character's discovery of his goal. At the end of the first act, Conrad signals his initial commitment to his goal by cooperating with Dr. Berger for the first time. All of the elements that will oppose his getting well are set up in the first act. One is his own mind, as represented by the nightmare that he has right at the beginning of the picture. Another is his mother's hostile attitude. Others are his father's relative ineffectuality, his estrangement from his friends, and, as a result of all of these elements, his lack of a supportive environment. These all escalate in the second act. Again, take the time now to reread the outline and follow each of these story strands and you'll see how they organically grow in impact and are woven together at the end of the act. Here the fragile progress he'd made is shattered when he finds out that his friend has killed herself. It's the moment of truth: either he will kill himself, too, or he will finally confront the truth, assisted by Dr. Berger. In the third act, we see him take the latter course and see its consequences. Each of the story strands is resolved: he makes peace with himself, he finds friends and a supportive environment, and his crisis has caused his father to see his own life more accurately and to assert himself. There is no happy ending as far as his relationship with his mother is concerned, but at least honesty has prevailed over hypocrisy. And at the end Conrad is not only strong enough to be better able to take care of himself, he's also strong enough to offer comfort to his father.

It looks easy, doesn't it? All you do is find an interesting central character and give him a goal, plant the seeds of opposition to that goal in the first act, escalate the opposition in the second act leading to a moment of truth, and resolve all the elements of conflict in the third act. Unfortunately it is easier said than done, but knowing that this is the structure you are striving for gives you a solid foundation for your script writing.

A terrific story will work if we understand and care about the people to whom it is happening. How to create such three-dimensional characters is explored in the next chapter. First, as will be our practice throughout this book, we'll cap off this chapter with an informative chat with a professional—in this case a specialist in plot construction, feature writer Tim McCanlies.

TIM McCANLIES

Tim McCanlies is one of Disney's hot new writers. His first script, *Brothers in Arms*, is due for release in 1988. *The North Shore*, actually his second script for Disney, was released in July of 1987.

What's your approach to choosing a subject?

Well, not what I think will interest other people. It's got to interest me. I've got to have passion for it. Otherwise, it won't come across. Characters are of great interest to me; guys that are going through a moral crisis of some kind. A moral crisis against an action backdrop.

I want my characters to go through a lot, to have a lot of very tough decisions to make. Additionally, I like to mix comedy with drama, because I think that most accurately mirrors real life. When you've got a real character, with problems that can be identified with, you've got comedy, you've got drama—you've got a real person!

Do you think of the character or the dilemma first? Or do they occur at the same time?

Usually the character first, then the problem. I think, when somebody asks you what a movie's about, you should always be able to say, "It's about a guy, or a woman, who . . ." You shouldn't want to discuss the subject matter, or a particular shot or gag or whatever—you should want to talk about the main character, and what he or she had to do or decide or overcome or deal with.

And there's somebody or something out there working against the character.

Oh, sure, that's conflict. Otherwise, thirty pages into it . . . (Yawns deeply)

As interested as you are in character studies, a movie must still tell a story. How do you set up your conflict, your plot . . .

I've done it a variety of ways. I usually have a very good idea of where I'm going, because I always come up with the ending first. Then I come back to the beginning. Then you have the range of your character's actions mapped out—you have the guy before and after, so to speak. A lot of times the ending, or even just the last shot, can give you a feel, an atmosphere, a tone, mode, or whatever that can dictate how comedic you'll get, how dramatic you'll get, how "real" you are.

Now a lot has been written and said about three-act structure. I do believe all movies have a beginning, middle, and end, and so I tend to structure my stories that way. That doesn't mean, however, my first act will be exactly thirty pages, although somehow it usually seems to work out that way.

So you know going in what your third act is, and you take a while to set up character and story in your first act—all that's left is making it tough for your main character to get to that ending you're aiming for.

Exactly. And that second act, for me, is the most fun, because as you say the first and third act have such clearly defined functions. The first act you have to set up the problem or problems, introduce all your characters—there are so many things that you've got to do, there just isn't room for the fun stuff. And the third act is almost an extended scene in a way—the chase, the fight, etc. But in the second act you really get to cut loose, find out who this character is, see his or her changes.

In some ways I look at TV shows like "Hill Street Blues" and like them a lot, because they seem like they're all second act.

When you plot these stories out, the old analogy is that you get the character up a tree, throw rocks at him, and then get him down. Do you plan the "rocks" in a certain way?

Certain scenes, by their very nature, have to be in a certain place. In my *Brothers in Arms* script, the basic setup is two detectives, brothers, one an older country sheriff, one a Dallas Homicide lieutenant. Their youngest brother is framed by arms dealers in Monte Carlo, and he goes off to clear himself—followed closely by these two, "noodging" each other all the way.

Now, I knew I wanted to have a scene putting them on horseback in Monte Carlo. A big chase through the streets, that kind of thing. It wasn't big enough to be my ending, to resolve anything, so really the only place for it was towards the middle of the second act, where it's kind of like the big moment that sets up your third act—it brings a lot of elements together. So I always knew where that scene would be.

I also knew that I couldn't put it at the exact middle of the second act, because to have your big scene there results in the rest of your second act going downhill. And second acts should build and build, allowing you one last chance to catch your breath before the third act and the big final scene that's going to resolve everything.

How do you keep all these scenes organized?

I use a computer program to outline my scripts before I start writing. On one level I can view the overall story in terms of acts, with one line representing each scene. I can then delve into each scene through a separate sub-file, open it up and see what actually happens in that scene. But it's nice to be able to get an overview, to see the whole script as a series of one-sentence summaries of scenes.

Now, in progressing from your outline stage to actually filling in your scenes, I'd imagine your ideas change.

Oh, sure. I've gone into movies knowing exactly what's going to happen in each scene, and then I've gone into others not really having set acts, even. The second way's a lot harder, but sometimes you discover things, too. You throw out a lot, but in a way it's kind of enjoyable, not knowing what's going to happen.

But even when you know specifically from Day One what each scene will be, aren't there times that you reach the second act and say, "None of these scenes work, they're gone!"?

Yes. It's usually more of an opportunity to do something better. When you're writing scenes, you're always looking toward the next one, finding a chance to build to what's coming up. Sometimes an opportunity that you hadn't foreseen comes up, and you jump on that. Then of course you have to go back and fill in the roots for that scene, and so on.

You seem to think in very visual terms—horse chases in Monte Carlo, things like that. It's not so much, "Here's my story of such-and-such," as it is, "Here's a scene I can see, and here's another, and another . . ."

Yeah, that's true. I am always impressed with anybody who can do a *Breakfast Club*, with characters in a room for the entire movie. I think of that kind of thing and just say, "My God, I wouldn't know where to even begin tackling that!" It's nice to be able to just power it out with talent, but to me you're going in with one arm tied behind your back.

I'm very action oriented, because I like action. I think very visually, and my story ideas lend themselves to a lot of action.

In writing this action, how much detail do you go into? Do you juice the script up a little?

I try to use as many action verbs as possible. I try to make it as vivid as I can. I notice now, after looking back on some of my older scripts, that I write much more succinctly than I used to. To me, more than four lines of action in a row is a lot. People read very quickly in this business, and they tend to skip over large blocks of print. If they come to a twenty-line paragraph, they ain't gonna read it! A lot of time, if it isn't dialogue, they don't see it! So sometimes I find myself saying more in dialogue than if I was actually shooting it.

Another way writers get around this problem is, if they have a big block of action, they'll put things in caps, or at least underline things—all with the intention of holding the readers' interest, making them actually read the action lines.

A lot of writers break the action into smaller blocks.

Right, I do that too. And in my action sequences even when there's a lot going on the characters are talking to each other the whole time, and that breaks it up a bit. One of the problems I ran into in *Brothers in Arms* when writing about the younger brother was that he didn't have anybody to talk to, so there were long blocks of description. To try and break that up I had him talk to himself! Also, since he was in France, I could have him say things to people that they wouldn't understand—and he of course would know that, and kind of have fun with it.

It's interesting that in writing a screenplay you not only have to worry about the people watching the movie, but the people reading the script who just don't have time to give each script the careful read it may require.

A reader, a studio story analyst, is someone who has to take home seven scripts a weekend! That's a standard number, from what I understand—and they have to do a written report on each, with suggestions and notes. That's a lot of work. So I try to make it as vivid, colorful and interesting as possible. I also try to stick to what you'd see on the screen. No internal monologues, "He thinks," "She suddenly understands," things like that. I've seen scripts where writers have spent pages describing things no director could ever direct. "He looks in her eyes, and in them he can see the smoldering fire of too many years gone by . . ." And the director thinks, Jesus God, how am I ever going to show that!

Maybe a whole lot of back light! (Laughter)
Right, and incredible soft focus techniques!

As an action writer, you have to be very conscious of pacing. After all, you don't want your audience completely exhausted after the first fifteen minutes.

That's very true. I'm also very conscious of transitions. The old rule of beginning a scene as late into it as you can is a good one. And I always try to end each scene on a good note. I go into it thinking, what is the purpose of this scene, what has to be accomplished? Each scene has its own arc, its own story.

I try to start each scene with something interesting already going on. I don't like to do direct exposition, I like to kind of come in the back door, find a subtle way for the scene to complete its purpose.

So, in essence, you approach each scene as a kind of "mini-movie," with its own beginning, middle, and end?

Yes, I think I do, although I may not show the beginning. I try to fill each scene with as much as possible. I think sometimes writers tend to throw in scenes to advance the plot. John walks into the living room and says, "Mary's dead!" I try to approach that scene by saying, "Now, where could they be that's more interesting than the living room? And what would John be doing when he discovers Mary's dead? How can he tell us Mary's dead, without just coming right out and saying it?" You see, you have to take a great deal of time with each scene, to cram as much in and keep it as interesting as possible.

And still make it fulfill the purpose—to provide the impetus and motivation for the next scene, and the next, and so on.

Right. Every scene has to build to the next. Sometimes I'll write a scene, and I'll absolutely love it, but I'll get a funny feeling in my rear end that I'm getting off the track. And I'll have to dump it. That's seat-of-the-pants writing, and I think most writers work that way. I don't sit down and say, now I'm gonna write a dramatic scene. I just feel the way with my characters, wrestle with the problems they're facing, and see what comes out.

Afterwards, when the first draft is done—that's the time to go back and pull out your English major stuff and clean the scene up, or move it around. In a way you have to be two people.

I have friends who have been English majors, have never written anything, then all of a sudden they write a novel. They have a real big problem because their critical sense is so much more finely developed than their writing ability, they hate everything they write. They get no pleasure out of writing, so they quit writing! On the other hand, I've been lucky in that my critical sense has developed at about the same speed as my writing skills, so I've always liked my writing, always enjoyed it—and then, later, I can go back, apply my critical knowledge, and say, "Oh, that's shit!" But the important thing is to suppress that sense throughout the first draft of your scenes, and just write from the guts. You can keep it, fix it, or throw it out later.

CHAPTER 4

How to Create Three-Dimensional Characters

THERE IS AN OLD ADAGE AMONG scriptwriters that if your characters don't come alive on the page, they won't come alive on the screen. When scripts are rejected, one of the most frequently cited reasons is that something is wrong with the characterization. The problem is stated in a lot of different ways:

> I didn't care about the characters.
> The hero wasn't somebody I could relate to.
> I didn't believe in these people.
> I couldn't figure out what makes these people tick.

However it's said, it usually boils down to the fact that the characters weren't three-dimensional. In this chapter we'll see how you can create characters that come alive in the minds of the people who read your script. We'll look at how you can quickly get to know your characters inside and out, and how to reveal their attributes to your audience. In screenwriting, what your people say is as important as what they do, so we'll also cover how to write dialogue skillfully. At the end of the chapter you'll read interviews with two writers who have created some of the most memorable characters of stage and screen.

• WHAT MAKES A CHARACTER THREE-DIMENSIONAL?

Someone you meet briefly and about whom you know very little doesn't seem quite as "real" to you as a good friend does. You may make a surface judgment about the acquaintance based on appearance and first impressions, but the lack of information and the lack of shared experiences makes it difficult to go beyond that. In the case of the friend, you know that person's background, likes and dislikes, sense of humor, political attitudes, tastes, and a thousand other things. Your goal as a scriptwriter is to leave your audience feeling that they know your central characters almost as well as they know their friends. They won't necessarily always like your people, and in certain types of stories you don't even want them to like them. If you saw the *Godfather* movies, for example, you wouldn't necessarily want to have Michael Corleone over for dinner, but you certainly have a sense of what makes him tick. Think back to *Patton, Julia, Lawrence of Arabia, In the Heat of the Night*, or your own favorite film, and you'll find that your impressions of the central characters are very strong long after you've forgotten the plot details.

For the audience to know your characters well, *you* have to know your characters well, and often scriptwriters don't. They know only enough to make the characters serve the needs of the plot. That makes the screen characters seem flat. Let us give you an example of this in the form of a brief exercise. Take five minutes to write a page of dialogue between a husband and wife having an argument because the husband came home late from work and didn't call to let his wife know.

Finished? Now take another five minutes to write a page of dialogue between your father and mother having an argument because your father came home late from work and didn't call to let your mother know.

Whenever I (Wolff) have asked students to do this exercise in my workshops, the second set of dialogue pages have been far superior. They've been specific, frequently laced with humor, and full of convincing attacks and defenses. The first set of pages often have been stereotyped and weak. Why? Simply because most of us know our parents well and can draw upon that knowledge. Unless you automatically based your first exercise on two particular people you know, you had little to go by and probably you focused more on the argument itself than on the people having it.

• HOW CAN YOU GET TO KNOW YOUR CHARACTERS?

Some writers recommend that you write a complete biography of your major characters in short story form. It's a good idea but it takes a lot of time, and when you're itching to start writing your script, taking a week or two to write lengthy biographies is frustrating. Also if you want to refer back to a particular point about one of your characters while you're writing your script, having to wade through a thirty-page narrative can be unwieldy. Instead, try the questionnaire below. It's an adaptation of the type of form included in *The Art of Dramatic Writing* by Lajos Egri (the most recent edition of this book was written some twenty-five years ago, and it addresses itself to playwriting rather than scriptwriting, but we still recommend it very highly). Use the questionnaire as a guideline; if you feel like expanding on some aspect of the character, use as many pages as you like, and if additional pertinent questions occur to you, add them.

CHARACTER ANALYSIS

1. Name:
2. Sex:
3. Age:
4. Physical appearance:
5. How does this character feel about the way he or she looks?
6. Describe the character's childhood in terms of:
    a. relationship to parents
    b. relationship to siblings
    c. relationship to the other key people in his or her youth
    d. lifestyle while growing up
    e. education
    f. childhood activities (hobbies, interests)
    g. location(s) where he or she grew up
7. Describe the character's education during and after high school, as well as any military service.
8. Describe the character's current relationship to:
    a. parents
    b. siblings

c. other key people from his or her youth

9. Describe the character's romantic life (married? involved?) and any relevant background (e.g., previous marriage, affairs).

10. Describe the character's sex life and moral beliefs.

11. Does the character have kids? If so, describe his or her relationship with them. If not, describe his or her attitude toward children.

12. What is the character's religious background and current religious belief?

13. What is the character's occupation?

14. Describe the character's relationship to his or her boss and coworkers.

15. How does the character feel about his or her job?

16. What are the character's hobbies or nonwork activities?

17. Describe the character's philosophy of life.

18. Describe the character's political views.

19. Sum up the main aspects of the character's personality, including whether he or she is optimistic or pessimistic, an introvert or extrovert, and so forth.

20. What is this character proud of?

21. What is this character ashamed of?

22. Describe the character's state of health.

23. How intelligent is the character?

24. Summarize the character's relationship to the other major characters in the screenplay.

If you write brief phrases answering these questions you'll have a well-rounded picture of your characters in a form easy to refer back to. Now you know how these characters function in life. You must also know how they function within the specific story you're choosing to tell. As we discussed in detail in the last chapter, the heart of any script is conflict, and conflict arises when someone wants something and someone else or something else tries to prevent him from getting it. Therefore the following questions should also be answered:

25. What is this character's goal in the script?

26. Why does he or she want to achieve this goal?

27. Who or what is trying to stop this character from reaching the goal? Why?

28. What strengths of this character will help him or her in

the effort to reach the goal? What weaknesses will hold him or her back?

Based on what you know about the character, you should be able to decide exactly how he or she acts and reacts in each of the major story developments in your script. Since dialogue is such an important component, you should be equally aware of how your character speaks. For that purpose, answer these questions as well:

29. How articulate is the character?
30. Does the character have an accent or dialect? (If so, describe it.)
31. Does the character use slang or professional jargon? (If so, describe it.)

When you've covered these 31 questions, you'll know your characters thoroughly. Naturally not all of this information will show up in your script; actually, only a small fraction will. However, the very fact that you know these things will be reflected in what the characters say and do, and how they say and do it, and therefore will enrich your script enormously.

• IS IT A GOOD IDEA TO BASE YOUR CHARACTERS ON REAL PEOPLE?

Up to a point, yes. As you saw if you did the exercise suggested earlier, you can benefit by drawing upon your knowledge of real people. However, most good writers say that their characters are composites of real people they have known: the hero may have the wit of the writer's college roommate, the courage of the writer's Army buddy, and the unusual phobia of a man the writer once sat next to on a bus to Peoria. Drama is more organized and compressed than real life, so you shouldn't expect to find real people perfectly tailor-made for the demands of your script. But by picking and choosing traits selectively, you can create useful hybrids that come off as real people when you write your screenplay.

A word of warning is in order here. Not only is truth stranger than fiction, but people will accept certain things in real life that they'll scoff at in fiction. If you swear to your friends that you had an Uncle Ernie who ate golf balls for breakfast, they'll accept it if you're generally a truthful person. But if you create a character who eats golf balls for breakfast, most likely the audience will find it hard to believe. If you are writing something other than an outrageous comedy and you have something very weird that is important to include in the script, pave the way for it. Do some foreshadowing so that the event or trait won't be totally unexpected, and have one of the characters react in the same way that the audience is likely to react (with disbelief, shock, horror, or whatever). Then, when you deal with that character's reactions, you'll also be dealing with the audience's reactions.

• HOW CAN YOU MAKE THE VIEWER IDENTIFY WITH YOUR CHARACTERS?

If the reader is going to become engrossed in your script, he or she has to identify in some way with the characters, especially with your protagonist (and of course ultimately the audience will have to feel the same way). This isn't too difficult when your protagonist is a real hero—after all, *we're* all strong, courageous, right-thinking, and attractive, too. But what if the protagonist isn't such a wonderful person? What if it's Macbeth or a Mafia godfather or a bank robber? The important thing to remember is that even characters with serious flaws are still human and still motivated by the same drives as anyone else. One character wants to get his girl friend an expensive bracelet so he takes on an extra job; another character wants to get his girl friend an expensive bracelet so he holds up a jewelry store. In the former case we may admire the character for the means he uses, in the latter we may deplore the means. But in both cases we can identify with the motivation.

The best example of this, again, is in the *Godfather* movies. You don't admire or even excuse what Michael Corleone does, but you understand how he gradually gets involved in the family business, how he wants more power once he's tasted a little, how he wants revenge when his brother is killed, and so on. *Bonnie and Clyde* is another example of a film that gave viewers a lot of insight into the principal characters. If you know your characters well and reveal why they do what they do, the audience will go along for the ride.

This brings us to a special word about villains. These are the most one-dimensional characters in movies and especially on television. They do nasty things. Why? Because they're bad guys. And why are they bad guys? Because they do nasty things. What unskilled or inexperienced writers ignore is that real villains seldom are evil just for the heck of it. Even Hitler had reasons for the monstrous acts he performed—not valid reasons, not reasons that would satisfy anyone who has a regard for human life, but reasons.

If you've got villains in your script, give some information as to their motivation. This need not entail a psychological treatise or a long expositional passage; a clue or two will be enough. You're not trying to convince the audience that the villain's reasons are good, only that they exist (in other words that the villain, like every other human being, acts out of some need or desire).

A more sophisticated drama or comedy arises out of a conflict in which there are no villains. In *Kramer vs. Kramer* the parents clashed over who should have custody of the child but neither of them was a villain. Powerful mature scripts result when you pit two well-intentioned people against each other and reveal their intentions as well as their actions to the audience.

Viewers identify with your characters when they understand them and find their actions plausible. Let's say that our character is an intelligent young woman who's spending the night alone at an old mansion. So far she's found a mangled kitten, she's spotted drops of fresh blood on the carpet, and now she hears strange noises from the cellar. Assuming she's not certifiably insane, what would she do? She'd get the hell out of the house! What *does* she do? She goes down into the cellar! Why? Because the scriptwriter wants her to meet up with the corpse-like fellow who's been living down there for the last 112 years. In a certain genre of film the audience puts up with this type of nonsense because they don't take any part of the film seriously anyway. But even in horror films the better writer will give the character a plausible reason for each action. In this case, perhaps the woman is preparing to get out when suddenly she realizes that her dog has wandered into the cellar. If it has been previously established that this dog is like a child to her, we'll buy the fact that she'd risk going down there to get it.

• DO YOUR CHARACTERS HAVE TO CHANGE DURING THE COURSE OF THE SCRIPT?

All of us are changing constantly, although usually at a rate too slow to be noticed by us or those close to us. The changes are physical, emotional, and intellectual. We see them most clearly in others when we've been away from them for a while. This is why a twentieth high school reunion is such a bizarre experience—everyone else has aged while we've managed to stay the same. Once in a while we do see sudden drastic changes in others and usually they're motivated by drastic events: the father who finds God following the death of his son in a car accident; the woman who starts a new life after finding her husband and his secretary in Room 202 of the Bakersfield TraveLodge, and so on.

There is undeniably a certain fascination to seeing how people grow and change as a result of coming face-to-face with life's major developments. Dramas such as *Ordinary People* and *Terms of Endearment* have shown this process admirably and have been successful as a result. If your script deals seriously with realistic characters facing important challenges, it's almost inevitable that you'll be showing how they change.

Your task is to make the change believable. Again you'll have to use your deep knowledge of the character to give the audience clues as to why the changes came about. And again the audience will demand more of an explanation from fiction than they would from the daily newspaper or the weekly news magazine.

There are some types of films in which the characters are not necessarily expected to change or grow. Broad comedies, horror films, action-adventure films, and sci-fi adventure films fall into this category. Indiana Jones, for example, didn't undergo any meaningful character growth or change in the course of his adventures, but that didn't hurt him at the box office. If a fast-paced plot is the focus of your script, paying too much attention to character growth may only slow you down. However, if you're skilled enough to keep things moving at an exciting pace and still show how characters are shaped by the events in their lives, you'll have the best of both worlds.

Wonderful character construction goes for naught if the way your people speak makes them seem unreal. Therefore, let's turn to the subject of good and bad dialogue.

• WHAT MAKES BAD DIALOGUE BAD?

There are three major mistakes that unskilled writers make in their dialogue. The most common one is that they make all of their characters sound the same. How we say what we say is influenced by many factors, including where we grew up, the way our parents spoke, the degree of education we've had, how old we are, the type of job we do, and so on. A person who was a beatnik during his college years may still call something "cool," while a former hippie may still refer to it as "groovy," while a more recent youth may call it "radical." (This is intended as an example, not an exhortation to use outdated slang as a principal way of pegging your character's generation.) Once you've completed your thinking about your characters' backgrounds, consider how these facts affect the way they speak. A good exercise is to write one page of dialogue for each character on the same subject—let's say a recent news development. What they say about it will differ, and so should the way they say it. If your pages are too similar, go back to the source, your biographical notes, and try again. To really test yourself, give the dialogue pages to a bright friend and see how much he or she can infer about the speaker from what you've written.

This type of sameness of dialogue is what makes the worst sitcoms so instantly forgettable. The father's a wisecracking guy, the mother's a wisecracking gal, the children are wisecracking kids, and if the family dog could talk, he'd make wisecracks, too. It makes the writers' job easy because any joke they think of can be put into anybody's mouth. However, it doesn't make for good comedy. If you go back to the best sitcoms, such as "M*A*S*H," "Cheers," or "Taxi," you'll see that Radar doesn't talk like Hawkeye, Diane doesn't talk like Sam, and Latka doesn't talk like anybody.

The second major mistake is a variation of the first, namely that a particular person sounds the same no matter what the circumstances. If you're writing for James Bond, whose trademark is unflappability under the most dire conditions, that's fine; most other people will speak differently when they're facing imminent death than when they're announcing they're off to the K-Mart. Here the trick is mentally putting yourself into the circumstances you've created for your character, as well as recalling how other people have behaved and spoken at such times. For this and many other challenges that face the writer, taking a basic acting class is very helpful. It forces you to confront the problems of the people who will ultimately say the words you write, and gives you new tools for putting yourself in the position of your characters.

The third problem is that writers frequently load down their dialogue with exposition to the point that it no longer sounds the way people talk. In this regard the novel writer has a decided advantage. He can simply write, "Bob and Fred had known each other for twenty-three years." The scriptwriter, alas, often opts for that old standby, "How long have we known each other now, Bob—twenty years?" "Twenty-three, Fred." "It doesn't seem possible. Why, do you remember the time . . ."

You know that your exposition is clumsy when characters tell each other things that they would logically know already. If you find your people saying only slightly subtler versions of, "Marge, since you are my best friend I can tell you that my husband, Edward, has been drinking too much and that his job as manager of the Hackensack Steel Works is endangered," you know it's time to go back to the word processor. One way around this problem is to let information leak out slowly, at various times in the scene or over the course of several scenes. In real life we don't always blurt out what's on our minds directly and descriptively; more typically we broach a subject, withdraw, go back to it, beat around the bush, and hope that the other person will pick up the gist of what's bothering us.

Another useful device, unfortunately overused, is to put into the scene a character who doesn't know what's going on but has the right to ask a lot of questions—a cop or reporter, for example. As he learns all about Mrs. Monahan's three husbands who died mysteriously, so do we. This has become part of the formula of one-hour TV dramas. If you're writing something less formulaic, look for less predictable people who nonetheless can serve the function of interrogator: a new neighbor, a new employee, or a social worker, for example.

Sometimes the best way to eliminate excess exposition is to re-evaluate how much the audience needs to have spelled out. Give them credit for being able to fill in the blanks themselves. A student came to me with a long scene in which an old reporter has a drink with a new, young reporter. The former had once been at the top of his profession and now is back to working at a little weekly paper. The young reporter asks him what happened and the older man launches into a long speech about how he'd lost a series of jobs because of his alcoholism. I suggested that the writer cut that whole speech in favor of simply having the older reporter hold up his glass of whiskey and say, "This. This is what happened." The audience will fill in the rest.

Whenever you have vital information to impart, consider whether there's a way for a gesture or an action to take the place of dialogue. If a man is proud of his college degrees, show how prominently he displays his diplomas on the living room wall. If a mother is overprotective, show how she can't concentrate on the conversation she's having because she's nervously watching her little boy at play. If a man is unhappy with his job, show how he has to drag himself to work in the morning. All of these are more eloquent than dialogue and they take advantage of the freedom you have when you are working with pictures as well as with words.

• HOW CAN YOU MAKE YOUR DIALOGUE LIFELIKE?

Your goal actually is to write dialogue that seems lifelike but is not as fragmented as the spoken word is in real life. If you are old enough to recall the response when the transcripts of the Nixon secret tapes were released, you'll remember that people thought (1) this man's a crook, (2) this man swears a lot, and (3) this man's an imbecile because he can't seem to complete a simple sentence. Actually he wasn't any less articulate than most of the rest of us, but we have the advantage of never seeing our conversations transcribed. If you want to test this, tape any ordinary conversation, transcribe it exactly, and then have someone else look at the transcription and assess the "dialogue." They'll probably think you've written a scene featuring two idiots.

When writing dialogue, you have to use the hesitations, the stops and starts, and the repetitions of real speech just enough to make your words seem lifelike, but not so much that they impede the flow of meaning and the forward progression of the information you want to impart.

The other extreme gets writers in trouble, too: if all of your characters sound like William F. Buckley, they're not going to be believable, either. Similarly, lyrical dialogue that works in novels won't necessarily work in a script. The best examples of this have been the several attempts to adapt the novels of F. Scott Fitzgerald to the screen. His words, lively and expressive on the page, somehow seem stilted and leaden when spoken.

The best way to test your dialogue is to read it out loud yourself first, rewrite as necessary, and then have professional or amateur actors do a reading. You don't have to be in New York or Hollywood to do the latter; almost every community has amateur acting groups or community colleges or universities with drama departments. They're usually quite happy to set up a reading for you. Pay attention to the comments of the actors and try rewording speeches that give them problems. The playwright has the advantage of being able to rewrite during rehearsals. If you work with actors in the way suggested here, you can have some of the same benefits when you're writing for television and film.

• HOW CAN YOU CULTIVATE THE ABILITY TO WRITE GOOD DIALOGUE?

The subject of how to learn to write good dialogue is the one that most intimidates even the expert writers I've interviewed. To go beyond the general guidelines given here gets us into the realm of word placement, lengths of sentences, how to use suspense within a line, and so forth. These may be valid, but they break speech into such small components that it's easy to lose track of the overall sense, rhythm, and pace of dialogue. Because of this, some writers have said, "Either you can write good dialogue or you can't. You can't learn it."

However, you can improve your dialogue by paying attention to the major factors already discussed in the chapter, and by listening. Become a habitual eavesdropper. At the bus stop, in the coffee shop, in the grocery store line, at the bar, in the elevator—wherever people congregate—force yourself out of your own daydreams and listen to how people talk to each other. Think about what state of mind they're in and how this affects their modes of speech. Also be open to engaging in conversations with strangers. We have met fascinating people this way; on an airplane, a man who was on his way to Tulsa to visit his son, who'd just been convicted of murder; on a cross-country bus, with a real-life Willy Loman; in a little pub in Wycombe Marsh, near London, a veteran who refought his World War II battles on the table top, using salt and pepper shakers and the bottle of malt vinegar as props. You can learn a great deal from these encounters and since you're dealing with strangers you can walk away if the conversation gets too weird.

It takes an active type of listening if this process is going to help you as a writer. At the same time you're being entertained by what you hear you have to analyze it, to note the words used, the rhythm, the speed, as well as any colorful phrases to tuck away for possible future use. For example, there was the conversation between two young men, overheard in the neighborhood grocery store recently. One was complaining that his girl friend had found someone else. "He's short, he's ugly, he's a desk pilot—and he's rich," the injured young man said with disgust. Naturally the speaker was tall, not bad-looking, someone who worked with his hands, and apparently not rich. One striking thing was how to this young man being someone who worked behind a desk was in the same league as being ugly; the other was the term "desk pilot" itself.

Sometimes it takes some effort to place yourself where you'll hear the sorts of speech you need to employ in a particular script. If you are within driving distance of a larger city, you'll have access to just about any milieu. If you are writing a youth picture, start hanging around some of the music clubs (if you feel self-conscious, you can always say, "I'm here because my kid's in the band. He's the one with the purple hair and the safety pin.") If you are writing a cop picture, hang around some of the bars that police officers frequent (there's usually one near every precinct station). Just think: you can go to fascinating places and eavesdrop or start conversations and consider it part of your work; surely that's one of the great fringe benefits of being a writer.

The interviews that follow are with writers who have created some of the most vivid, enduring characters to appear on the stage or screen. When you wonder, as Alvin Sargent sometimes does, what your characters are up to even after you've finished your script, you'll know that you've followed in the footsteps of these skilled writers in creating truly three-dimensional characters.

STIRLING SILLIPHANT

Stirling Silliphant is a novelist and a film and television writer/producer. His honors include an Academy Award for screenwriting, an Edgar Allan Poe Award, and an NAACP Image Award. He was principal writer on "Naked City," principal writer and co-creator of "Route 66," and a contributing writer of "Alfred Hitchcock Presents" among others (for a total of more than 200 hours of original TV drama). The films he has written include *In the Heat of the Night, Charly, The New Centurions, The Towering Inferno*, and twenty-one more.

Mostly I'm going to ask you to discuss the craft of writing, but first a more general question. You were writing in the

Golden Age of Television—and to me those were the days of shows like "Route 66," "Naked City," and "East Side, West Side"—and you're writing now. How do the two eras compare?

I think a lot of the memory of that period is overrated. A lot of the shows were what I call tenement dramas. If you were to look at them today you would find them particularly naive or pretentious or overly socially conscious. I don't think that there were as many of them as brilliant as we like to think there were.

What there *was*, that prevailed in the 50's and 60's, was economic freedom which allowed for experimentation. The budgets were very small and as a result of that the risk taken was small; when you didn't have to spend a million or two or three million dollars on a couple of hours of television—you were only spending a few thousand—they would let you do different kinds of stories that might be off the mainstream. The result was that writers were encouraged to write and to create character. The emphasis in the writing was on character as opposed to narrative or action. In that sense, I don't have any doubt that that period was infinitely superior to the pap which is on most episodic dramatic television today.

The production, obviously, was very primitive. The sets were embarrassing by today's standards. From a cinematic viewpoint we've improved tremendously—what George Lucas and Francis Coppola and Doug Trumbull and people of that kind have been able to institute was just not dreamed of in those days. But for sheer writing, it was a writer's time, more than it was a producer's or special effects man's time.

Another factor that was important then is that there was no monolithic dictatorship, no control on the part of three networks, which now exists. That didn't really come into effect until the early or mid-sixties, when the networks took over total control of programming. Prior to that time, when I first started working, we didn't work for the networks, we worked for advertising agencies. There were maybe ten or fifteen big agencies that were producing programs. They would simply buy time. The networks were only in the business of selling time. If Procter and Gamble, for instance, had a budget of $200 million for television, they would buy from 8 to 9 on Tuesday night, from 7 to 8 on another night, and so on. Then they would turn over to their advertising agencies the responsibility of creating the programming that would go into those time slots. The result was that there were, around town, maybe ten or fifteen wonderful creative shops with agency people who were also writers and producers and creative people who would work with you. There was a great excitement in terms of story and style and themes. When that disappeared—when instead of twenty potential employers there were only three—you lost the freedom. You couldn't go with a crazy, offbeat idea to three people and expect to sell it. You *could* go to twenty people and someone maybe as crazy or even crazier than you might say, "Yeah, I'll go with that."

On top of that, when we were doing "Route 66" and "Naked City," one for CBS and one for ABC, my partner Burt Leonard and I had the creative control, not the network. The only right they had was to pay the agreed-upon license fee for the show and not put the show on—that was their ultimate control. But they had to let us make the show and the results of that were wonderful.

The world didn't end—there was less of an outcry about sex and violence than there is now.

Well, once you know you have no censorship, if you are a responsible, creative person, you tend to, if anything, censor yourself. You know you can't go out and flagrantly assault or insult the public. But on the other hand, you know that you can use concepts and language and themes that are daring and no one can tell you, "No, we don't want to do that." Those days are gone. In that sense, too, it was a golden age.

You mentioned that in those days there was more of a premium placed on character development. Is a character generally the starting point for your projects?

Always. I have never been a plot guy. However, unfortunately, the perceptions of me as it exists today in the industry and with the part of the public which is concerned with who writers are, are far different from my old ambitions for myself, and actually far different from where I'm guiding my career now.

I think I'm perceived as what they call a "money writer"—a guy who writes essentially commercially successful films, as opposed to what I was once known as, which was a writer of quality, character-oriented pieces. All my television work from those early years was character-oriented. My early films, films like *In the Heat of the Night* or *Charly*, were essentially character-oriented, as opposed to later films like *Towering Inferno* and *Poseidon Adventure*. Going back to comparing then and now, as a writer I find it more difficult today to do the things I did then, because of changing industry conditions. The only control you have is not to accept certain projects, and not have certain financial ambitions. The minute you decide that you want a certain thing and it's going to cost so much money and you have to earn it, you then put yourself in the position of having to do other than what you might personally prefer to do. But this is as old as time. You either write solely for money or you write solely for yourself, and it's very hard to have them both.

What kind of approaches do you use in creating three-dimensional characters?

I guess what I do is I try to find parallels or jumping-off points from people that I know or have known, or experiences that I have had myself. I try to find a character that I feel will allow me to express a certain theme or point of view—so I guess my characters start with the point of view of the whole story.

For example, I'm working now on a six-hour miniseries for ABC, called "The Looking Glass." It deals with, for lack of a better term, what they call the sexual frontiers of the 80s—attitudes of society toward marriage, open marriage, adultery, etc. I had to invent four basic characters for that story, because it's a story of two married couples who decide to all live together in one extended family.

You know you have two men and two women. How do you "invent" those characters? Well, I wanted one couple to be older, one couple to be younger; I wanted people who were essentially articulate as opposed to being, let's say, more physical. So I did not pick hard-hat type people; I picked professions where I would be able to have my characters say things, for the benefit of the audience, that I wanted to say.

I guess what you go through is a series of eliminations of what you don't want, to get to what you *do* want, as opposed to having a character spring full-blown out of your mind. If you were to write only three or four or five things in your lifetime, then you could probably afford the leisure to sit down and wait and think and create the person in your mind and then write his biography and do a total profile psychologically on him. But when you are a professional writer and have to deal with a continuum in your career, you have to get a little more organized than that.

Could you go into more detail on the anatomy of these characters as you created them?

In "Looking Glass," the next thing that went into the selections was where the story will take place—that obviously influences character. I decided that I wanted to get this in the middle of America because I wanted to be very sure that if I dealt with what, to mainstream America, might seem to be deviant behavior, that it couldn't be geographically blamed against being in L.A. or New York, where people seem to be able to do things that are freer. So I wanted to go into the heartland of America and deal with it as an American issue, not a freaky thing. That suggested a place like Kansas City or St. Louis.

I went to Kansas City and became enthralled with the city in terms of its beauty, its architecture, and, strangely enough, its sophistication. To my horror, I found that four people living together openly in Kansas City, Missouri, is considered "What else is new?" But if I just dropped a little bit south of Oklahoma, they'd all go to jail for ten years. That, of course, is one of the points of the story: the laws governing our sexual behavior and misbehavior in this country are extremely unfair. I think there should be one standard for all. I'm not talking about stronger federal control, but I sure as hell am talking about equality of treatment in the same country.

Now I know where they're from, and that helped govern what I wanted them to do. I wanted the younger woman to be essentially selfish, ambitious, an achiever and a professional woman. So I gave her the job of being at an advertising agency, but I wanted her to be modern, so I made her specialty film communication. I made her husband a professor at Reed in Oregon, which is a very liberal school. His specialty is the American novel prior to the Civil War. In a way, that relates to the story too, because the censorship and the controls that existed in American society at that time were very strong. Both of these people are just arriving at their new home in Kansas City from Oregon, he with a new job at the university, she with a job as vice president of an up and coming and powerful ad agency.

In terms of the other couple, I wanted one woman who was sort of like Mother Earth and yet very attractive. I saw her very clearly as one actress: Barbara Harris. I saw her as a lady who works in stained glass, but doing very creative, abstract, modern, slightly pornographic work, out of rebellion, more or less, against her traditional background.

Her husband I created out of a fascination with a job that's kind of exciting. All these cities have experts who specialize in attracting convention business and in staging conventions. These guys earn a great amount of money, anywhere from $75,000 in the small cities up to a quarter of a million dollars—more than the mayors make. They have to be very personable, kind of dramatic, hale fellows, and yet they have to be very, very bright. I also saw Gary, the older guy, as very sexual, into open marriage, a guy who really enjoyed relationships with new women and yet loved his wife very much. He wonders why you have to make a monogamous commitment physically. Is it not enough to make a monogamous commitment emotionally and spiritually and intellectually? He's a passionate advocate of this kind of freedom.

In a very short amount of time I was able to zero in on those four people. Once I had the basic shadows of the people I then really went to work on what their backgrounds were, and that deals with ethnic, religious, psychological, and childhood factors. Nine-tenths of that never appears in the material, but at least it prevents me from having them say the wrong thing or act in a way they wouldn't understand.

Once you have all that together, you have to throw it all out. We all pick up the newspaper and we read that the mother of three children has cut the throats of her children at night. She's a church-going lady; there's nothing in her background that could possibly explain her action. So you have to be careful in creating character and striving for something that's real not to lock yourself into inflexible, unchanging, unbending behavior, either in dialogue or in what they may do. But once I know what the limits are of the people, then I know where I can take them away from those limits, what I can do to create surprise.

And some of those surprises come from how the characters undergo some sort of growth in their thinking or behavior?

As the story evolves for these characters, the biggest burden of all is to change them and to evolve them and to resolve them. This is something which I would say in 90 percent—maybe 99 percent—of all screenplays, and certainly in 110 percent of all television plays, is very seldom done. And I very seldom can do it either, because you just don't have either the time or maybe the talent to do it the way you would do it if you were doing a play, working on it for three or four years. It takes time. But I do always conscientiously strive to make some kind of character evolution over the course of the drama. No again, you can't generalize on that. Suppose you've got a story with a very short time framework; *High Noon* is an example of that. You're not going to evolve that character beyond a point of view. I mean, he's going to defend the town, he's going to kill the heavies, and at the end he's going to throw the badge on the ground. To me that is an incident, not a total dramatization. "The Looking Glass" takes place over a period of roughly three months, so it's not going to allow me, within the structure of reality, a hell of a lot of character change. Too much change itself could be called bullshit. They say a person is pretty well locked in by the age of two. So don't misunderstand when I say that a thing that doesn't change is wrong; I just think that the burden of the writer should be always to say, "What would the effect of these events be on this given person?" That is really all you have to be concerned with, both in a narrative sense and in a character sense.

In the very successful kinds of action pictures that you've done—Poseidon Adventure, Towering Inferno, *and so on—obviously there isn't as much time to develop characters. Are there techniques to cope with that problem?*

There are, and they're all horribly transparent and awfully superficial, and I have to admit, in retrospect, kind of dreadful. I hope never to have to do them again. But when you do what we call disaster films—and frequently they are that in every sense of the word—you're dealing with eight, ten, fifteen people who are only there to survive or be killed. They have no other possible reason to be in the story except to get you hooked, so that when we throw them out of an elevator or off the top of something, everyone says, "Oh God!" I'm being very cruel about it. Actually I think *Towering Inferno* was a pretty good flick and I have to remind myself that it was nominated by the Academy as one of the best films of the year.

The strokes have to be very broad and very quick and therefore very superficial. The minute you take time to go deeper, you're going to slow the story down and get people too interested in one person versus another. It's a chart job more than anything else. You have to see how it all balances. In *Towering Inferno* we had twenty-five characters, of whom twelve or fourteen were principal, foreground characters. I once made a note when I was working on that script that I had seven pages for each person—of course there were overlapping moments where two people would cross. But there are not scenes of great dramatic intensity, you're just whipping things by.

You do stereotypes and then change them a little bit so they're kind of off the wall and stylish. But essentially if they are not recognizable stereotypes, people have trouble with them—they have to know who they are so they can follow the story.

In retrospect, do you feel you got stuck in that genre?
Yes. I have no apologies for *Towering Inferno* or *The Poseidon Adventure*, but once I went on further into that genre and began to make a career out of it, I almost hit the point of no return. I don't think that a writer should allow himself to do more than one of any type of thing, actually. Unfortunately, the industry tends to categorize writers like it categorizes everything. The minute I finished writing *In the Heat of the Night* I was approached by six other producers to do so-called Black stories. The only other one I did, and it happens to be one of my favorite films, was *The Liberation of L.B. Jones*, Willy Wyler's last film, based on a very important, powerful book by Jesse Hill Ford. It did nothing at the box office, but it was a very, very powerful film about racial relations in this country. I also did the three *Shaft* films, but I don't consider them in the Black-White realm; they were strictly fun, strictly cop shows.

Since we're talking about the way that you handle characters in different genres, now you're writing novels, which is yet another approach. Is novel writing something new for you, or is it something you're coming back to?
Something I'm coming back to. I began as a novelist. What brought me out to Hollywood twenty-seven years ago was that a novel I wrote was sold to a studio. Now, I hoped that they would ask

me to do the screenplay, because actually I had written it first as a screenplay and then rewritten it as a novel. That never happened, they refused to even talk to me about doing the screenplay. But that gave me the money to come here from New York and stay here.

I prefer the novel form above all else. Now I have signed a contract with Ballantine to do three paperbacks, a series of books based on the same character. I'm having so much fun writing them. It's so wonderful in a novel to be able to go on, as long as you think the reader will have any interest, with memory and introspection, points of view, social commentary, irony—all the things that you cannot afford to do in a screenplay, except through some character occasionally. In the novel, everyone knows that's the writer talking, even though it is the hero speaking. There's no one else in there— there's no director, no producer, no studio, no committee, no story editor, no actor . . . it's all you, so it's the ultimate ego trip. And, actually, that's all writing is, isn't it? It's what you think and feel; except screenwriting, television writing, is not that at all. That is a professional exercise in manipulating the committee.

Each of the types of writing that you've done has its own structure. When you write scripts do you do it with an emphasis on the traditional three-act structure?

No, except in television. In television you must think structurally because you know you're locked into segments. If you think in a nonlinear form in television you have to know at least where you can get out for the commercials, that is compulsory. In a two-hour episode on ABC television, we do seven acts. You know that you've got about a hundred pages, each act is fourteen or fifteen pages, that's it.

Forgetting television, no, I do not think of a movie at all with any kind of act breaks. I think a film has to be either an incident or a canvas. *Reds* is a canvas, *Dr. Zhivago* is a canvas. If in a canvas you had acts it would be boring, you would be looking for the next curtain break. It's not like the theater at all. What you're interested in doing is taking a character and following him to his high moment, whatever that may be. In an incident film, such as *High Noon* or *Towering Inferno*, an event is about to take place, you meet the people who are involved in the problem, you create the problem and you extend it and you solve it.

It's classic in the sense that it all follows the prescriptions of Greek drama, but in a film you have to be very clever to hide those act breaks. I hate it in a film when I can see the mechanics behind the thing.

In all of your experience you've obviously learned how to cope with the suggestions or demands of the committee that is, as you said, part and parcel of scriptwriting. How do you do it?

I have been very lucky all my life to be absolutely and totally objective about my writing. And if I could knock any kind of sense into a new writer it would be the need to be that way—that would be the most important single thing I could impress upon a person. For some inexplicable reasons, whether it's genetic structure or my folks just raised me right, I have no self-defense mechanism about my work. It's not written in marble and there's more wherever it came from, so why should I say "This is the only way to write it?" If I have written something and I'm still tentative about it and someone looks at it and says, "That ain't it, baby!" that's not going to help; but if they say "This is not your best work, have you considered approaching it from *this* angle," I'm the first person to look for that.

I love rewriting my own work and I'm constantly rewriting it. I will even go back and rewrite my scripts that have already been made into films. I'll find a script on a shelf, I'll open it up, and say, "Jesus, what a piece of shit this is," you know, and start changing dialogue—mostly cutting dialogue. As writers we all tend to feel that the actor is going to miss the thing and we'd better give him a lot to say.

Can you offer any advice for writers who do have a problem dealing with suggestions or demands from the director or the producer or whomever?

One of the things I would try to get straight in my head in a story meeting is whether the people I am meeting with are genuinely able and talented, or are assholes. Now, if they are assholes, I would have no advice except that if you need the money, listen; if you don't, leave.

If they are people you respect—and I would hope that we all have to work for only such people—then you must force yourself to

listen, not only to what they are saying but also to what they are try·
ing to say. Very few people are able to sit with a writer and tell him
what they really want; otherwise they'd be writing it.

I would say most writers tend to go to these story conferences
with a very defensive attitude, swearing to get in there and fight like
hell for what they've got. That is not the way to go in. The way to go
in is to see what the other guy has to say. You will find ninety times
out of a hundred that his criticisms are not really that much. I've
been told sometimes by a producer on a first meeting, "We have
such problems here! Stirling, you missed, you really didn't get it."
Then you go into the meeting and the guy says, "Why did you call
this character Monty?" You say, "I don't know. You don't like the
name Monty?" "No, I had this uncle named Monty—can you call
him Jack?" And that's it.

Now of course I'm making a little light of this, it could be a lot
worse. They could say, "Your third act is absolutely off target." For
example, ABC said to me that the third episode of "The Looking
Glass" is out of balance with the first two. And they were right. I
went off deliberately—or at least partly deliberately—on an experimental path to try something, and it didn't work. But it's very simple
to bring it back.

If you find you can't live with their suggestions, you have to
tell them right then and there, or you have to say, "I have to go think
about it." Sooner or later you're going to have to bite the bullet on
the confrontation with your employer or your producer. If they truly want to take a character that you have written, to change him into
something you don't believe in, then that's a different matter. One
time an important network executive suggested that we inject a
sense of danger into a character by having her open a drawer in
which we see a gun. I can't tell you what a preposterous idea that
was—it had nothing to do with that character. The director was
with me, and while I was getting ready to counterattack, he, with a
wonderful sense of humor, said, "I've got a better idea. Why don't
we have her run over a Mexican in a pickup truck?" Needless to say,
the executive grasped the point, and dropped it. But at a certain
point you have to hit back hard, and if you can do it with humor
that's better than getting uptight.

***You are known as a prolific writer. I imagine this comes
partly from experience, but is it also an attitude?***

Yes, it's an attitude that stems from a very disciplined, even compulsive childhood, but I'm no longer a compulsive writer. The reason that I've never had any stress is that essentially I'm very lazy. My idea of a great time is get on my boat and disappear. I don't really like work and discipline and schedules and the whole studio system. But because I have personal ambition in terms of things that I want that cost money, and because I realize that one of the ways I can make money is writing, I force myself to have schedules. Over the years, if you do that long enough, you develop an inner timetable.

On top of that because I'm really very realistic and I hate bullshit more than anything, I appreciate that the act of doing anything is simply the act of doing it. If you want to do a painting or you want to write or you want to write music, you just sit down and start doing it. Sooner or later you'll have something. It may not be any good, but you'll have it done. In the act of doing it time and time again, if you're serious about it, you'll begin to learn things about it. And after a while it becomes easier.

At what pace do you work now? Can you tell us a little about your working methods?

I map out five pages a day, thirty-five pages a week. Thirty-five times four is enough to make a movie. So that means I should be able to write a screenplay in four weeks, assuming that I have everything—the story, the characters, the research—and I'm just sitting and actually writing scenes. What happens is, in effect that's a little too ambitious, so I keep revising the schedule and the four weeks become six weeks or eight weeks, but to take more than eight weeks for the first draft would be reprehensible. Of course then you might spend a year or two or three revising it. I imagine that in the case of a film like *Reds*, Warren probably spent months and months on the screenplay because it's a difficult piece of work. There's a particular scene later in the film, between Jack Nicholson and Diane Keaton, in which they confront each other honestly about themselves—it's probably one of the most brilliantly written scenes of human confrontation I have ever heard, seen performed, listened to in my life. With a scene like that, either you write it in hot passion, instantaneously, or you slave over it for months.

When I'm talking about a television show, that kind of craftsmanship is not involved. It's not permitted; they don't expect it, they don't want it. If you can't write five pages a day, say twenty-five pages a week on a five-day week, on a television drama, then you are not a professional. If you're a professional, they may or may not be good pages, but you can write them.

What I do is I write them and the next day I go back, edit them, throw them out, start over. By the time I've finished the first draft I have probably edited each of those five pages thirty or forty times—and then it's still the first draft.

And this is the approach you use for whatever specific type of script you're working on?

Well, because of the experience and years of doing things, when I know that I have to write a two-hour television script or a six-hour miniseries, or a motion picture, or whatever, I know what is involved in the mechanical make-up of that particular item. I know how many pages it takes and I know what my own pace is. When I start the actual writing I make up a schedule and, as I said, I write seven days a week. Because I have so much free time and because I am so lazy, I can't take Saturday and Sunday off—that would be unconscionable because I take Monday, Tuesday, Wednesday, Thursday, and Friday off, during the day. I'll go out in the morning and go swimming in the pool or walk around the Tiburon path—we live in San Francisco—and it may be around three o'clock that I'll settle in and work like a dog for three or four hours. That doesn't sound very disciplined, but I guess what I mean is that I won't go to bed that night without doing my work, but I'll try to put off as much as I can. That's in the early stages of any particular work. Once it gets going, then it's very easy to go right to it. You're hungry to do it— once you've got it moving, as you know, you've got to get to it, nothing can keep you away. And anything that gets in the way of it, you're ruthless about pushing out. You become totally preoccupied, you drop everything, you cancel engagements, you just stay in and do the work. That's the best time.

ALVIN SARGENT

Alvin Sargent is the Academy Award-winning writer whose scripts include *Ordinary People, Julia, Straight Time, Paper Moon, The Sterile Cuckoo, The Effect of Gamma Rays on Man-in-the-*

Moon Marigolds, The Stalking Moon, Bobby Deerfield, and his personal favorite, *Love and Pain and the Whole Damn Thing.* This is the first interview he has granted on the craft of scriptwriting.

In general, how do you view a project when you start out?

Feeling something. Finding that place to begin, free-associating. Weeks, months of free-associating: scrambled notes, scrambled ideas, but somehow sooner or later connected with the sense of what the movie should be. Sounds disorganized, doesn't it, but then I'm not very organized. I can't wait to be old enough to retire and go back to playing with the typewriter in the basement. Back to the hobby, not the career.

Do you begin with the emotions of the characters rather than the dynamics of the plot?

Well, I think about what this story means to me, how I am affected by it, how I want to project that on paper. Paper is the great enemy. Getting something from your head onto the page is the hardest part. New writers get ideas and can tell you what they want. They can describe some dialogue in a scene that's very good, they have a sense of character, of what the scene is about, of how it moves. But then—and this happens to me, too, sometimes—something will happen between the time that you know what to say and decide on how to put it on paper. The problem of that transition to paper somehow or other has to be eliminated. It has to be, I think, as if it were a Xerox machine so that the image moves directly onto the paper. I guess that's the way I work. I structure later, after I have all this goop from my mind down on paper, just exactly as I feel it, immediate acceptance, not edited and polished in the mind. Don't prepare something before the paper gets it.

What's in this goop?

People talking to themselves or with each other, without necessarily any connection to the story. I do a great deal of free-associating. Talk, for pages and pages, I don't know what's going on.

Several months go by, suddenly you've got a big pile of stuff as if it were a basket of material, pieces ready for the quilt. I find something alive—I hope. I think too many people are too organized; they've got it all worked out, instead of hearing their characters first. Don't be afraid to write words that don't even connect. Sometimes when I'm writing and nothing's going on, I'll just write anything: "cow . . . dog . . . book . . . the man shaved" and then try to get something in my head related to what I'm writing. Sooner or later, maybe after pages of it, something begins to show up. Of course you must feel something to begin with, and that is very concentrated work, to cut off from outside and simply feel something—anything will do, anything.

Does this process of free-associating take longer than writing the script?
It *is* the process of writing the script.

Does most of this material end up in the script?
No, not most. Sometimes I know I'll use things. That's very satisfying—I absolutely know it's going to be a scene in the movie; maybe the beginning, maybe the final scene. The beginning of a movie for me is always more difficult to find than the end of the movie. It's very hard starting. It's like telling a dream or a joke— sometimes you say, "Well, let's see . . . how do I begin?" People can tell the same story and all end up at the same place, but the beginnings are always different.

Going back to characters, what I've admired so much in your work is the "realness" of your people. It sounds as if the process of free-association you've been describing really puts you in touch with them.
Over a period of time, I begin to understand them, to think about them not only in terms of where they are in the story. But I'm sure this is the case with most writers. I think about where these people are today, even when I'm not writing. What are they doing now? Are they on the road? Are they eating dinner? *What* are they eating for dinner? Do they ever get together? They're in my mind, they're people I met somewhere. But now I'm home in my house, away from the typewriter, and they are somewhere in their lives. Sometimes I'll go to bed at night, wonder where they are, how they are, think about the fact that I'll see them tomorrow. Trouble is, sometimes they don't show up for work. (Laughter) You go to the typewriter and you say, "Where are they? What time is it? Why

aren't they here?" Sometimes they never come back, and so sometimes I fire them.

It seems to me that so often films are not satisfying because the characters in them are "types" rather than people, and that probably goes back to the writer not knowing them well.

Yes, and even if you know them well, you want to know them better. You want to know things about them that nobody else knows. In real life you go home sometimes and say, "I spent the day with so-and-so, and I've known him for ten years but today I found out a lot of things I'd never known—things I hadn't paid enough attention to, or things he never let me see." They show up on page 85 sometimes, so never show pages if you can help it.

Do the characters ever surprise you?

Oh boy! You write somebody that you can trust but you don't know them so well that they can't surprise you. It's wonderful! Hopefully, it's more unpredictable than an audience is prepared for. I remember in *The Sterile Cuckoo* there's a scene in which the boy is wondering where his girl friend is. Well, I didn't know where she was, either. And I loved not knowing, but I knew she was somewhere. When they'd first met, they'd stayed in a rooming house across from his dormitory. One night he gets up, walks around, sits at the window. He sees the light on in the room where they'd both stayed four months ago. This boy and I both looked at this light in the window across the street and said, "I wonder . . . is she there?" She was.

If you don't allow yourself the pleasure of working at it—and that doesn't mean you have to be as disorganized as I am—then you don't give yourself the freedom to find the surprises. Rigidity is the mother of rigidity.

It sounds like this unpredictability and freedom is your source of joy in your writing, and also gives your characters their spark.

People don't know how they're going to behave, and those who do know exactly how they're going to behave during a certain period of time are not very interesting to watch. Beth in *Ordinary*

People knows exactly how she's going to behave, until certain circumstances arise over which she has no control, and then she panics, and that frightens her. And her behavior becomes drama, whereas earlier she was more of a fascination, I guess.

I said before that a screenplay is like a joke or a dream—it moves fast, it's filled with emotion and with drama. A dream takes great dramatic license, it can do anything it wants to, and it's very exciting. Jokes, too, they move fast, they're cut well. People aren't afraid not to explain everything that happens in the story of a joke. You say, "Mr. Schultz walked down the street and saw two elephants and walked into the bar and had a drink..." You don't have to tell everything about the street and Mr. Schultz and his wife; we can follow the story without that. So although you may know all about the characters, that gives you the freedom to be even more selective about what you reveal about them in the screenplay. I don't think I just made clear sense ...

Anyway, it's very exciting to be ridiculous. I wish I could be even more so than I am. Jump! Jumping is a lifeline, not the suicide or the predictable. It brings you to life. Take the character and put him where he least wants to be. If it's honest, it'll be worth exploring.

And eventually the process does lead into a structure, right?

Hopefully. Maybe I'm just urging people to free-associate and fool around because I'm not very good at sitting down and organizing the structural elements. I wish I could do it, I wish I were more of a storyteller. I wish I could get an outline early. Usually the outline I get comes halfway through the process. I go through the pile of scenes and notes and I find things that'll work, and finally I know the characters and the scenes I'll need, and I begin to put it all together.

Are you influenced by knowing which actors will play the roles?

It never matters to me. I don't care. It's not usually worth knowing. However, when I wrote *The Sterile Cuckoo* it was valuable to know that Liza Minelli was going to play the young girl. She was nineteen when I met her—there was a freedom in her that was wonderful and very much like Pookie Adams. But usually it doesn't matter. It may even be a hindrance because I'd be writing for that actor rather than the character.

Do you do much rewriting?

Ninety percent. But I have to be careful. Sometimes I do a rewrite and make the script tighter and leaner, smoother, and I say, "This is better." But it's not better. It got polished to death. It's as if we all walked around polished all day, saying perfect things. We all meet somewhere, the door opens exactly on time, it's all very neat and polished. I think polished is one of the worst words in the language of writers. Slick! There's even accomplished slick, which tries to fool us and often does. But slick is polished. The truth is, too often I'm guilty of all this stuff.

But even when you've handed in the best version you can do, other people can change it. How do you feel about that?

I want to retire to Martha's Vineyard . . . Sometimes a director will say, "We don't need this line," and I'll say, "We do need this line." He'll say, "Why?" and I'll say, "I don't know." When you start taking out a little of this and a little of that, it's not the same. Nobody should fool around with that stuff, or at least they should try to understand or see what is valuable. Audiences "get it" without knowing why they get it. We don't always understand why something works, but we know when it does. Rhythms, maybe. Natural confusions.

Has the process of having things changed bothered you over the years?

It hasn't bothered me enough. I'm an easy target. I'm too happy to have a parking space. I think I was a better writer before I had a parking space.

So far it hasn't bothered you enough for you to become a director. Are you tempted?

Yes, if I didn't have to show up every day.

What would you tell aspiring writers?

I think you have to write every day. It's necessary exercise. It doesn't have to have anything to do with your work, but probably it will, even though you may not see it right away. I used to do it more than I do, and I've suffered for not doing it enough. But I get lazy and I don't work hard enough, and consequently sometimes I feel a lack of freedom, so I have to begin working out every day on that damn paper. The truth is I love paper. There is nothing more wonderful than fresh reams of square-edged, three-hole typing paper. I like to buy six or seven reams before starting—pile them up somewhere and go into a state of disbelief when I'm down to the last one. Of course I waste a lot of paper, but I save that, too. Because sometimes in the desperation of the last minute there is life in what seemed to be a waste. So don't throw anything away.

CHAPTER 5

How to Write Outlines and Treatments

OUTLINES AND TREATMENTS ARE intermediate steps on the way to writing the script. They are narrative summaries of your story, much shorter than the script will be. The outline that you create in order to help you structure and write your story, and that nobody but you will ever see, can be in any form you want. But if you are writing an outline or treatment that will be read by others, there are specific format guidelines you should follow, and those guidelines are what we'll be discussing in this chapter.

• DEFINING OUR TERMS

An outline is a brief narrative summary of the story of the script you have written or intend to write. Outlines are from five to fifteen pages long, double-spaced. Because they are so brief, they usually do not include sample dialogue.

A treatment is a somewhat longer narrative summary of the story of the script. Their usual length is from fifteen to thirty pages, double-spaced, and typically they do include some sample lines of dialogue.

Both outlines and treatments differ from short stories in that they are written in the present tense rather than the past tense. For example, here are a couple of lines that might occur in a short story:

> Henry paused at the door, turned, and suddenly began to weep. Eliza heard his sobs and ran in from the kitchen. Embracing him and gently rocking him back and forth, she asked what was bothering him.

Here is the way the same lines would be written if they were part of an outline or treatment:

> Henry pauses at the door, turns, and suddenly begins to weep. Eliza hears his sobs and runs in from the kitchen. She embraces him, rocks him back and forth gently, and asks what is bothering him.

If you've written short stories or novels or even articles, writing in the present tense may seem awkward to you initially, but you'll get the hang of it soon enough.

• WHEN ARE OUTLINES AND TREATMENTS REQUIRED?

Regardless of what form of scriptwriting you choose as your focus, initially you will need a full sample script that demonstrates your capabilities. If someone is impressed by that script, he may then invite you to present (or "pitch") ideas for additional possible scripts. If an assignment results from that pitch meeting, the first thing you'll have to write is an outline or treatment.

Let's take a look at how this works in terms of feature films. Let's say that producer X has read our sample script, *Nuns on a Rampage*, and loved it. He doesn't want to buy it because his company already has a nun picture in the works (*Nuns on Motorcycles*), but he wonders if we might have other ideas to present to him. We go in and pitch two other feature ideas, *Killer Children from Outer Space* and *Rabid Dogs in Suburbia*. He likes the rabid dogs idea, presents it to his boss who also likes it, and he gets the OK to put it into development. At this point we may already have given him an outline of the idea, one we wrote while working out the story because we wanted to give him something that would help him present the idea to the higher-ups at his company. Next we sign a contract for what is called a "step deal," meaning that we will proceed step-by-step and be paid for each step as we go along. If the producer feels that it's not going well, he can stop at any step along the way, pay us for the work already done, and do what he wants with the material we've turned in so far. The steps normally are a treatment, a first draft script, a second draft script, and a polish. Although the producer already has the brief outline, he'd like to see the story in greater detail before he gives us the OK to proceed with the script, so he asks us to write a treatment. As soon as he sends us off to do the treatment, his company is obligated to pay us whatever amount our agent negotiated for that step of the process. If the producer hates the treatment he can cut us off at this point and bring in new writers, but he still has to pay us for the treatment. The process is the same for television movies. If you get a sitcom or one-hour series assignment, the first step will be writing an outline that is six to eight pages long for a half-hour show and roughly double that for an hour-long show. The person who reads your outline should know who the major characters are, what the central conflict is, who or what is trying to stop the central characters, and how the conflict is resolved. They should also know enough about the main characters that they can picture them in their mind. So basically what you are putting into this brief form is all of the major points that we discussed in the chapters on characters and structure. Stick to the most important points only—there just isn't space in an outline to go into great detail.

For a look at a completed outline that was penned by Wolff for a Movie-of-the-Week project, refer to the outline of "Two Guns" in Chapter 7.

• WRITING TREATMENTS THAT SPARKLE

While the outline functions as a rough sketch of your story and characters, the treatment is your chance to add color and detail. It is usually about twice as long as an outline, and offers a more complete description of characters, settings, and plot twists. The treatment is the all-important in-between step that will determine whether or not the person paying you asks you to go on to the next step: writing the script itself. Many professional writers hate doing treatments because there is so much riding on a work that inherently provides an imperfect means of giving an accurate idea of what the script will be like, due to the completely different format and shorter length. However, treatments are a part of the business, so you might as well learn how to make the most of them.

The first requirement, of course, is that the treatment expand on the outline, while telling the story accurately and clearly. Additionally, however, you now have a chance to more fully employ your writing skills in using lively language to make the treatment come alive. Here, for example, is one way a sequence might be described:

> Rombouts finally catches up with Elias, cornering him in an alley. Elias tries to escape, but Rombouts knocks him down and the two men fight energetically until both of them are worn out. The exhausted Elias notices a fire escape and starts to climb up.

Pretty dead, isn't it? Let's try again:

> Finally Rombouts corners Elias in an alley. Elias rushes him, but Rombouts' tackle brings them both down and they go at each other in a furious, no-holds-barred, bone-crunching struggle until both are too weary to throw another punch. Elias looks up and sees a possible lifeline: the fire escape. His every muscle screaming with pain, he pulls himself up.

This version is much better, and only a little bit longer. The key to making treatments sparkle is to use lively language that evokes images in the mind of the reader. To say that two men "fight energetically" is bland. To say that the fight is "a furious, no-holds-barred, bone-crunching struggle" gives a much more specific and interesting mental image of what goes on. To say that someone notices a fire escape and begins to climb it doesn't bring a very specific image to mind. But saying he "looks up and sees a possible lifeline: the fire escape" cues us to see it as he does (wasn't your mental image this time of a fire escape as seen from below?), and to feel about it as he does (a possible lifeline). And to say "his every muscle screaming with pain, he pulls himself up" gives us a much more vivid notion of how he feels and what that ascent is going to look like than saying, "exhausted, he starts to climb up."

The same use of colorful and specific language will enliven your character descriptions. Instead of saying that Al is "a somewhat cynical middle-aged man who sells cars at an unscrupulous used-car lot," try "Al is forty and dedicated to P.T. Barnum's proposition that there's a sucker born every minute—a philosophy he exercises every day at 'A-1 Used Cars,' where he earns his daily bread."

Another luxury offered by a treatment, as opposed to an outline, is the chance to include some dialogue, which is woven into the narrative itself. How the central characters talk should reveal something about their background and nature. Let's look at a few examples:

> Len looks deeply into Patsy's eyes. "How did you feel when I asked you to marry me?" he asks. "I was in hog heaven," she says.

> Len looks deeply into Patsy's eyes. "How did you feel when I asked you to marry me?" he asks. "Well, I immediately grasped the fiscal advantages of such a union," she says.

> Len looks deeply into Patsy's eyes. "How did you feel when I asked you to marry me?" he asks. "As though every wish I'd ever had since I was a little girl had come true," she says.

We've exaggerated a bit for effect, but certainly each of these responses calls to mind a different Patsy. Since you'll be limited in the number of lines of dialogue you can include in a treatment, make them count: employ them at key points in the story, use them to tell us something about the person speaking, and make sure that the dialogue is as well written as the dialogue in the final script will be.

• SAMPLE TREATMENT

To give you a better idea of what a treatment looks like, what follows is the treatment for a motion picture that one of us (Cox) has co-written for a production company.

There are a few things to note about this treatment. Since the film is to be a broad comedy, the treatment was written with a light-hearted tone as well. Before this treatment was written, the project and especially the major characters had been discussed in detail with the producers (in fact, this treatment reflects the input of the four people on the production team and the executive producer), so the character descriptions in this treatment are rather brief. Finally, each writer has his own style. In this case, Cox likes to specify "CUT TO" and "DISSOLVE" and other cinematic transitions to help the reader visualize the flow of the picture. This is an option, not a requirement.

CAMP WILDLIFE
A TREATMENT
by Kerry Cox

We OPEN with a CLOSE UP on a digital display of a clock on a computer screen. As it clicks over to 7:00 we hear the WHIR of the disc drives, and a PROCESSED VOICE, smooth as honey: "Mornin', lover man. Time to rise and shine, mmm-hmm." A light clicks on as a mechanical arm telescopes out of a stand, reaches over to the bed, and yanks the covers off PRINTOUT, a slender black youth who's sleeping like a dead man. "C'mon, sugar, big day today," purrs the computerized voice, as the mechanical arm reaches to a CD player, slides in a disk, and presses the "Play" button. A BEAT, and the room is SHATTERED by THUNDEROUS MUSIC.

On the music, we begin a MONTAGE of quick cuts that will introduce our characters as they prepare for camp. At first, all we see are tight closeups: a suitcase being filled with food, a cigarette being crushed next to a half-eaten doughnut, a huge butcher knife being stropped to hair-splitting sharpness, several shades of lipstick being sampled on one pair of lips, and so on.

Within the montage we also see TAYLOR, the camp director we'll meet later, cramming a bunch of rubber rafts into a storage shed. It's a struggle, but he finally triumphs—only to have the door spring open and trap him in an avalanche of rafts.

We also get a very quick look at the camp bus passing a four-wheel vehicle on the long, winding road toward the camp. The vehicle has a very unusual and somewhat unsettling emblem on the side of the cab.

Once the campers have all assembled, FRED TAYLOR steps to the podium to address them. He explains that he's replacing the former camp director, who felt the rigors of camp life to be too demanding and decided to return to his old job as an air traffic controller. Taylor goes on to say that he's heard all about the traditional raft race held each year at this camp, and they can just forget it. After all, when "They" come, what good will a silly little rubber raft be? One of the campers remarks that they may not need rubber rafts nearly as much as a rubber *room*, as Taylor goes on to warn them about the impending invasion of Communist armies intent on destroying the American way of life.

Taylor is supported in his ranting by HARRIS PALERMO, an R.O.T.C. buzz-head who idolizes whoever's in charge, regardless of their sanity. As Taylor continues, he expertly and quite nonchalantly fends off various spitwads, paper airplanes, even an apple that he catches and chomps on absent-mindedly.

"And be well-warned," says Taylor. "They *are* coming." At that instant we hear the THUP-THUP of chopper blades, and Taylor hits the dirt, screaming, "Incoming, incoming!" It's a couple of seconds before he realizes it was just a small model being remote-controlled by Printout.

As quickly as he hit the dirt, Taylor is back on his feet and in full vocal stride. "I know what you're thinking . . . 'Us? Ready? How, Mr. Taylor? How can we soft-handed, jelly-bellied, wet-behind-the-ears babies hang in there when the going gets rough?' Well, I'll tell you how . . . SURVIVAL!"

For a lengthy moment we view the proceedings through a BINOCULAR POV. Someone we can't see is watching.

Before the meeting breaks up, the campers learn that they'll be put through what basically amounts to a basic course in survival training as opposed to all the horsey-back riding and arts and crafts advertised in the brochure. And the culminating event: an "Encounter" game, setting cabin against cabin.

We meet our male campers in a slow 360 PAN of the cabin. Palermo, their counselor, is obviously going to have little or no control over them, particularly in the case of the brooding EDDIE, who flicks a burning cigarette at Harris when he's told to put it out. Our other characters:

BRAD- Good-natured and quick-witted, he's the voice of sanity in the group.

TWINK- A walking appetite with a very dry, sarcastic sense of humor.

PRINTOUT- The computer genius who immediately sets about connecting up a bank of equipment that would do NASA proud.

LARRY- The daydreaming Walter Mitty, who drifts into his first fantasy when a couple girls walk by outside. We'll soon see that Larry is a young man whose mind is completely overrun by a classic case of raging hormones.

EDDIE- He wants nothing to do with anyone. In the opening montage, we saw him arrive at the bus on the back of a Harley chopper.

MURPH- A jock with a real blood revenge going against Sally, his counterpart in the girl's cabin.

As we catch a snippet of conversation from each boy, some action is being played out on the floor. It's an Atomic Sit-Up, wherein a towel is placed across a boy's face as he strains against it to do a sit-up. At the appropriate moment, a bare posterior is placed in the flight path, the towel is released, and the boy's face—enough said.

Next, we meet the GIRLS. Their counselor is JANET TERHUNE, who assures them that any trouble they have sleeping can be dispelled through some Zen deep breathing exercises she learned from some guy she met in line at a Burger King.

SALLY cranks out a tough aerobics workout, while RITA has DEBBIE unpack her makeup suitcase. Rita mentions that she has no intention of doing any deep breathing all by herself. Sally insists they should all get into top shape so they can trounce Murph's cabin in the Encounter game, figuring the male ego would crumble after being beaten in war games by a bunch of girls—and then he would be all *hers*!

The dining hall at dinnertime is where Rita makes her first somewhat obvious move at Eddie, who seems a lot more interested in Debbie. THE BUTCHER, the camp cook, encourages the campers to take heaping portions of the unrecognizable main course. After one look at him they choose between the lesser of two evils, and decide they'd better eat.

Eddie is fending off Brad's attempts at civility. Murph is showing no restraint over his disdain of the food as he yells over to Sally that the mashed potatoes taste exactly like the dirt she and her team will be eating during the Encounter game. Then, just as he prepares to flip a huge spoonful of mashed potatoes at his nemesis, The Butcher's huge hand reaches into frame, totally covering Murph's hand. It takes the spoon from him, reverses it, and gently feeds the mashed potatoes to a suddenly hungry Murph.

Back in the boy's cabin after dinner, Printout proudly announces that he's managed to use his computer modem to tap into the food supply warehouse, and the boys happily order everything from steak and lobster to Twink's favorite, chocolate oatmeal. However, while placing this order, Twink takes a hand and accidentally increases the order from three cases to 333,333 cases—and hastily enters the order before the others can see.

Murph remembers he's left his letterman's jacket in the cafeteria, and, despite Brad's teasing about The Butcher being out there in the darkness, goes out to get it. Suddenly he comes face to face with his jacket, hanging in shreds, swinging from a rope.

We CUT to LOUD BUZZERS AND BELLS going off as Palermo bursts through the cabin door, raking his baton against the legs of the beds, exhorting his crew to come to life. We contrast this with Janet, over in the girl's cabin, as she cosmically awakens the girls to the glory of a new morning. BACK TO the boys, where Printout's computer gives a reading of the weather, the breakfast menu, and the temperature of the shower water.

But, it appears that information is only academic, as Taylor informs them of the rigorous enduro course they'll have to pass through in order to earn their breakfast.

And rigorous it is, as kids belly-whop through mud, scrabble under barbed wire, muscle their way along rope bridges, and clamber over large walls. All with Taylor's encouragement, of course: "Just think of the mud beneath your feet as a seething pit of liberal politicians just waiting to give your parents' entire income to the first Save-The-Whales goofball with an open hand, and you'll SURVIVE!" Janet, on the other hand, has her own method: "Find your center, girls. Visualize your goal. Summon the energy from *within*." "I'm about to summon up something else from within," says a panting Rita.

Thanks to Palermo's agility (not to mention his strong back) Taylor's feet never touch the mud as he continues to yell his own peculiar brand of encouragement. In spite of this, things start deteriorating quickly, as Twink loses his pants on the barbed wire, Rita does a belly-flop into the mud, and Eddie succumbs to severe smoker's hack. INTERCUT throughout we see a hand slip in and use a diamond-wire on a couple of bolts supporting a large wall. When Twink's turn finally comes to scale the wall, he's awfully hesitant. But, urged on by an abusive Palermo, Twink takes a running leap, and brings the wall crashing down on Harris. Taylor is quick to point out Harris' survival capabilities, but expresses disappointment when the battered counselor lapses into unconsciousness.

We CUT TO The Butcher's quarters, as Taylor makes his tentative way in to discuss the possibility of giving the kids something for lunch. As he searches for the big man—"Oh, Mr. Cooo-oook . . ."—he spots a hockey mask, a chain saw, and various other horror film spoofs. While examining the chain saw Taylor is startled by The Butcher's sudden entrance, and accidentally fires it up, sawing through several pieces of furniture before it's finally brought under control by The Butcher's simple flick of the "Kill" switch.

In the meantime, Palermo is teaching the boys to dig a proper ditch. "My mother could dig a better hole," he sneers, prompting Brad to ask, "You make your mother do this?"

Janet tutors the girls on the ins and outs of baiting a fishing hook. Sally readily skewers her worm, while some of the other girls aren't quite so eager. Rita substitutes a wad of gum, and sure enough, she's the one who gets the first bite. After landing the flopping critter, everyone wonders what to do. "I'm not sure," says Janet. "Perhaps we simply wait for its life force to drain." At that point, Taylor crashes into frame, grabs the tiny fish, and holds a pistol to its head. "It has to be this way, ladies. Survival of the fittest. In a situation like this, it's either him or me, and I choose . . . meeeee!!!" His scream is cut short as his footing gives way and he plunges into the stream.

From the swirling water we DISSOLVE TO the swirling punch being poured at the "Get Acquainted" dance. Taylor does his lounge lizard best to hit on first aid instructor NURSE BRONSON, a gorgeous creature who sets Larry's hormones into overdrive.

At first, the dance is a typical camp dance—boys on one wall, girls on the other—until Sally grapples Murph into a slow dance. Larry isn't dancing, but it's not for want of trying. He's turned down with alacrity by every girl in the place, including Debbie. It's interesting to note, however, that she only turns him down after Rita expresses her opinion of him: "And now, representing other life forms . . ." Rita is hot for Eddie, calling him, "Dangerous . . . I swear, he looks just like Billy Idol."

Larry approaches Brad about his girl problems, and Brad tells him they sense his desperation. He needs to settle down, maybe take a couple cold showers, do some push-ups. Larry protests that he's tried doing push-ups *in* a cold shower, and it doesn't seem to help. Eddie has some advice: "Ever thought of just getting laid?" Larry looks at Brad—he hadn't thought of that.

Eddie heads over to Debbie, asking her if she wouldn't like to step outside where it's a little more quiet. Debbie is completely out of her league, and she knows it. She somehow manages to put him off, although she unwittingly makes it sound more like a raincheck than a turndown.

In the meantime, Palermo has managed somehow to talk Janet into an evening stroll, saying, "You know who you remind me of? You know that girl . . . the one in the movies? You know who I mean? You look just like her." "Thank you," says Janet, just as they hear some NOISES in the bushes nearby. Against Harris' better judgment they investigate, only to come face-to-face with The Butcher, who insists they return to the dance. "No telling who—or what—might be lurking out here," he intones. Harris hastily agrees, dragging Janet back inside.

Back inside at the dance, it looks like Larry has finally found a dance partner when he starts to lead Nurse Bronson toward the floor, only to have the LIGHTS SUDDENLY GO OUT! At first there is nervous laughter, and the usual hoots of kids in the dark. Suddenly, a LOUD VOICE BOOMS into the room: "Stay out of these woods!" followed by the crash of broken glass as rock after rock smashes through the windows.

There is a stampede for the door, but once the kids are outside they're thrown back by the WOOSH of a huge object bursting into flames. It's a structure in the form of the emblem we saw in the opening montage, painted onto the side of a truck, and it's fully ablaze. As the campers all stand in stunned silence, the fire reflecting on their faces, Brad turns to Twink. "Know any good campfire songs?"

THE NEXT MORNING, Taylor and HUNT MCQUADE, the local sheriff, are discussing the events of the night before. As Harris counts double-time cadence for his cabin, first running forward, then running backwards, Mcquade reflects that perhaps the campers have taken a dislike to Taylor's rigorous survival program. Taylor comments that he's a veteran of many camp pranks, and never before have they cut the camp's phone wires. He doesn't think the kids were responsible. Mcquade promises to ask around, but suggests that Taylor should maybe ease up a little on the kids.

That day, during aquatics training, Murph accuses Sally of shredding his jacket. He even thinks she had something to do with last night's pranks, in an effort to scare the boys out of the woods. Sally retorts that she would never go to such lengths to scare boys, they were born scared. This of course leads to a diving competition, which Murph painfully loses with a five meter belly flop that practically knocks him unconscious.

Nurse Bronson, in the meantime, instructs a class in CPR, using a dummy to demonstrate mouth-to-mouth. We watch from Larry's POV, as he drifts off into another daydream. This time he's the CPR dummy, and Nurse Bronson applies mouth-to-mouth that quickly turns into something much, much more. He awakens when he's stampeded by volunteers willing to demonstrate the crosschest carry on Nurse Bronson, who has leaped into the pool to act as victim.

In the hills surrounding the camp, we see a glint of the sun off metal, and then go to BINOCULAR POV. "Wouldn't mind jumpin' in that pool myself," says a voice we haven't heard before. "Lemme take a look," says another voice, and there is a brief tug-of-war over the binoculars. All at once the binoculars are dropped, and we JUMP CUT to The Butcher snapping his head around at the sound. He quickly lifts a pair of binoculars to his eyes, but sees nothing. At least, not at first. After a moment, he sees something swinging in a small tree, just a few feet off the ground. We can barely tell that it's a rabbit caught in a snare trap.

During the following couple days of survival training Murph tries to pump up the boys for the Encounter game. The campers learn to eat bugs, build shelters, sprint through the woods, and ride horses. In fact, it's at the horse stables that an interesting event occurs. Debbie happens to notice Eddie's fear of horses, which she mentions to Rita. "Big deal," says Rita. "I mean, can Rob Lowe ride a horse? Who knows? Who cares!?"

At one point, Nurse Bronson calls for volunteers as she demonstrates the proper method for sucking the poison out of a snakebite wound. Palermo pushes a reluctant Larry forward, and when Nurse Bronson puts her lips to his arm, the poor guy passes out cold.

Amidst all of this we get a quick glimpse of a rabbit caught in a snare trap. As a large pair of hands reach into frame and begin to pry apart the trap, we pull back to reveal The Butcher, as he tenderly frees the little animal. Spotting a spent rifle cartridge, The Butcher picks it up, sniffs it, and carefully surveys the woods. Suddenly he hears the crack of twigs and commotion in the bushes—but it's just Sally and Murph, dashing through the underbrush in an impromptu race. All parties concerned are a little startled by this sudden confrontation, as he tells the kids, "Best if you don't play in this area." Murph counters with macho fearlessness, until The Butcher takes a branch and trips one steel-jawed trap after another, set all around their feet.

While learning the approved method for creating a campfire, Eddie tries to kindle a spark or two of his own out of Debbie, apologizing for coming on a bit too strong at the dance, saying that he just gets a little carried away with really attractive girls. As Brad passes by he catches some of this, and we can see from his expression he's a little pissed off by Eddie's attitude. On the other hand, Rita was within earshot and does everything she can to encourage Debbie to give Eddie a chance. She goes so far as to throw one of her ever-present romance novels at Debbie, insisting that if she ever did any reading she'd see how retarded and immature she is.

We get another quick look at The Butcher, this time as he gazes down from the top of a hill at a small cabin tucked away in a box canyon. There are several MEN walking the perimeter, almost as if they were guarding the place.

INSIDE THE CABIN we get our first look at the SURVIVALISTS, and discover them to be a sort of John Birch group gone insane. They're a bit ridiculous, a bit dangerous, but not one bit intelligent, and they're all concerned about what their leader will say regarding their botched efforts to scare the campers away.

As night falls, romance is in the air back at the camp. Palermo once again manages to get Janet off by herself, only to have Printout's video-camera-equipped model helicopter relay the entire attempted tryst back to the hysterical boys at the cabin.

An entirely different situation develops when Debbie meets Eddie at the horse stables, and, feeling the pressure of her peers and knowing that this is what they all do, she allows herself to be seduced.

The CUT AWAY from that quiet scene jolts us abruptly into the beginning of the Encounter game, which begins with a tearful, moving speech by Taylor. He's just so darned proud of his little soldiers! "Now, of course," he says, "the chances of actually being injured or killed are not as great as in a real war—but it's a start!"

THE ENCOUNTER GAME consists of a fast-paced MONTAGE SET TO MUSIC. We see Murph, decked out in his best "Rambo" fighting uniform, get blasted between the eyes by a paint pellet before the game is two minutes old. In fact, Murph spends every other minute of the game wiping paint from yet another direct hit, incessantly screaming "You missed!" at the invisible enemy.

Debbie and Rita are teamed together, when Debbie tells her friend of her experience with Eddie. She's shattered when Rita reacts with disgust instead of pride, and she bolts off into the woods.

A short distance away, Larry finds her, and makes an effort to lend some comfort. She'll have no part of it: "What is it?" she demands. "You want some too? I guess everyone in camp will be lining up, right?" Larry has no idea what she's talking about as she breaks into tears and races off.

With the Encounter game still in full swing, Murph has taken Twink on a shortcut designed to outflank the girls' cabin. Unfortunately, like most shortcuts it leads nowhere, and the boys find themselves good and lost. They come to a cave, and with the curiosity inherent in all kids they investigate, only to find an enormous cache of weapons. They make radio contact with Printout, only to be suddenly and mysteriously cut off as they cry out for help.

The game comes to a screeching halt, as all gather around Printout's video monitor. He sends the helicopter on an aerial recon of the woods, but there's no sign of the missing boys. Then, The Butcher appears, and points to an exact location on the map. "Try here." Printout sends the chopper to the quadrants on the screen, and we can see Twink and Murph being escorted into the Survivalists' cabin. The apparent LEADER of the group is there, and through computer-enhanced blow-ups we can see . . . it's Hunt Mcquade, the Sheriff.

Knowing now that the local police are not to be trusted, Taylor feels it's his duty to get his campers back—especially since they prepaid their tuition in full. He is prepared for battle by his trusty lieutenant Palermo, whose only wish is that he could go along, instead of having to stay back and defend the women and children (sure it is).

CUT TO the Survivalists' cabin, where Murph and Twink wrestle against the bonds around their wrists and ankles. It looks like Murph has managed to free one hand, and he sidles over to Twink, back-to-back. After a couple moments of fierce effort, he succeeds only in tying himself to Twink.

In the front room, the Survivalists are at a loss as to how to dispose of their captives. They've seen the illegal arms stash, they know of the secret bomb shelters all around the cabin. That's exactly the kind of information the Survivalists don't want getting out, so when the Big One is launched by the Russkies, they won't be beseiged by people with less foresight, without shelters of their own. Mcquade figures they'll just have to wait until dark, kill them, and get rid of the bodies.

Back at camp, Printout predicts a 98 percent probability that Taylor will screw up the rescue attempt. Brad agrees, and convinces the rest of the boys that they have to help. Eddie is the only one who won't get involved. In the immortal words of Humphrey Bogart, "I stick my neck out for nobody."

The boys succeed in mobilizing the entire camp into action, including all the junior counselors, Palermo, Janet, and the girls' cabin. In fact, the only holdout other than Eddie is Debbie, who's too embarrassed by the whispered innuendos and sly jokes some of the boys subject her to. It's then that Janet shows another side of herself, revealing a person who knows she's different, but accepts herself for what she is. She tells Debbie that she must be the same. She has to admit she made a mistake, and live with it. She needs to regain control of her life.

Meantime, Taylor is off, swearing to return with his shield or upon it. JUMP CUT to Taylor swinging upside down from a foot snare, his assorted weaponry cascading to the ground like rain. JUMP CUT again, and Taylor is tossed into the back room of the cabin, along with Murph and Twink. He tells the boys not to worry, that everything's going according to his master plan.

Knowing that time is of the essence, Brad has organized the campers and counselors into various units, each given specific chores. Since there are no real weapons on the grounds other than the paint pistols used in the game, they have to be inventive. So, we see clothing being painted, potatoes being thrown in bags, pots and pans counted and dispersed, and all kinds of activity that looks purposeful, even though we can't figure out what the ultimate use for all these items will be.

When a helping hand is needed for last-minute preparations, Debbie finally shows up, much to Janet's approval. Both of them head over to the stables to get the horses, taking all but Thunderhead, the riding counselor's horse, who's gun-shy and just plain hard to handle. Before they leave they see Eddie, and Debbie lags behind, telling Janet she'll catch up, and turns to confront Eddie. He's as smart-assed as ever, wondering if she came back for an encore. She asks why he's not helping, and he repeats his stance that it's none of his business. She tells him she thinks he's just afraid—not of getting hurt, but of getting involved or showing any feeling. He laughs off her pop psychology, and she leaves him there, alone with Thunderhead and his thoughts.

THE ASSAULT BEGINS. The Survivalists are suddenly pelted by empty lipstick cannisters (thanks to Rita) filled with something that spews a foul-smelling smoke into the room. Printout's helicopter drops cannister after cannister down the chimney, until Mcquade finally fires a gun up the chimney and wounds the chopper, which goes whining off into the distance.

During the diversion, Larry and some boys lead a paint gun assault on the back of the cabin, only to be repelled by Survivalists firing real bullets. Mcquade sends several men out into the woods, in spite of the Russian, Black, and Mexican VOICES booming through the woods (which are caused by Palermo and company speaking into Printout's synthesizer).

One by one, the Survivalists out in the woods are ambushed by the resourceful kids, who use everything from bows and arrows to slingshotted phony nail tips to overcome the men. Janet has an apparent assignment to gather a certain form of herb, which she sets about doing as Brad drags Palermo off the synthesizer. The poor confused goof was screwing up so badly he was starting to sound like Max Headroom on acid.

The Butcher has backed a huge truck up to the bomb shelter area, and proceeds to dump an enormous amount of some goopy substance right into the open holes.

Back at camp, Eddie listens to the distant sound of automatic gunfire.

We see one confrontation after another ending in the kids' favor, until Larry and Debbie are both outsmarted by a Survivalist who spots their primitive rope snare. He holds it in front of them, wondering if he can hang both of them with one rope, when Debbie suddenly WHISTLES, and we hear HOOFBEATS. The rope straightens with a jerk, tightening around the Survivalist's wrist, and he's dragged screaming off through the bush. Debbie's horse has come through.

Brad isn't so lucky, however. Instead of a trusty horse, he's stuck with Palermo, and when they're confronted by a Survivalist with a knife that makes The Butcher's knife look like a Boy Scout special, Harris panics and runs. Brad is left with nothing but his paint gun to defend himself with—until the man kicks it out of his hand and way out of reach. It looks like the end, until EDDIE comes whooping into frame, barely clinging to Thunderhead's back, and scoops up Brad while knocking the crap out of the Survivalist. Still at full gallop, they head for the cabin, The Butcher suddenly appearing alongside.

Together they smash in through the back door, and before any of the Survivalists can get into the room, The Butcher hurls his knife into the space between the door and the floor, where it acts as a highly effective doorstop. Taylor, who has managed to tie himself to Murph and Twink, is finally freed, just as Janet has her girls fire flaming arrows spouting unusually thick smoke into the front of the cabin.

From a distance, the campers watch as the captives make their escape out the back, and the smoke drives the Survivalists out the front. Strangely enough, the men are all LAUGHING, barely able to control their hilarity. Janet explains the effects of the herb, which basically acts as a powerful laughing gas. "Must be some really good shit," remarks Eddie.

Mcquade somehow manages to usher his hysterical men into their bomb shelters, only to have them find themselves suddenly swimming in tons of chocolate oatmeal (remember the excess ordered by Twink?). He's furious at first, but the men just look so darned *funny* in there, what else can he do but jump in and join them?

Nobody's laughing a few minutes later, when the campers have the Survivalists in a line, covering them with their own weapons. Taylor can't resist rubbing in their victory, and when he gets too close to Mcquade the big man suddenly grabs him, holding a spring-loaded knife to Taylor's throat. Mcquade orders Eddie and Brad to untie the rest of the men, but before they do we see Larry go off into another DREAM. In this dream he tells Debbie to faint, which she does, and in that moment of distraction Larry leaps up and grapples with Mcquade. He's unable to overpower him, but keeps him busy long enough for The Butcher to come over and give Mcquade a solid thunk on the noggin.

Suddenly he wakes from his dream, only to find himself surrounded by cheering campers! And there's Mcquade, down on the ground and out for the count! Debbie gives him a big hug and kiss, and Larry sees that sometimes dreams *do* come true!

At that moment we hear the staccato thumping of helicopter blades, and we see the little helicopter loom over the nearby hill—followed by three Huey combat choppers, all carrying National Guardsmen.

As the cleanup begins, Taylor is quick to assume credit for the rescue. Larry remains silent, explaining to Debbie that everyone's entitled to their dreams. And hopefully, one of Taylor's dreams is to soar with the eagles, because when one of the choppers takes off, a trailing rope tangles around the camp director's foot, and off he goes into the blue yonder, much to the delight of the campers.

END

CHAPTER 6

How to Write Feature Film Scripts

IN THE PREVIOUS CHAPTERS we've described all of the ingredients that you need in order to write a good feature script: an interesting and salable idea, a structure that develops that idea into a plot with a beginning, middle, and end, and three-dimensional characters who will make the story come to life. If you've assembled all of those elements and used them to write an outline and/or treatment, the final step now is to write the script itself.

• THE BASIC FORM OF A FEATURE SCRIPT

Comedy feature scripts are usually from 95 to 115 pages long, and dramatic scripts are from 105 to 125 pages long, with each page equaling approximately one minute of screen time. Scripts include both dialogue and a description of the action. As we'll discuss in more detail below, scripts do not concern themselves very much with camera angles and camera directions.

Feature scripts are written in a series of scenes. A new scene begins every time there is a change of location or a change of time. For example, if a couple is talking in the kitchen and then they move into the living room, the latter would signal the beginning of a new scene. Also, if we see a couple talking in the kitchen in the morning and then still talking there that night, the latter would also be a new scene. A new scene begins with a line that indicates whether the scene is inside (INT. for interior) or outside (EXT. for exterior), where it takes place, and whether it takes place during the day or at night. These lines look like this:

INT. THE SUPERMARKET—DAY

EXT. THE BACK YARD—NIGHT

Following the line specifying the nature of the scene is the description of the action. This is written in the present tense. Here's an example:

INT. THE LIMOUSINE—DAY

George and Helen ride in the back. George opens the small refrigerator and sees it is full of miniature bottles of booze.

When it's time for your characters to talk, you center the character's name and write it in capital letters, and below that, with reduced margins, you write the dialogue. It looks like this:

GEORGE
This is the first time I've been in a limo. Jeez, look at this—booze!

In this chapter we'll give you the exact specifications of the format of feature scripts (margin sizes, and so on) but this overview is designed to familiarize you with the basics, and to make it easier for you to read the sample script segments in this chapter. Now let's look at the key components of feature scripts.

• WRITING EFFECTIVE SCENES

Just as a script has a beginning, middle, and end, so does each individual scene. This does not mean, however, that each scene has to begin at the very beginning of the sequence it represents. For example, if your scene is about a wife who is trying to tell her husband, at dinner, that she doesn't want to go with him to his mother's house this Sunday, you don't need to start with the salad. We can join them mid-meal:

INT. DINING AREA—NIGHT

Carla and Fred are in the middle of their dinner.

> CARLA
>
> More potatoes?

> FRED
>
> No thanks. I'm getting fat.

> CARLA
>
> No you're not. Did I tell you that Fran called?

> FRED
>
> Uh uh. What about?

> CARLA
>
> She wants to get together with me. A girls' night out, I guess. I think she's depressed. I feel sorry for her.

> FRED
>
> What does she have to be depressed about? Al is pulling in fifty grand a year.

> CARLA
>
> Well, I think I should see her. Trouble is, the only night she's free is Sunday.

> FRED
>
> Well, that's out of the question. Did you tell her we always go to Mother's?

> CARLA
>
> Yes ... She said would it be such a big deal if I missed just once.

> FRED
>
> She's a damn selfish woman. Mother would think you were mad at her if you didn't come. You told her no, didn't you?

                    CARLA
Uh, well, more or less.

                    FRED
Good.

At this point we might go on to another scene. We didn't see the beginning, middle, and end of their dinner, but we did see the beginning, middle, and end of Carla's attempt to tell Fred that she didn't want to go to dinner at his mother's place that Sunday.

As you'll recall, the general shape of the entire movie is that a character has a goal, meets mounting opposition, gets to a moment of truth, and ends up either reaching his goal or failing to reach it. The same pattern applies to scenes.

In this case, Carla begins her quest when she says, "Did I tell you that Fran called?" This is how she's broaching the subject. She hopes that if she uses Fran's problem as an excuse, Fred will not object to her missing the dinner with his mother. She runs into opposition almost immediately; Fred is not sympathetic to Fran's situation. Carla, again using Fran as a screen, floats an idea: would it be such a terrible thing if she missed a night, just this once? More opposition from Fred. Then the moment of truth, when he asks her whether she told Fran no. The resolution: Carla caves in, says she more or less said no, and Fred says "Good," signaling that as far as he's concerned, the subject is closed.

You can turn the scene around and realize that Fred has a goal, too, whether he's consciously aware of it or not. In this case, Fred is trying to protect the status quo: Carla always goes to Mother's with him, and he doesn't want that changed.

Most of the time you will not formally plan every scene in this kind of detail. Generally you will know what you want to achieve and doing so will owe at least as much to instinct and impulse as to any intellectual process. But when a scene isn't working, it's good to be able to take it apart to see whether any of its constituents is missing. You can examine what each of the characters wants (whether or not he is conscious of it), and what actions he takes in order to get what he wants.

We got to the heart of the scene pretty quickly, but there were a couple of lines first that didn't address the point (she offers him potatoes, he declines and says he's getting fat, she denies it). These brief opening lines are there for two reasons: to give the audience a moment to get used to the new setting (they will not listen carefully until they've had an instant to get used to where they are whenever a scene changes) and to make the dinner conversation more realistic.

Notice also that we only used a line of description of the action at the beginning of the scene, indicating that they are halfway through dinner. Since they keep eating throughout this scene, we could have added much more in the way of action: he sprinkles salt on his peas, she butters her bread, he pours himself some wine. But unless we have a particular reason for describing a specific action, we can leave it to the director to come up with that kind of movement. Of course if we wanted to establish that her husband's bullying is driving her to drink, then we might want to end the scene by writing that she pours herself a large glass of wine and continues eating in silence.

Scenes can be of varying lengths, from only a few lines to many pages. Varying the lengths of the scenes will give your script a sense of rhythm, whereas having all the scenes the same length might make it monotonous.

Some scenes can be completely visual. If a father has lost custody of his child and misses her very much, one scene might consist solely of him watching her, unnoticed, as she comes out of the school building at recess and playing jump rope.

Sometimes you will surprise yourself by realizing that you can throw out a scene with a lot of dialogue and replace it with a short visual scene. Whenever possible, do it. Going back to the divorced father, what would be more effective: having him spend five pages telling a co-worker that he misses his little girl, or showing the scene described above, with tears coming to his eyes as he sees his little girl playing happily?

• THE IMPORTANCE OF SETTINGS

Many newer writers don't give much thought to the settings of their scenes. They're missing an opportunity to enrich their material. You should always strive to maximize the visual interest of your screenplay, and you should keep an eye open for ways to use your setting to reinforce the point of a particular scene.

To cite an example, one of us (Wolff) recently wrote a screenplay in which a father has a talk with his grown daughter, who has not been acting in a very mature way. First of all, it seemed important to get the characters out of the house—a lot of scenes have already taken place there. The father asks the daughter to go for a walk so they can talk.

This was logical, in that her little children were around and it would make sense that the father would want to talk away from them.

They begin their talk, and when it gets to a crucial stage he leads her over to a children's playground and asks her to sit down. The only seats are little toadstool chairs designed for children, and this is where they discuss what she's doing with her life. Since the point of the scene is that the father is trying to get her to grow up and take responsibility for her own actions, having the scene take place on a children's playground underscores that message in the mind of the viewer: father and daughter are out of place there, just as her immature actions are inconsistent with her age.

Not every scene must have a setting that comments on the action, but when you can come up with one that does, so much the better.

At the very least, the setting should be visually interesting. You needn't go into great detail when describing a setting, but giving a description of one or two specifics as well as an overall summary can be helpful. For example, you could write, "The living room is typically middle-American" or you could write, "The living room is typically middle-American: the painting above the couch is a Norman Rockwell print and the magazine on the coffee table is *TV Guide*." The second description is only a line or two longer but it presents a much richer image to the reader.

Remember that the better the reader is able to visualize what you have in mind, the more likely it is that she'll be absorbed by the script. Be brief, but give the reader enough information to allow her to conjure a mental picture.

• DESCRIBING THE ACTION

Just as you should strive for interesting and powerful images when describing a setting, you should find the most effective ways of describing action. We touched upon this in the chapter on writing outlines and treatments, but it's important to reiterate it here.

Many times newer writers will concentrate so much on making their dialogue powerful that they expend no effort on describing the action. Both should be given attention. No need to become flowery or poetic, but look for specific images and use your imagination a bit. Here's a pair of possible descriptions.

"Larry sits down at the dinner table. He looks hungry and takes the first possible opportunity to help himself to the chicken."

"Larry sits down at the dinner table. He eyes the food like a vulture, and immediately grabs a drumstick."

Clearly the second description comes to life while the first one is bland.

• DESCRIBING THE CHARACTERS

The first time you mention a character in a screenplay you type his or her name in capital letters and give a brief description. This is what gives the reader a visual image of the character, so it's particularly important that you do a good job, especially where your central characters are concerned.

The same guidelines apply to character descriptions as to setting and action descriptions: make them colorful and specific. Again, a pair of examples, one bland, one better:

"HARRIET is a housewife in her twenties. She looks exhausted as a result of having to take care of three infants and is no longer as attractive as she once was."

"HARRIET is only in her twenties and once was beautiful, but the strain of dealing with three bawling babies has taken its toll."

In his excellent book, *Adventures in the Screen Trade*, William Goldman points out that scripts are read by actors as well as by producers and suggests that the writer keep this in mind when writing character descriptions.

If your lead character is an over-the-hill cop, you could write, "SAM HART is a paunchy, middle-aged cop who's burned out" or you could write, "SAM HART is middle-aged and carries a paunch, and he suffers from the same problem that a lot of veteran cops do: after twenty years of trying to do the right thing and being kicked in the teeth for it, he doesn't care any more."

The second will sound a lot more appealing to an actor because it suggests that there is a noble reason for Sam's current ignoble state. It also gives a character insight to anyone else reading the script. Naturally this assumes that the description is accurate—we're not suggesting that you make up a flattering description if that would be inconsistent with the nature of the character.

Don't get hung up on specifics of physical description unless they play a part in the plot. If one of the characters later is revealed to be a murderer, based on the discovery of a red hair under the fingernail of the deceased, then by all means specify up front that the character is a redhead. Otherwise keep the descriptions general. If you tell us that the hero is a tall, athletic man in his early thirties, that's enough about his appearance; we don't need to know the color of his eyes, his exact height, or his blood type.

• NO CAMERA ANGLES, PLEASE!

If you've been reading older books about scriptwriting, you probably are under the impression that you have to learn lots of terminology such as "pan," "tilt," "zoom," and so on. Don't.

For over a decade now, the trend has been away from the use of such terms in scripts. They are all ways of describing what the camera does, and that is now clearly recognized to be the responsibility of the director, not the writer.

If you see such terms extensively used in a script, the odds are you are in possession of a shooting script, that is, one that is a generation beyond the script that the writer did initially. A director may make such notations and then have the script retyped to incorporate them.

Once in a while you may have to call for a CLOSEUP (all camera angles and descriptions are written in capital letters), but usually you can use the specific way you phrase the description of the action to suggest the way the scene would be shot.

For example, let's say you write: "Jack digs into his pocket and digs out the spare change. It's a quarter and a dime. It looks like he's about to cry, but then suddenly he laughs uproariously. He hurls the coins away. They arc through the air and land in the water."

There's no mention of camera angles at all, but if the audience is to know that all Jack has is a dime and a quarter, the director will have to show a closeup of Jack's hand. If we are to see how his facial expression changes, a long shot is out. If we are to see the coins land in the water, obviously a shot of the water will be called for. In the old days all of these would have been spelled out technically, but no longer.

• THE IMPORTANCE OF DIALOGUE

We have already discussed dialogue extensively in Chapter 4, so we will only touch on the subject here. As we pointed out there, in order for characters to come across as three-dimensional people, they have to *sound* like real people.

The key to making people sound real is knowing them inside and out. Once you know your people and know, via working out the structure of your story, what you're going to have them do, you may be surprised to find how relatively easy it becomes to make them speak.

People reveal themselves by what they say in a manner that goes far beyond the literal meaning of their words. Going back to the sample dialogue we used earlier, when Carla says that her friend Fran is depressed, her husband says, "What does she have to be depressed about? Al is pulling in fifty grand a year." His words are about Fran and the income of her husband, but they also tell us a lot about Fred.

Obviously Fred feels that money is the key to happiness and he can't understand how someone who has money can be depressed. It makes him come off as insensitive and unsympathetic. At the same time, we may surmise from this that Fred probably has never had much money himself, or he'd know that it isn't a guarantee of bliss.

This is a dimension of dialogue that you must consider, because it can work for you or against you. The reader (and viewer) won't consciously analyze the impression your character's dialogue is making on him, of course, but some kind of impression will be registering nonetheless.

• THE FEATURE FORMAT

What follows are the specific format parameters that you can use in writing your feature script, and they are followed by several pages of a feature script written by one of us (Wolff). Looking at the sample script pages will help clarify the points. The guidelines pertain to the scripts that you turn in to your agent or producer, not to a shooting script which is put together by the director, shot by shot.

MARGINS AND TABS. To facilitate the typing of your feature script, it's best to set your margins and tabs to the points you will be using frequently. For a pica typewriter (the type size preferred in the industry), the settings are:

17—Left margin (this will allow enough room for hole-punching)
28—Dialogue
35—Parenthetical directions
43—Character's name (above the dialogue)
66—Transitional instructions (such as CUT TO: or DIS-
     SOLVE TO:)

72—Page number (in top right-hand corner)
75—Right margin

CAPITALIZATION. The following are all in CAPS:

INT. (for interior) or EXT. (for exterior), the scene locale and DAY or NIGHT;

A NEW CHARACTER the first time he or she is introduced in the narrative;

The CHARACTER'S NAME above the dialogue;

SHOTS, CAMERA DIRECTIONS, & SOUNDS (i.e., CLOSEUP, CAMERA PANS ACROSS THE ROOM, there is a BANG and Murphy slumps in the corner);

LINE SPACING. Use the following guidelines:

Single space
    —the narrative (which includes the scene description, charac-
        ter actions, camera directions, and sound cues)
    —between the character's name and dialogue
    —the dialogue itself
Double space
    —between the scene locale and the narrative
    —between the narrative and the character's name (above the
        dialogue)
    —between the speeches of the different characters
    —between the paragraphs of long narrative passages
Triple space
    —before starting a new scene.

Always leave an inch to an inch-and-a-half at the top and bottom of each page. An airy feeling facilitates smooth reading.

BEATS AND PAUSES. The screenwriter always attempts to compose dialogue which is as natural sounding as possible. In some cases, that means the character talks in incomplete sentences, pauses for reflection, or perhaps changes his mind in the middle of a speech. Such breaks in speech can be indicated in the dialogue by three dots, a (pause) or a (beat). They all achieve the same effect, so which you use really is a personal preference. However, they should not be overused.

NUMBERING YOUR SCENES. As you'll see, our sample pages don't have numbered scenes. It's not a bad idea, though. The advantage is that it allows you to identify the scenes easily for rewriting purposes. If you decide to number your scenes and the page ends in the middle of your scene, type the word (CONTINUED) in parentheses at the lower right-hand corner of the page. Then on the top left-hand corner of the next page, type the scene number and CONTINUED: (with no parentheses). Double space and continue typing the scene.

THE TITLE PAGE. The title page has the following features: The title in caps, in quotes, and underlined, is centered about 2½ inches from the top. Centered eight to ten spaces under that is: Written by or Screenplay by, and four spaces under that, the author's name.

In the bottom left-hand corner is the draft number (i.e., First Draft, Revised Draft, Final Draft) and the date. However, indicating the draft number is more appropriate when a script has been commissioned, and indicating the date of a spec script may just make people aware that it has been circulating for a long time. An alternative is to use an unobtrusive code (A, B, C) to help you keep your drafts straight.

In the bottom right is the agent's name and phone number, or the name, address, and phone number of the writer.

REGISTRATION NOTICE. You should register your scripts with the Writers Guild (see Chapter 15 for details) and note on the title page that you have done so. However, you should avoid large copyright notices and other references to whatever measures you've taken to protect your material; these tend to suggest paranoia.

CUT TO: and DISSOLVE TO: It is understood that when a scene is concluded and a new one begun that there must have been a cut. Therefore, it's not necessary to type it every time. Occasionally, it may be valuable to use the transitional instruction, DISSOLVE TO:, to help the reader realize that a period of time has transpired.

Suppose in your script a man is being released from prison and he promises the warden: "In two years I'll be a prosperous man. You won't recognize me." The next scene is two years later with the man going into a bank, wearing an impeccable business suit. After the first scene, you should type DISSOLVE TO: on the right-hand margin, and after double-spacing, EXT. 1ST NATIONAL BANK—DAY—TWO YEARS LATER on the left margin.

FINDING PROFESSIONAL SCRIPTS. If you live in the Los

Angeles area, there are several places where you can look at scripts. The Academy of Motion Picture Arts and Sciences Building at 8949 Wilshire Blvd. in Beverly Hills (278-8990) has a library on the 4th Floor that is open to the public for reading and study. Hundreds of produced screenplays are available for your perusal on the premises (they cannot be checked out). There is no charge, but your driver's license must be left with the librarian while you take your script to your table. The library is open during business hours each weekday except Wednesdays.

Another script library can be found at UCLA in the Theater Arts Library located on the second floor of the University Research Library. Nonstudents must get a reference card at the main desk (no charge) and present the card at the Theater Arts Library. Scripts cannot be checked out. Call 825-4880 for library hours.

If you're not near L.A., you might try the communications department of the nearest college. Alternately, you can buy scripts by mail order. Check the classified ads in the back of a current issue of *American Film* magazine for names and addresses of places that sell scripts.

The following scene, written in feature script format, should serve as a good reference for you in formatting your own script.

SAMANTHA

I know you don't mean that. You and me are friends.

Howard softens a little, but he'll be damned if he'll show it.

HOWARD

You'll be in the women's penitentiary by the time you're eighteen.

INT. FANCY FRENCH RESTAURANT—NIGHT

Howard and Laura arrive. She's impressed.

LAURA

My goodness, when you said dinner, I didn't imagine a place like this.

HOWARD

It was Lou's idea. I was thinking of a deli . . .

The Maitre d' approaches, gives them an up and down look (they're not really dressed for this place), sighs, and escorts them to a table near the kitchen doors.

LAURA
Howard, if you want, I'll tell Sam she'll get the spanking of her life if she tells anybody about your arrangement with Roger.

HOWARD
No, I promised . . . besides, do you think a spanking would stop her?

LAURA
(laughing)
No.

Their snobbish French WAITER arrives.

WAITER
Bonsoir. Your first time here?

HOWARD
Yeah.

WAITER
(condescendingly)
I thought so. My name is Jean-Paul. I'll be your waiter. I'll be serving you.

HOWARD
Our names are Howard and Laura. We'll be your customers. We'll be tipping you—maybe.

The Waiter gives them menus.

WAITER
(to Howard)
Let me know if you need help with the French.

Howard gives him a dirty look and the Waiter leaves. Laura looks at the menu.

HOWARD

I'm sure the police and the insurance people have been all over this case. But can you think of anything they might have missed?

LAURA

I refused to talk to them at the time. But one thing did strike me as strange.

HOWARD

What's that?

LAURA

A month before all this happened, Peter got a call in the middle of the night. There was some sort of problem with Len Connelly in Spain. Peter went over on the next flight.

HOWARD

Who's Len Connelly?

LAURA

He was Peter's best friend. They grew up together. Len was an outsider. No friends, no family except for his mother. Peter took him under his wing and they were practically inseparable. Len went to Europe about six years ago to travel and work—I guess to find himself.

The Waiter returns.

WAITER

Have we decided?

LAURA

I'd like a small dinner salad with oil and vinegar dressing, and the coq au vin. And a glass of white wine.

WAITER

Very good, Madame. And has Monsieur made up his mind?

HOWARD

Monsieur would like white wine, small salad, French dressing, and a burger.

                    WAITER
                    (loudly)
Monsieur, La Feuille de Choux does not serve hamburgers!

Heads turn, Customers AD LIB expressions of shock and contempt.

                    HOWARD
I see. Does La Fooey de Shoes serve steak tartare?

                    WAITER
Of course.

                    HOWARD
Then bring me that. Immediately, please. Don't wait for the coq
au vin.

                    WAITER
Very well. Although most people consider it rude to begin before their companion.

                    HOWARD
Thank you for that insight. Go away.

                    (The Waiter
                    leaves. Howard
                    turns to Laura)
So what happened in Spain?

                    LAURA
Peter was over there for a few days, and when he came back he
wouldn't talk about it. We had a big fight. We needed the money
he used for airfare for other things.

                    HOWARD
Where is Len Connelly now?

                    LAURA
I don't know. Somebody said they saw him in town once, but he
never came to see Sam and me.

                    HOWARD
Hmmm.

The Waiter arrives with the steak tartare.

> WAITER
>
> Is this satisfactory?

> HOWARD
>
> Perfect. Hang on a second.

Howard mashes the raw egg into the raw ground beef and forms the beef into a big patty with his hands as the Waiter looks on in horror. Laura GIGGLES.

> WAITER
>
> Monsieur!!

Howard hands him back the plate.

> HOWARD
>
> Medium rare, please.

We conclude this chapter with interviews with two top feature writers, Colin Higgins and Larry Gelbart. Both men boast a long and impressive track record in writing movies that gain both critical and box office success, and what they have to say about structure, characterization, and even the use of comedy in feature writing is valuable advice for us all.

COLIN HIGGINS

Colin Higgins was born in New Caledonia—a French Island in the Pacific—to an Australian mother and an American father; he was the second of six boys. He grew up in Australia in the 50s, then moved to the San Francisco Bay Area in the 60s. At 19 he dropped out of Stanford, hitchhiked across the country, and studied acting in New York. Then he volunteered for the Army and spent three years in Europe.

After his discharge, Higgins studied at the Sorbonne in Paris, then returned to Stanford for his B.A. degree. After graduation, he worked as a seaman on a ship sailing to the Orient, before enrolling as a student in the UCLA Film School in 1967. For his Master's thesis, he wrote a script called "Harold and Maude," a screenplay that "Paramount Studios bought in one weekend," Higgins recalls.

Higgins went on to write *Silver Streak*, wrote and directed *Foul Play*, co-wrote and directed *9 to 5*, and scripted and directed *The Best Little Whorehouse in Texas*.

There's been criticism of some new writers that they don't have the life experiences to call upon in their writing. Certainly in your case, you've had enough adventures to keep you at the word processor for a few more decades.

A lot of my experiences have been invaluable. But that's not to say that I can't lift the experiences of other writers. (laughter)

I suppose your own life is your best resource. It's funny looking back ten or fifteen years to my travels around the world and saying, "Ah yes, when I was in Florence . . ." I sound like an old man looking back over his life!

Experiences do help you as a person, and consequently as a writer. The three years I spent in the Army were terrific in stabilizing me, making me more adult. When I came back from Europe, I felt more mature than my classmates. I had seen the world. I had lived in Paris and seen it all.

When did you come to Los Angeles?

1967. After graduating from Stanford, I sat down and asked myself what I really wanted to do. I decided I didn't want to continue as an actor, that I wanted to come to Hollywood with all its glamour and promise of success. But I didn't know anything about film—I was just aware of the studios and the movie stars and the glamorous aspects.

So I enrolled in the graduate program at UCLA and learned about film, which was another expanding experience for me. I learned about film as an art form—the basic stuff—what you can do with two images by putting them together.

You wrote Harold and Maude while you were at UCLA?

Yes. I had made two short films at UCLA that had gotten some exposure—I had managed to sell them to a packager of student films. It was my impression, however, that the studio execs and producers would look at these films and say, "Great little short, but can you do a feature?" What they wanted was a feature, and I figured that I could give them a feature if I wrote a script.

Why do you think** Harold and Maude **has enjoyed such long-term popularity?

Ruth Gordon used to have a saying that the basis of every love story was "having someone to tell it to . . . and the beauty of *Harold and Maude* was that these two misfits had someone to tell it to." I guess that's as good an answer as any.

Although you mention that you used screenwriting as an entry to becoming a director, you've become quite a well-respected writer.

I now feel comfortable calling myself a writer, but for many years I didn't call myself a writer. I had such enormous respect for writers that I knew I didn't deserve the classification. My idea of writers were giants like Hemingway or Faulkner. The way I would get around comparing myself to them—extremely unfavorably, I might add—was that I would not refer to myself as a writer. Therefore, that negative part of my ego that wanted me to fail had nothing to attack. That little voice would say, "You can't write; you can't do it because you're not Hemingway." And I would return with, "I never said I was a writer." I just told myself that I was putting some images down on paper.

Can you tell us the process you go through when you write a feature? What's your starting point: an idea, a character, or is there no general rule?

I'll start with an idea—a premise I can sum up in one line—and characters that I like who I feel will provide conflict or an attitude I can play with. Then I research and outline extensively.

Where the story comes from I don't know. On a metaphysical level, I do believe it's already written in some other dimension. So all I have to do is get out of the way. But that's easier said than done.

Do you structure your scripts in terms of a three-act paradigm?

I have an ingrained sense of structure, a sense of when certain things should happen in the course of 120 pages. I know that you should have the characters introduced and the problem set up by page 20 or 30, and the escalating conflict with the twist around page 60. Trip up the characters, send them in another direction. Basic stuff like that.

Do you lay out your plot on index cards before you go to first draft?

I usually write a treatment of ten or twelve pages, and jot down notes of some of the scenes, or particular lines of dialogue that I find funny.

One of the major problems that I see in many comedy features is that the comic scenes are too episodic, and not integrated well into the storyline. Do you know what I'm getting at?

Sure. I'm usually able to avoid that problem because the comedy I do involves realistic people in improbable situations. I don't just devise set-ups for jokes. I don't write jokes very well.

I get comedy from the attitudes of the characters—taking a Gene Wilder and putting him in the men's room with Richard Pryor, and having Pryor turn him into blackface, and trying to get him on a train. This is a totally improbable thing, totally ridiculous. But the way you make it work is you give the actors very credible attitudes. So Gene's attitude is, "This will never work," and Richard's attitude is, "This has gotta work because we gotta get on the train." And so Richard tries to teach Gene how to get rhythm. (laughter)

That's one of my favorite comedy scenes of all time. How much of that scene was on paper, and how much was improvised?

Oh, the whole thing was on paper. I remember I was living on Beverly Glen in a one-bedroom apartment, and sitting at my desk laughing as I wrote that scene.

Or the scene in *Foul Play* in which I had Dudley Moore taking off his clothes, while Goldie Hawn doesn't see that he's taking his clothes off—and they play that double entendre. She's at the window and asks for binoculars, and he says, "Oh, you're into that?" And I'm laughing to myself and thinking, "What am I writing here? What can two people possibly do with binoculars?" (laughter) But Dudley just played it out. And if you keep the attitudes consistent between the two people, then it becomes hysterical.

Those are the scenes I like to do—those long, improbable scenes in which one thing builds upon another. In *9 to 5*, I had Lily and Jane and Dolly throw a dead body in a car and have a policeman stop them.

But I make sure that these comic scenes advance the plot, that they stitch in perfectly with the fabric of the story.

To me, getting the narrative flow is simply a case of seeing the movie in my head, and playing it over and over again. So you know the story from all different angles. And when you see an opportunity for comedy, you're ready. You say, "Oh, if that character were the nurse, then I could do the whole hospital schtick . . ."

When you play a scene in your head, do you envision a particular actor or actress? Do you stick in a Gene Wilder or Richard Pryor?

I wrote that role in *Silver Streak* for Richard. I had never met him, but I used to listen to his comedy albums. And I got his patterns down, his comic rhythm.

Actually the role that Gene played I had written for George Segal; in fact, that's why his name is George. After Gene got the part, I adapted the part somewhat for him.

Did Arthur Hiller get the movie up on the screen the way you envisioned it?

No, but I don't think a director should try to translate the writer's vision absolutely. I like what Arthur brought to the film. If I, as a director, tried to get exactly what I pictured in my head on film, I would be limiting myself. When I write a scene, I sometimes sketch out the set so it becomes real for me. But when the Art Director comes in to talk about the movie, I'm not interested in bringing out my sketches. I can always go back to those. But I want new and better stuff. It's a collaborative process.

It's like an actor working with me during rehearsals—going over the dialogue and making the material play as effectively as possible. I don't like changing things on the set. But I want the actors' input during rehearsal.

I understand that you were brought in as a script doctor on the 9 to 5 project?

Well, Fox already had a script by Patricia Resnick, and Lily, Jane, and Dolly were already set to star. They brought me in to do a rewrite and direct.

I knew immediately that the story wasn't right. The biggest problem I felt in Pat's draft was that the women actually kill the boss. To me that gave us much too dark a comedy. There had to be a way for our stars to have their cake and not ruin the light comedy tone.

So, producer Bruce Gilbert and I went to Cleveland and spoke to a group of women about their jobs as secretaries. We heard a number of horror stories about low pay and sexual harassment and bad working conditions. It was like a union meeting. Very dull.

Finally, I asked these women if they ever fantasized about killing their bosses. Well, you wouldn't have believed it. The place went wild. I heard one terrific story after another about how they would do away with their bosses in a fantasy way, and I knew we had the key to our story: Lily, Jane, and Dolly would each fantasize about killing their boss never expecting to pull it off. But a humorous universe makes it happen and the women end up paying for their upset of world order, as they used to say in Elizabethan comedy.

Any advice to aspiring screenwriters?

What always surprises me in reading material from new writers is the pervasive lack of professionalism in the presentation. Regardless of the merits of the story itself, the script should be presented in such a way that it's easy to read.

The job of the screenwriter is to run the film in the reader's imagination. And nothing should get in the way of that. The format should be consistent, including your scene headings. Pay attention to grammar—not out of some old fustian sense of conformity, but because it works. Good prose is the only way to have a reader envision an exciting film. For example, I can't believe it when I find a sentence without a verb. Verbs are some of the best tools for creating pictures in the imagination of the reader.

What a screenwriter should realize is that executives who buy the scripts go home each weekend or to Palm Springs with a stack of a dozen scripts. It's up to you to make yours the most exciting, appealing, fun-filled reading experience possible. The worst thing you can do is direct the film on paper. There's nothing more boring to read than a shot-by-shot description of the action.

When I write a script, I write in the best prose possible—writing that will vividly create the film in the mind of the reader. Later, I'll do a script for the director and crew with a lot more shots and scene numbers and stage directions.

For example, take the opening page of *Great Expectations* by Charles Dickens. As you get involved in his marvelous prose on the first page, you are shocked when Pip is abducted by the convict. If you saw the movie, you were shocked as well. But if you read the screenplay, written in the shot-by-shot method, you wouldn't feel the shock at all. It had lost all the flavor that Dickens intended. My point being, it's better to incorporate some of that exciting Dickensian prose into your script to conjure up images and emotions in your reader's head. That's the job of the screenwriter.

LARRY GELBART

Larry Gelbart's impressive list of feature credits includes *The Wrong Box, Movie, Movie, The Thrill of it All, Neighbors, Oh, God!* and *Tootsie*. For the stage he wrote *Sly Fox* and co-wrote *A Funny Thing Happened on the Way to the Forum*. He was also one of the creators and writers of the TV series "M*A*S*H," and created "United States." Among his honors are a Tony for *Forum* and a producer's Emmy for "M*A*S*H."

People usually are interested in the point at which a writer considered his or her career to be truly launched. What was that point for you?

It was the experience I had in co-writing *A Funny Thing Happened on the Way to the Forum*. The stage play, that is—I didn't have anything to do with the movie, except squirm. At that time I'd already done a lot of writing; one-liners for comedians, stand-up spots, sketches, interview material for a half-hour radio show. Then in television I did largely variety. The first situation comedy I ever tried was "M*A*S*H," so my whole background had been in variety. With sketches running no more than 8 or 9 minutes one never got the feeling that one could write something that had to sustain itself over a longer time. So when Burt Shevelove and I finished our work on the book of *Forum*, I knew I could do it—with a lot of help, but I could do it. That's the first time I really permitted myself to think of myself as a writer, not just a clever monkey who could turn out material in a comedian's voice, rhythm, and style. In *Forum* we took a place that didn't exist and created characters that were uncast at the time of the writing, and *then* it went to performance, rather than being tailored to a performer from the start.

You've written for stage, film, and television. What are the relative advantages and disadvantages of these media, from the writer's standpoint?

The best thing about television is that, like a good meal, you can serve it when it's hot. There are not those interminable waits of weeks and months and maybe even years that can happen to you in pictures. In TV you can write something on a Friday and begin to shoot it on a Monday, and sometimes you do some very good work under pressure. The disadvantages we all know, and I won't go into them; at this point in my life I'm afraid they outnumber the advantages. Probably the most satisfying is the theater, because there your work is considered yours and pretty much left alone. It's a collaboration as the other two are, of course, but there's less of a presumption that everybody else knows better than you what you meant when you wrote the material. It's the first and probably the last refuge of the writer.

When you come up with a new idea, is it usually apparent to you right away for which medium it is best suited?

Yes, pretty much. For instance, when it comes to anything in longform, I just wouldn't think of television because the idea of breaking up something that takes two hours to tell with forty commercials is an abomination. It puts an unnatural burden on the writer; it's like calling time-outs in a game just to fit in the commercials. When I have an idea for a series—and I know I've had my last one—I know where that goes. Whatever that little selector is inside that tells you where a project ought to go, it works. Unfortunately, when you live out here you tend to think of everything in terms of television or film. If you live in New York you think of most things for the stage. Even though I live here [in L.A.], I've been lucky in having moved around so that I think of that stage option, too.

Many new writers who want to write feature films wonder whether they should try to get into TV first, to get experience and some money. Do you think that's wise, or is it better to go directly to doing features?

I would say, work away at trying to get a feature sold. The TV market is so variable, it's very likely you'll be coming in with last year's goods. Usually people write on speculation for a show that they know, which rarely impresses the people who are producing it. Original writing, like a feature script, always shows you more about somebody's talent than a script for a series, which tells you more about somebody's ability to pick up trademarks and punch-lines and character traits that, in the case of a hit series, have been established for four or five or six years.

If you get used to doing TV, it can be difficult to make the transition to features. The big thing about getting off "M*A*S*H" was trying hard to make things work beyond 24 minutes and 20 seconds—getting back to a more demanding form.

Also, with a screenplay you've got a better piece of material on your hands. It can be a theatrical motion picture, it can go on the network as a movie for TV, or on cable. And if you're still interested in a series, you can use that as a sample to say, "This is what I can do."

Let's talk about some of your feature scripts, beginning with* Neighbors, *an adaptation. What is it in a book that makes it seem adaptable, and how beholden are you to the original?

The process of determining whether or not something is adaptable is almost an unconscious one. If you're reading a book and suddenly in your mind you're seeing it on a screen as a film, something in it has taken over and permitted you to think that way. Truly, I think the only novels that I've ever read that I wanted to do as screenplays were books I picked up and read for pleasure, rather than ones I looked at hoping to find a movie in them.

In the beginning there's a good deal of respect for the source material, but after a time you do begin to feel you can add to what the author's given you without replacing him or her. In this case, Tom Berger, who wrote *Neighbors*, had a great visual sense to start with. He wrote me a letter and said he hoped I would depart as much as possible, that it's the screenwriter's function to take off from the book. So I think he got his wish, and I got mine, which was to preserve the intention of the original. Usually people talk about "opening up" the action of a book when you adapt it. We didn't really open it up that much; one of the wonderful things about the book is that it is a bit claustrophobic, and I didn't want to lose that.

Do you have a preference in terms of doing adaptations versus originals?

As I get older I'm beginning to wish I'd done more originals, but it's only at this point in my life that I feel I can do originals and I'm less and less attracted to adaptations. I think the dependence on adaptations comes from a long experience of collaboration, of counting on someone else—even if you say to yourself, "He's no help at all—but he's there." In the same way you count on the structure and content of what you're adapting, even if you change what's there. I started in this business at a very early age. I was sixteen when I started writing professionally, and I'm in my fifties now, so it's taken a long time to get away from early and long-standing habits.

Do you have any advice for a writer looking for something to adapt—should he or she be looking for something obviously cinematic, or just a good novel with an interesting storyline?

I think that any aspiring writer is probably wasting his or her time by looking at anything current. The agents and the independent producers get a look at new books in manuscript form. With new books, it's likely they have all been seen, bought, or passed over. It would be terrible to, in effect, fall in love with somebody you didn't have a chance with.

But there are wonderful, wonderful things in the body of literature that have never been touched. I was lucky, along with Burt Shevelove again, to have been touted onto a book called *The Wrong Box* by Robert Louis Stevenson and his stepson Lloyd Osborne. Happily it was in the public domain, and happily we didn't have to talk any company into seeing in it what we saw in it. What we finally asked Columbia Pictures to do was to look at a finished screenplay and then of course they saw the possibilities in it.

Another of your feature films, Oh God! *was also an adaptation. How did your involvement in that project come about?*

In the beginning there was David Susskind. David and I did a number of television specials back in the 50s and we always talked about doing a feature together. He had bought the rights to *Oh*

God!—almost everybody at one time or another owned the rights to that book. It was a favorite of a lot of folks, but it never got to the deal stage. I read it and thought it could be a picture.

My original thought was that Mel Brooks and I would co-write it, Mel would play God—even though it would mean a demotion for him—and Woody Allen would play the part John Denver played. I was going to direct it, partly to eliminate the issue of which one of *them* would direct it. Mel was all for it, but Woody didn't want to do it. He had done *Love and Death* and treated certain subjects in it in a way that was much more faithful to his philosophical outlook than *Oh God!* was.

Mel to me was always the obvious choice for God because the book smacked of the "2000-year-old man" routines that Mel used to do with Carl Reiner. Well, Mel began to wonder whether this idea could really go the distance—and I'm still not sure he wasn't right.

I went ahead and did the screenplay without anybody in mind and I handed it to 20th Century Fox, with whom Susskind and I had made the deal originally. They were disappointed by how gentle I'd made it, they were looking for something more off-the-wall. Fox said no. It then went into turnaround, which is a place I find myself a lot, and Warner Brothers picked it up. My only contribution from that point on was to suggest that George Burns play God.

By that time I didn't want to direct it because, frankly, I still feel as though the movie is a first draft. I never felt I licked all the script problems, and I didn't want people asking me, on the stage, questions that I couldn't answer in my own office, about why certain people were saying certain lines and where it was going and so forth.

It did strike us that Oh God! *could easily have been more bitingly satirical. Was your choice to go the more gentle route a personal one or a commercial one?*

There weren't any commercial considerations. Mostly I was treating it gingerly because I don't know where I am on the real-life Oh God situation. I wasn't worried about offending anybody and I wasn't worried about attracting anybody to it. I guess I didn't always confront the material head-on; I just tap-danced a lot, and that's where the gentleness comes in.

I never think about the commercial aspect of anything. I don't know what anybody likes, I just know what I like, and it's that old story: if I do, I hope there are another twenty million people with money in their pockets who'll like it, too.

You said Fox didn't like the script because it was gentle and not off-the-wall enough. It seems that there are cycles in comedy that affect what they buy, right?

Sure. If they're buying *Animal House* and Mel Brooks, really wild stuff, they'll look at a gentle comedy and say, "This is the wrong time for this." But that's another reason to write something *you* think is wonderful, not something you're guessing they'll think is wonderful. Write the best way you can, and don't think about the market too much.

Can you tell us the process you go through when you write a feature—what's your starting point: an idea, a character, or is there no general rule?

No general rule. It tends to be just the beginning of an idea that I'm interested in developing. Yet I've come to learn that there's a great deal of action in character, and that your character may take you someplace you originally didn't dream of going, in terms of plotting.

As you write, do you relate to your main character by picturing a specific actor in the role?

No, I relate to them as living people, but I don't put a face on them. The only time I've written for an actor has been in the theater. Once Zero Mostel said he would do *Forum*, many of the changes we made began to reflect the man who we knew was going to say the words. The same was true of *Sly Fox*. In rehearsal, the more I was in George C. Scott's presence, the more that character became those parts of him that are so dynamic and powerful.

Of course, on *Tootsie*, Dustin Hoffman had been with the project a lot longer than I had, so that was a screenplay that was totally spoken for.

So you feel it's a mistake to visualize your protagonist as a certain actor. Why?

Chances are you're not going to get the actor you want.

And by tailoring it, you may have made the rhythm so specific that it may not work as well with another actor?
Exactly. And it may be a feeling that you'll always have about it, that it wasn't done the way you heard it and saw it. But if that helps you, do it—these tend to be very personal things. It could be, too, that I'm reacting to all those years when I did write for specific performers, so now I welcome the opportunity to write for myself first, and then make the adjustments that will help make it the actor's person, too.

How do you approach a new project in terms of the structure of the screenplay?
As I said, I've been spoiled by doing so many adaptations, in which a lot of the groundwork has been done for me. In a great sense I'm an aspiring writer myself; I have yet to face what a lot of your readers are facing. I have an idea, now I have to get a structure, I want to do an outline, and a step outline, I want to know who my characters are, and so forth. I haven't chickened out, but I've certainly taken the easy way over the years.

Do you think in terms of the three-act structure?
I've never thought of a movie as three acts. My stage experience has been to think in terms of two acts. In "M*A*S*H" we only thought of two acts.
I sort of write to taste. If it feels good, if that indefinable measuring system you have is in balance, it's right. It may not check out to be a true one, two, and three act-er that meets certain requirements, but I can't help it. I can't do it any other way.
In terms of structure, I just know when you're in trouble at the end it's because you were in trouble in the beginning. There's no point in writing the end over and over again; you have to go back and see how well you've given yourself the opportunity to finish successfully. That's why the theater is really the most marvelous place for a writer, because the vacuum is gone. You know from night to night, in rehearsals and try-outs, where you're making it and where you're not.

There is the philosophy that says, "Get the story right first, you can make it funny later." Do you agree?

It's good to know where you're going. You're certainly not bound to any outline, no matter how detailed it is. If on page 3 it starts going in a wholly different direction, terrific, you go with it if it's better than what you had planned. Certainly I never think beforehand about how I'm going to make it funny—that comes in the writing.

I think the only major thing I consciously learned about being funny was on "M*A*S*H." There it was possible every week to examine a specimen, so to speak. It wasn't something where you went away and had to wait sixteen or eighteen months before you saw another one, as is the case with features. I saw that in the editing process we were losing a lot of stuff that I thought was funny. We had to, for time reasons, technical reasons, performance reasons, or even writing reasons. What I began to realize was that the one thing that never went away was exposition. And so, in almost the only conscious rule I've ever given myself, I've made it a point thereafter to make the exposition entertaining. Not necessarily funny—if it can be funny, fine, if it doesn't want to be funny, don't try to force it. But those parts of your script that are essential for your story to be told had better be terrific. A large percentage of the other material is expendable.

Can you give us an example of how to make the exposition more entertaining?

One thing you can do is give your character an amusing piece of business to do, if what he's saying sounds like the reading of the rules at the Academy Awards. If it's so technical, you hide the nuts and bolts. But other than that, just break your head to say it in a way that's diverting, so that you're coating the medicine.

I know I may be asking you to intellectualize comedy, but are there any other approaches of yours that you can tell us?

Contrary to most comedy construction and to the way I learned to use comedy, more and more the characters that I now write seem to say funny things in the middle of the sentence rather than at the end. There'll be an observation and the sentence will go past it, to emphasize that the characters don't think they're being funny. They're just being colorful or making a pithy remark, but not marking it as a punchline. When I watch some of the old "M*A*S*H" episodes I'm a little embarrassed at the frequency and sheer number of jokes. It's like a young lyricist showing you he can rhyme, and rhyme internally, and rhyme your ass off. Again, for me that's a legacy of working for performers who look at the page of material and count the number of jokes. I think sometimes it destroys the reality of a situation when someone says something so apt and witty and bright. Now I try not to overload a page with one joke after another. Also, you come to know what else you can do that's entertaining, by way of expression and performance.

One problem with a writer—with this writer, anyway—is that I sit here and write and I have to fill in every moment in the script. I can't pan across the room and go for the visual stuff the audience will eventually enjoy. I need to make sure that the readers—the producer, director, the actors—feel that everything works terrifically. Therefore my scripts tend to be very full, and I may go back later and thin out some of the parts and possibly build up others.

II

APPLYING THE CRAFT

CHAPTER 7

How to Write Movies-of-the-Week

A RELATIVELY NEW FORM, the television film has become a popular mainstay of network programming. Networks find that by the time a feature film has played in the theaters and been exposed on all the cable channels, the audience that wants to see it on free TV is much diminished. The answer? Make their own movies. These days each network produces between fifty and a hundred such telepictures per year. Increasingly, the pay-TV outlets like HBO and Showtime are also producing original films, to supplement the features available to them.

There are few differences between writing a feature script and writing a Movie-of-the-Week (MOW). Let's look at the differences that do exist.

• BUDGET SIZE

Probably the clearest distinction between feature films and films made for television is how much they cost. As of this writing, MOWs are produced for between one and two million dollars. If the budget is much over that, the project will not be considered for television (exceptions are the miniseries). If your script will be expensive to shoot, perhaps because it requires exotic locations, difficult special effects, or a few thousand extras, forget about trying to sell it to television. If your project can be made for two million or under—meaning no exotic locations, wild special effects, incredible stunts, or other unusually expensive elements—then it might be good for TV or as a low-budget feature film, and other criteria will determine which would be your best bet.

• SUBJECT MATTER

In recent years television films have taken over the realm of "social drama." Very few feature films have been made about social problems, such as child abuse, AIDS, wife-beating, drug abuse, and so forth, while almost every week you have been able to see such films on and made for television. There are some signs now that that trend is petering out, as did the earlier predilection to air "disease of the week" films (people nobly battling cancer/epilepsy/blindness, etc.). So far, no new trend is developing, but undoubtedly one will. As a newcomer, your best bet is to look for stories outside of the current trend anyway. Writers who are already very active in this field will be approached by producers who have their ears to the ground, and will come up with variations of whatever type of Movie-of-the-Week is in vogue. Your strategy should be to come up with stories that demand to be told, whether or not they fit today's subject matter fashion. In any season, the networks will take a few chances on some offbeat material as long as it is special enough. The only point to keep in mind is that there are certain things that films can show that TV can't. Also, you should be aware that networks like films that seem controversial but usually stay away from ones that are truly controversial. For example, doing a film about child abuse is not controversial—who's in favor of child abuse? Doing a film about abortion that really takes a stand one way or the other would be controversial—and therefore has a slim chance of getting on the air. The networks seem to agree with the late Don Marquis' observation that, "If you make people think they're thinking, they'll love you; but if you *really* make them think, they'll hate you."

• LENGTH AND STRUCTURE

A feature film can be from 85 to 135 minutes long. A movie made for television has to fit exactly into a two-hour slot, which means that it must be exactly 94 minutes long (the remaining minutes are used for commercials and promotional announcements).

The structure of a television film is identical to that of a feature film in story terms. That is, to build your story you can use the three-act (beginning, middle, and end) structure discussed in Chapter 3. However, the technical structure is different since allowances have to be made for commercial interruptions. For this reason a TV film script is broken down into seven acts, each one approximately 14 minutes long. Actually, the acts can vary by as much as 5 or 6 minutes as long as the total is 94 minutes.

One thing to keep in mind is that you don't want any act to end exactly on the half-hour or hour, since at those times programs will be starting on other channels, and you don't want to tempt the viewers to switch over.

Since each act will be followed by a commercial, the networks like to have a little climax at the end of the act, something that will motivate the viewers to stick around while the commercials play so that they can see what will happen next. Not every act break has to be a big cliff-hanger, but if you watch some television movies you'll see that most writers do try to build to a moment of heightened tension or interest just before the commercials start.

If you write an outline of your Movie-of-the-Week idea it's helpful, although not mandatory, that you indicate where the act breaks come in. When you eventually write the script, you'll do the same.

• SELLING YOUR TV MOVIE IDEA

The vast majority of television films are made as the result of a network commissioning a script after it has heard the idea for that script. Very seldom do the networks buy a finished script. The reason for this is that network executives like to have "input"; that is, they like to make suggestions right from the start that they feel will help tailor the project to their requirements.

Therefore, it is not a good idea to write a spec script for a Movie-of-the-Week. Instead, for your writing sample write a feature film script. Then come up with ideas for MOWs and be prepared to present them verbally ("pitch" them). You don't take these ideas directly to the networks. Instead, you approach production companies who do MOWs (normally your agent would set this meeting up). If they like one of your ideas, they will go to the network with you and together you'll pitch the idea. If the network likes it, they will determine whether they will approve you as the writer, or whether they want the production company to hire someone else. If you have a terrific writing sample and the full backing of the production company, you may be approved even though you have no credits. It can be an uphill battle. There are a number of writers experienced in the two-hour form that the networks like to use over and over. However, even they had to be first-timers once, so don't assume you don't have a chance. If the network does insist that the company hire someone else, you will still get paid and probably will share the story credit. (This may sound like they've stolen your idea away from you, but they haven't. You've been paid. Of course, you don't have to sell the idea, that's up to you.)

If you are hired to write the script you will be paid between $35,000 and $60,000, assuming you do two drafts and a polish. As a first-time writer, it will probably be somewhere nearer the bottom of that scale. Even if they commission you to write the script there is no guarantee that they won't bring in another writer later to do rewrites, and no guarantee that the project will get on the air. Currently the networks air about one out of three projects that they develop as far as the script stage. However, your script fees will be paid whether it airs or not (a production bonus may be part of your deal, so that you will earn more if it does get on the air).

To give you an idea of what a Movie-of-the-Week outline looks like, we are including an outline of a project called "Two Guns," which Jurgen Wolff pitched initially to Taft Entertainment. They optioned it, and then Wolff and three producers affiliated with Taft took it to the network, which approved its development into a full script. A number of plot changes were made along the way—the outline you are about to read was the "pitching" outline that Wolff used to sell the project.

This outline has one somewhat unusual feature, a prologue. Because the subject matter of this proposed telefilm didn't fit into any of the usual convenient categories (disease of the week, woman struggling in a man's world, male-oriented action-adventure, etc.), Wolff thought it would be useful to lead off with a short scene that would reflect the tone of the entire movie and that would establish that his main character, Wyatt Earp, would still be portrayed as a tough guy even though he would be in his later years.

As you read the outline, notice the way that mini-climaxes are used at the end of each of the acts.

Following the outline, we present an interview with Len Hill, a top producer who sells MOWs but also has the benefit of at one time having been a network buyer of telefilms.

TWO GUNS
outline for a television film
written by Jurgen Wolff

PROLOGUE

Los Angeles, 1919, on the last night before Prohibition will close the city's bars. At one of them, a man in a long black coat keeps an eagle eye on the last-night revelry. Although he is no longer young, he still has the bearing of a dangerous man. This is Wyatt Earp, one-time gunfighter, now about to be unemployed.

A young gangster type gets too far out of hand and drunkenly knocks into him. Wyatt calmly asks him to quiet down. "What's your name, grampaw?" the younger man demands.

"Wyatt Earp."

At first the younger man thinks this is a joke, but once he realizes he's confronting the survivor of the shootout at the OK Corral, he drunkenly insists on a gunfight. He pulls aside his jacket and draws a pistol from his shoulder holster. He tugs at Earp's long waistcoat and it parts—Wyatt is wearing a holster holding his Ned Buntline special, a .45 Colt six-shooter with a foot-long barrel. Wyatt tries to talk the younger man out of the gunfight, but fails.

Finally Wyatt agrees to the gunfight but insists that his opponent know the rules. "Hell, I didn't know there was rules in the Old West," the young man says with a laugh. Oh yes, there are rules, Earp says: they'll have to start back to back, walk ten paces, then turn and fire. They stand back to back. As soon as the young gangster turns and starts to pace, Wyatt turns and uses his gun to knock him unconscious. "You knocked him out when his back was turned!" one of the spectators exclaims.

"That's one of the rules," Wyatt says with a smile.

ACT I

When the Los Angeles saloon where Wyatt Earp works as a guard closes down with the advent of Prohibition, he is once again on the lookout for a new job. He's been a gunfighter, a sheriff, a stagecoach guard, and a private detective—and, if you believe the rumors, a claim-jumper and a racketeer. What's left for the man who survived the shootout at the OK Corral and has lived to see the automobile replace the horse?

There are groups of cowboys riding in Los Angeles; these days not to hold up banks, but to appear in the silent Westerns that are all the rage. Producers like Thomas Ince and stars like William S. Hart are sticklers for authenticity and like to use real cowboys and Indians as actors and extras. As Wyatt drinks bootleg liquor with the ranch-hands, he starts thinking: who is more authentic than he is? He introduces himself to the head of Cosmopolitan Pictures, Samuel K. Bright, a tycoon of shady reputation. Bright orders a screen test.

Earp, a terrific story-teller and actor in real life, freezes when the cameras start rolling. The screen test is a fiasco, but Bright asks him to stay on as a stunt consultant, overseeing the handling of the horses for Bright's biggest picture yet, *The Fall of Rome*.

Earp takes the job but, not far into shooting, tragedy strikes: during a spectacular chariot race the horses break loose from their harness, the chariot goes out of control, and the blond starlet of the picture, Lila Crest, is killed.

An on-the-spot investigation shows the death was caused by improper rigging of the horses—Wyatt's responsibility. The Police Chief arrests Wyatt for manslaughter. Wyatt protests that the rigging was all right, that it was just an accident. The Chief says that's probably true, but the studio is owned by Martin Parker Williams, a reclusive multi-millionaire who has his finger in every major industry in California, and Mr. Williams doesn't like bad publicity. The studio needs a scapegoat for the starlet's death. "And how much are they paying you?" Wyatt demands. "Quite a bit," the Chief says with a smile as he closes the cell door.

ACT II

The bail is set at $5000, which is about $4900 more than Wyatt can afford. As he sits in his jail cell, reading the paper, something on the sports page catches his attention. He scribbles out a note, calls for the guard, and asks him to take it to the gym downtown. By way of payment, the guard can have either a silver dollar or Wyatt's autograph. He takes the dollar.

In the gym downtown, young Jack Dempsey is training for a championship fight as a contingent of reporters look on. One of them is an older man dressed in the Eastern style—a bit of a dandy, but just as capable of handling himself as any of the pugilists. This is Bat Masterson, former gunfighter and now well-paid sports writer for the *New York Telegraph*, out here on assignment. The prison guard finds him and gives him Wyatt's note. Bat reads it and laughs. He asks the guard to tell Wyatt that he'll come by to see him after he's gone back to his hotel for dinner and a bath.

That night Bat goes to see Wyatt in jail. These two men are old friends but below the surface is a sense of competition that is always present when a good man suspects that he has met a better man. Bat questions Wyatt: "Were you drinking the day of the accident?" "Of course I was drinking," Wyatt shouts, "but no more than usual! Can you get the $5000 or can't you?" Masterson can, but it represents his life savings and his entire retirement fund. Grudgingly he agrees to put up the money, but it will take a couple of days to get it wired out from New York.

Bat stops off to see the judge to arrange the details. The judge is a fan of Bat's, and offers to release Wyatt to his custody and to waive the bail. Furthermore, he can let Wyatt out right now. Bat says no, a couple of nights in jail builds a man's character.

The next day, Bat starts checking around about the accident. He goes to see Ruth Benson, the dead starlet's roommate, and senses that she is afraid of something. He charms her into confessing her suspicion that Lila's death was not an accident. She has no proof, only the knowledge that in her last days Lila had been fearful and recently had said, "Soon I'll be rich or dead." But although the women had been roommates and friends, Ruth knows surprisingly little about the secretive Lila.

Bat also tracks down the man who'd been working with the horses on the day of the accident. He refuses to tell Bat anything, and it's obvious that the man has something to hide.

Bat returns to the jail and springs Wyatt. He tells him that he's found out that he thinks Wyatt was set up. For a moment Wyatt is pleased that Bat was so fast to start the investigation. Then a thought hits him: "If you *hadn't* found anything fishy going on, you weren't going to go bail for me at all, were you?" "You're as suspicious as ever, Wyatt," Bat says with a smile—but he doesn't deny it. And he reminds him that since it's his $5000 at stake, he's going to be giving the orders.

Their investigation uncovers the fact that Lila had been having an affair with studio head Samuel Bright; maybe what she said about soon being rich or dead meant that either Bright would get a divorce and marry her (making her rich), or have her killed if she pressed the issue or exposed their affair.

As soon as Wyatt starts asking questions about Lila, the studio head orders him off the lot and instructs the guards never to let him on again.

ACT III
The two men go to the Dempsey fight together and each bets on the opposing fighter. They talk about their strategy in finding out what's going on, and get into a squabble—right at the point Dempsey knocks out his opponent. Bat won his bet but missed the knockout punch that he's going to have to describe in his article. Wyatt goes over to one of the other reporters who's furiously scribbling his story, distracts him, steals the notes, and gives them to Bat.

The next morning, Wyatt and Bat ride in with a gang of cowboys working on a Cosmopolitan western. When the guards recognize them and try to stop them, the cowboys take on the guards, proud to be fighting alongside two legends of the west. During the free-for-all, Wyatt slips away and makes his way to Bright's office. Bright is always surrounded by bodyguards, but he calls them off and invites Wyatt into his inner sanctum. He admits he was having an affair with Lila but says if he killed every starlet he slept with there'd be no one left to appear in his pictures. His wife knows of his habits and the public will never hear of them because he has the city's newspaper editors in his pocket. Wyatt realizes that Bright is a bastard, but is telling the truth.

Bat and Wyatt go with Ruth to Lila's funeral, a lavish Hollywood affair paid for by the studio. Both Wyatt and Bat are charmed by Ruth and go out of their way to be gallant to her. She wonders why Lila's family isn't there—Lila had told everybody that she came from a wealthy family, but none of them are present. Bat thinks this is suspicious. He checks with the funeral parlor owner and finds out that Lila's body was claimed by someone named Rosaria Sanchez.

One of the attendees of the funeral is Margo Lawrence, the glamorous mistress of tycoon Martin Parker Williams. Formerly an actress, she is now the leading hostess in the west, and an invitation to El Dorado, the hilltop retreat of Martin Parker Williams, is the ultimate achievement. She approaches Wyatt. Obviously she is fascinated by power: in the case of Williams, the power of money and influence, in the case of Wyatt, the power of a man who has killed and backs down to no one. She makes a point of introducing herself and invites Wyatt to a party at El Dorado. Bat tries to horn in, but obviously she finds him too polished to be of interest, which irritates the hell out of him.

Wyatt and Bat go to see Mrs. Sanchez, the woman who claimed the starlet's body; she lives in a poor Mexican neighborhood where many of the servants reside. Rosaria is a simple older woman who says she was the housekeeper for Lila's family. She was the starlet's substitute mother, since Lila's real mother was a society lady with little time for her children. When Lila became an actress the family disowned her and she changed her name. Wyatt presses her for the family name, but she refuses to tell. While Wyatt is talking to her, Bat is unobtrusively snooping around and spots an inscribed photo of Rosaria with a white family, and from that gets the family's name.

He goes to see the wealthy family, which shows no signs of grief . . . not surprising, since it turns out they have no daughter and never did. They do remember Rosaria, who was their housekeeper some years before. They remember her as a kind woman who worked hard to support herself and her daughter.

Bat goes back to see Rosaria. She won't open the door, but he tells her that he knows Lila's secret. She looked white and created a fictional white background so she'd be acceptable to people like Samuel Bright—but in fact she was Rosaria's daughter, wasn't she? The only answer is the old woman sobbing from behind the door. Bat gently tells her that Lila's secret doesn't matter any more; she is at peace now.

ACT IV

In the meantime, Wyatt is picked up by the police and taken to see the Chief. To his surprise, he's told the charges against him have been dropped on orders from on high. The studio head? Higher, the Chief says. "Any conditions?" he asks the Chief. No conditions, the Chief says, but of course now that there is no crime, it would be foolish to keep poking one's nose into these affairs. Wyatt nods and says he can take Bat's $5000 back to him. "What $5000?" the Chief asks. "You were released on his recognizance." Silently watching the proceedings is a very tough-looking man named Drummond.

When he gets back to Bat's hotel, the furious Wyatt finds the door locked. He pounds on it and Bat says he'll be right there. When he opens the door, Ruth is inside getting dressed—obviously she fell prey to Bat's charms rather than to Wyatt's, which doesn't improve Wyatt's mood any. He confronts Bat about the $5000, which Bat just laughs off. Wyatt tells him, "You never did tell the truth. That time in Dodge City I got into a gunfight with Billy Murdoch because of your lies, and ended up having to kill him!" Bat counters, "You didn't kill him, I killed him!" "The hell you did! I killed him . . . wait a minute . . . Wild Bill Hickock killed him." "Oh, yeah," Bat admits.

This abates the argument, and Wyatt tells them about the development with the police—that apparently Martin Parker Williams had put out the word to spring him. Bat says he's glad the whole thing is over. Now he can get back to his true line of work, sports writing, and Wyatt can go back to whatever he's going to do next. Wyatt is outraged: as far as he's concerned, his name hasn't been properly cleared and obviously the dropping of the case is intended to buy them off. "It worked," Bat says as he counts his money. Ruth is astonished that Bat would stop even though now it looked more and more like Lila was murdered.

Wyatt immediately makes use of this, telling Ruth maybe she fell for the wrong man. If anybody is more vain than Wyatt Earp, it's Bat Masterson, and this ploy works in getting Bat to agree to stay for a little while.

Bat and Wyatt get duded up for a party at El Dorado. Wyatt catches Bat touching up his hair with shoe polish and whoops with laughter. "That's the god-damnest thing I've ever seen, a man putting paint on his hair!" he says. He watches for a moment more. " . . . Does it work?" he asks with genuine interest.

At El Dorado Margo Lawrence greets Wyatt with great affection—indiscreetly so, perhaps. When he is introduced to Martin Parker Williams, Wyatt thanks him for clearing up the little confusion about his arrest. Williams looks blank—but Margo doesn't. It's clear that she was the higher-up who interceded. Williams looks displeased with his mistress's interest in the old gunfighter. Watching all the proceedings with an eagle eye is Drummond, who is Williams's head bodyguard, and who'd been at the police station.

Bat and Wyatt mingle with the guests and Bat can't help trying out his considerable charms on Mary Pickford and some of the other female stars. Even though he's caught up in flirting with these beautiful women, he does notice that Margo and Wyatt disappear upstairs . . . and when they come back down, Wyatt looks like a cat that swallowed a canary—or a man who has just tied up the score.

Bat and Wyatt go back to see Rosaria, but when they get to her shack, she's no longer there. They track her down and find her living in a comfortable little bungalow. She got the money by selling some land that her father had gotten via a Spanish land grant. Her father had left it to Lila, and when Lila died her mother inherited it. She sold it for a pittance, but it was worthless land, too far outside the city of Los Angeles to build on. They don't yet know how, but Bat and Wyatt are convinced that this land is the key to the young woman's death.

Act V

Back in L.A., Wyatt goes to the land office, but he can't find out who bought the land. Key documents are missing and no one seems eager to help him find them. On his way back he's picked up by the police again, but this time the chief watches as a bunch of officers work Wyatt over, with the lead taken by Drummond. The Chief tells Wyatt that the up-and-coming city of Los Angeles doesn't need a couple of over-the-hill gunfighters poking their noses where they don't belong. He suggests that Wyatt join his friend Bat when the latter goes back East. Otherwise they won't be alive much longer.

The bruised and bleeding Wyatt makes his way back to the hotel room . . . where he finds Bat in much the same condition, being tended by Ruth. "It appears we have 24 hours to get out of town," Bat tells him. "Then we'd better do it," Wyatt says. "I'm getting too old for this." Ruth is upset, tells them off, and stalks out.

At the train station, policemen watch approvingly as Wyatt and Bat get on the train heading East. They get off at Pasadena, and they buy tickets for the next train back to L.A. While they wait, they spot a poster for Buffalo Bill Cody's Wild West Show. They look at each other—if Bill Cody joined them, it'd really be a hell of a gang. They make their way to the show's campgrounds. But when they see Cody he's a drunken old man who is now a parody of the real Westerner he used to be. He advises them to abandon this thing in Los Angeles and join him in his Wild West Show. Disgusted, they leave. It's a shame, Wyatt says, that some people don't know when to die. They unpack their Ned Buntline Specials (.45's with 12-inch barrels) and get on the train back to L.A. "Feels good to have these back on again," Wyatt says. "Yeah," Bat agrees, " . . . but it seems to me they used to be lighter."

Back in L.A., Bat and Wyatt stake out the land Rosaria had sold, and soon encounter a surveying party. Bat and Wyatt kidnap the head surveyor and threaten to string him up if he doesn't reveal the purpose of the work. Once he knows who they are, he cooperates. He reveals that the railroad is coming through here, completing a vital junction to Northern California. As everyone knows, the railroad is owned by Martin Parker Williams. Afterward the man asks whether they really would have lynched him. They might have, Wyatt says wistfully, just for old time's sake. They release the man. They realize that they are on to a case that could rock the country with scandal—and one that pits them against the most powerful man in California.

ACT VI

Bat and Wyatt are heading back to town that night when
suddenly they are surrounded by twenty armed railroad police
led by Drummond. The two gunfighters finger their holsters, but
realize that even in the old days they were never up against odds
like this. They are taken to El Dorado.

At El Dorado the two men are ushered into the presence of Martin
Parker Williams and Samuel Bright. Williams says that he's
unhappy with their conduct, but that the death of two
once-famous gunfighters would draw unwelcome attention.
Besides, he has a better idea. Williams says that he wants his
studio to make a great Western picture—re-creating the gunfight
at the OK Corral, with Wyatt starring. Bright nods and says
Wyatt's earlier screen test meant nothing; with proper coaching,
Wyatt can be a fantastic actor. And, most important, the film will
make Wyatt a hero around the world—he's already a legend, but
this film will immortalize him. The picture will show the shoot
out as it really was, based on Wyatt's account. And it won't
bother with extraneous details, like the fact Wyatt narrowly
escaped a murder conviction for his part in the event. Wyatt's
salary: a quarter of a million dollars. And they will also require
Bat Masterson's services as a consultant for a couple of
weeks—for a hundred thousand dollars.

Of course both men know this is a naked attempt to buy them off,
but when Martin Parker Williams offers to buy a man's soul, he
knows just what to bid. A hundred thousand makes Masterson's
$5000 retirement fund look pretty puny. And Wyatt has always
appreciated money and fame, but immortality, even on film, has
particular appeal. They agree to the deal. Afterward they bullshit
each other that this is a great way to keep on looking into the
case—this way they'll be on the inside and Williams and his men
will be off their guard—but we can tell that neither is completely
sure of the other—or himself.

The OK Corral is re-created on the studio lot. Bright has cast
Drummond and the rest of Williams's bodyguards as the
cowboys who face down Earp and his cohorts. The cameras are
about to roll on the showdown scene. Williams is on the set,
watching. Bat is behind the scenes, and suddenly he discovers
that a prop man has substituted real bullets for the blanks in the
guns of the men facing Wyatt. He rushes out just as the scene is

starting and stops it, with the excuse that the public will want to see Wyatt using his Ned Buntline Special. He gives it to Wyatt and says, "Make it real." Wyatt understands. The men opposing Wyatt start sweating. They look to Bright. He looks to Williams. Williams nods for them to go ahead.

ACT VII

Before the cameras can start rolling, Drummond and the bodyguards draw their guns—but Wyatt is faster, and so is Bat, who backs him up. Once again bullets fly at the OK Corral, and once again there are bodies in the dust, including Drummond's. The bodyguards are all dead. Bat grabs Bright and puts a gun to his head. The terrified Bright blurts out that he was only following Williams's orders. Wyatt and Bat advance on Williams, who is without a bodyguard for the first time in years and who drives off in his Model T. Bat shouts that they can follow him in another car. Wyatt says he must be kidding. Wyatt and Bat saddle up and follow Williams on horseback, out of the studio gates into the city. Wyatt shouts to Bat, asking him where the gas tank is on that contraption. Bat tells him. Wyatt plants a shot squarely into the gas tank and it explodes, sending the car out of control. It hits a tree, and when Wyatt and Bat get to it, it's a burning wreck that is also Williams's coffin. Wyatt looks on philosophically. "He should have taken a horse," he says. "I've never known a horse to explode."

At the train station, reporters besiege Wyatt and Bat. The land will be restored to Rosaria Sanchez, Bright will go to jail. Ruth is there to say good-bye to Bat as he heads back East, and a woman in a black dress and veil is there to see Wyatt. She takes him aside. It is Margo Lawrence. With Martin Parker Williams dead, she will need a strong man to oversee the empire she has inherited. Is Wyatt interested? "Sounds like a lot of indoor work," he says. "Flattered, yes; interested, no." He kisses her and she leaves.

As Bat's train starts to pull out, Wyatt shakes his hand and thanks him for his help. He says it's good that Bat is almost as fast a gun as he is, or else the scene at the OK Corral would have come out differently. "*Almost* as fast?" Bat exclaims. "I'm faster than you are and always have been!" "Bull!" Bat yells. "I guess we'll never know," Wyatt says. "I guess we won't," Bat says quietly as the train pulls away.

THE END

LEN HILL

Leonard Hill and Phil Mandelker established Hill/Mandelker Films in September of 1980. Following the death of Mandelker, Hill established Leonard Hill Productions. The company produces telefilms and also theatrical films. Previously, Hill had been Vice President, Motion Pictures for Television, ABC Entertainment. There he was responsible for the development and production of approximately 100 TV movies, including *The Jericho Mile, Elvis, Friendly Fire, Attica, Amber Waves,* and *Off the Minnesota Strip.* A 1969 summa cum laude graduate of Yale, Hill also served as a writer for "Adam 12" and has held posts at Universal, MTM, NBC, and Paramount TV.

In the last few years, TV movies have become more ambitious and willing to deal with a wider range of subjects. Do you think there is now any difference between the topics of TV movies and features?

No, outside of spectacles, I don't think there's an appreciable difference.

When you were at ABC, how extensive a presentation did you require before you knew whether or not you wanted to go ahead with an idea for a TV movie?

That was a function not merely of the presentation, but of the presenter. If a well-known writer came in with enthusiasm for a specific idea, there was probably greater trust than if a writer or producer with whom we'd had less experience came in with the equivalent presentation.

What is critical to success in selling an idea to the network is an understanding of the network market. I was constantly amazed by how many people would come in and show a considerable ignorance of that body of work, which had developed over the years, that is the television movie. A lack of familiarity with the body of past work makes it impossible to sell. I would encourage anybody who's thinking of writing movies for television to immerse themselves in what is presently being broadcast. In that is, if nothing else, a history of mistakes that are not to be repeated, as well as familiarity with a vernacular, an idiom, to which network executives have become accustomed. The first requisite of an effective presentation is familiarity with what the networks have presented in the past, a knowledge of what's worked and what hasn't.

What's the best way to gauge what has worked and what hasn't?

The most important thing is the writer's own opinion of what works and what doesn't work. Having arrived at that, the writers should inform themselves of the commercial success or failure that any given picture enjoyed. You may love a particular type of film that's been presented on television, yet if it has been clobbered the last three times the network has attempted to program it, they're not going to be in the mood to buy it—you're wasting everybody's time going in to present it.

But with TV it seems harder to judge commercial success because to some extent the rating will depend on what else was on.

Absolutely. It's a very difficult thing to determine. There are cases when a 31-share movie is more successful than a 40-share movie, depending upon the strength of the competition on that particular day.

The fact that this is a difficult thing to evaluate is one of the many reasons as a network we had taken the policy that there needed to be a track record on the part of the production entity that was bringing in the idea. There had to be some filtering process that would allow the certainty of that sophistication.

So the writer is wise to affiliate with a production company, rather than trying to go directly to a network with an idea?

The numbers game insists on it. There are six or seven thousand Writers Guild members, compared with maybe five television movie executives at each network. There has to be a reduction device, some filtration process. That device has, at least in the experience I had at ABC, been the production entity. There are roughly 150 entities with whom we had familiarity. And our statement to the writing community was, "That 150 represents a lot of alternatives; find that company that you think best understands your style and ideas, and allow their credibility to be the endorsement for your idea that is necessary to gain network presentation." [Note: Refer to Chapter 20 Resource List for publications that list the addresses and phone numbers of production companies.]

I understand that networks have lists of writers with whom they prefer to work. When a production company came to you with a new writer, what was your response?

It depended upon my evaluation of the credibility of the production entity. If a company that I held in high esteem came in and said, "We have found a writer for whom we have great regard, who has never had any produced network or feature credits, but we think is perfect for this idea and whom we will support," and if they offered as evidence two or three scripts that writer had written, then we'd go ahead with the writer.

What surprises me is the number of writers who have written outlines but have never written a screenplay. They expect on the basis of an outline to be considered seriously for a scriptwriting commission. I think that's unrealistic.

Can we talk about the elements of a successful pitch for a TV movie?

Certain aspects of a successful pitch have already been discussed: the credibility of the production auspices, the past history of generically similar projects, and the passion evident in the presentation. Those elements aside, it is necessary to evaluate the basic story notion in terms of both its suitability vis-à-vis the TV movie form and in terms of its salability both in terms of packaging and promotional opportunity.

To address the question of suitability, there are certain questions that can help the writer focus on whether the idea is truly a movie, as opposed to a novel or a play, or a short story.

The first question: Does the idea allow me to show a character in transition? The incidents of a movie should be structured in a way that allows a character to reveal himself or herself, and through that revelation to grow and change. Reflections and observations are insufficient; incidents should be catalytic—forcing the protagonist to respond, not merely observe.

The second question: Can the audience identify with my protagonist and the protagonist's plight? Identification is, in my opinion, particularly critical on television, where the viewer is seeing something that is not larger than life, due to the size of the box.

Can you elaborate on what makes for good identification?

Let me give you an example in the negative—a story such as Frederick Forsyth's *Day of the Jackal*. The protagonist is an assassin paid to kill the Prime Minister of France. As a viewer I cannot identify with his profession, the location in which he operates, nor with his plight. So I'm reduced to being a passive spectator, denied the access to the emotions of that character that would allow me to become an active participant. If a television movie doesn't get the active participation of the viewer, it loses a lot of juice.

OK, on to the third question the writer should ask . . .

It derives from the second one, and it's: Does anybody care—is there a rooting interest? If not, the yawn factor is considerable. One of the reasons we shied away from doing stories of the privileged people, people with wealth and power, is that no matter what device a writer might invent, the viewer's likely to say, "I should only have his problems! He's got money and opportunity; if he can't find happiness, I don't care."

The fourth question: Is the picture *about* anything? Is there a unifying theme, an attitude? If not, chances are you're writing what Aaron Spelling has called his own work: junk food for the mind. In the movie for television area, specifically, there is a need to balance the network programming. Thematic integrity of the material often escapes the series—and reasonably so. Theme is usually revealed through character transformation. Series, which insist on a protagonist who can come back every week, allow little character transformation, and as a result usually have trouble illuminating theme.

The final thing a writer should ask is: Is it a movie? Does it benefit from filming, or is it a play—something that can be confined to a small proscenium, presented without the benefit of the panorama, the color, the flexibility of filming? If it has movement and kinetic energy, that takes it from good storytelling to good filmmaking.

Isn't this last element something that can be consciously added—the way a writer will "open up" a play when adapting it for the screen?

Yes. *Amber Waves* could easily have been done in a belt facto-ry. But by choosing to set it against the wheat harvest, Ken Trevey added the visualization, the cinemagraphics that made it a special movie.

Of course it can go too far in the other direction. Lately I've been reading too many things which have a beautiful setting but say very little about the character. No one wants to read about the ship building industry *per se*, but it may be interesting to take a particular father-son theme, for example, and set it in the shipyards.

Is there any general way you can characterize the scripts that interest you the most?

I think all producers ultimately reduce their choice to one basic question: "Do I want to see this movie—is this something I'd go to watch?" There's not a common denominator of subject or period; we're not looking to do only sociodramas or biodramas or docudramas. We do desire to make movies that are emotionally effective, entertaining, engrossing, that provide insight and theme, that amuse, entertain, uplift, anger, provoke—that move people.

When you were with the network you told writers to go to the production companies. Now you run a production company. Are you receptive to new writers? And how do you screen them?

Part of that has to do with recommendations. One of the best ways to find new writers is through old writers. If I get a call from a writer with whom we've had a long-standing relationship and who says, "I've just read a new writer named so-and-so, you should meet with them, they've got great talent," obviously that's an immediate connection and introduction. But by and large I would counsel writers to find an endorsement, either an agent of credibility or another writer of credibility, who can provide the entree.

CHAPTER 8

How to Write Hour-Long Series Scripts

HOUR-LONG SHOWS, INCLUDING dramatic series, action-adventure series, and evening serials, have long been a staple of prime-time television programming. The reason is simple: a good hour-long show retains a large viewing audience for twice the period of time as a good sitcom. There is less tendency to channel-switch in the middle of an "L.A. Law" episode than at the end of a "Cheers"—and of course, all programming strategies are designed specifically to discourage channel switching. So, hour-long shows will always be around, and they offer a wonderful opportunity to anyone with a talent for drama and structure and a willingness to learn the rules.

As noted above, quite a variety of genres are currently being covered in the hour-long format. Aside from the longtime standard cop/private detective/courtroom drama shows, there are detective comedy/dramas such as "Moonlighting" or "Riptide"; family dramas (sometimes referred to as "Eight o'Clock Shows") such as "Highway to Heaven" and "Our House"; nighttime serials such as "Falcon Crest" and "Dallas"; and hybrids of all the above, of which "St. Elsewhere" and "L.A. Law" are perfect examples. But regardless of the type of show, certain rules and structural guidelines apply.

• WHAT'S THE STRUCTURE OF A ONE-HOUR SHOW?

Your hour-long script will be roughly sixty pages long, given the min-ute-per-page guideline applied to feature script format. It will consist of four acts, each one roughly fifteen pages long. Please note the opera-tive word, "roughly." Lots of dialogue will make for a longer script, while a script heavy on action will be shorter. The idea is not to turn scriptwriting into a mathematical exercise, but to be aware of the fact that your script has to allow the opportunity for commercials every thirteen-and-a-half minutes or so.

• HOW DO I STRUCTURE MY PLOT AROUND ALL THOSE COMMERCIALS?

Your story will have to be structured in such a way as to allow cliff-hangers of increasing intensity to be placed at the end of each act (ex-cept the last, of course). These cliffhangers are designed solely for the purpose of enticing the viewer to stick around for the next act—again, we don't want them changing channels!

What's interesting about the structure of an hour-long show is that, four-act format notwithstanding, in story terms you are still writ-ing a standard three-act plot. You'll create your conflict or problem, you'll complicate it, and you'll solve it, one, two, three. The challenge lies in getting the four-act format and the three-act structure to marry, or at least cohabitate in peace.

Act I

Assuming you're writing for an existing show, you won't be faced with the usual first act problem a feature script presents: intro-ducing the characters. Your protagonist is a known quantity, and your writing need only reflect the personality and character traits they've al-ready established in past episodes. By the way, if you can come up with something very interesting and new as a personality trait of the main character, you can take a big step toward making your script fresh and unique. Naturally you have to play off a weakness, strength, habit, or idiosyncrasy he/she may have displayed at one time or another, and not contradict his or her typical actions.

In Act I you should:

1. Establish any "guest" characters. In a script for "Murder, She Wrote," this would mean a quick look at everyone who might be a sus-

pect, and on "Moonlighting" it might be the wacky new client. Whoever this guest is, your first act should allow the viewer (and reader) to meet them, but not *know* them. A few hints at their personality is all that's needed, particularly if they are going to play the role of suspects in your story.

2. Establish the conflict. This is true not only for your "A" plot, but your "B" and maybe even your "C" plot as well ("B" and "C" being subplots to your main story, "A"). For example, in the first act of "Highway to Heaven," Jonathan and Mark will learn that a star basketball player is unable to read; in the first act of "Magnum, P.I." Magnum will reluctantly accept a case when he finds a friend is involved; and in the first act of "L.A. Law" Mike Cuzak will have a court case foisted on him with no time for preparation and little chance of victory.

The important thing to remember is to give your protagonist a goal, whether it be solving a case, finding a missing person, or avenging the death of a partner. The rest of your script will focus on making the attainment of this goal as difficult as possible.

3. Lay the groundwork. This is especially important in mysteries or detective shows, where a crime is committed in the first act, and the protagonist spends the rest of the show solving this crime. You have to be fair to your viewers. Therefore, you must be sure that any clues you'll depend on later are at least hinted at in the first act. They don't have to be obvious, and they certainly don't have to be fully explained, but they have to be there, somewhere. For example, if a glass of poisoned wine figures prominently in Jessica Fletcher's solution to a murder, be sure you've given your viewer a chance to see that glass right from the beginning.

You definitely don't want to jam *all* your clues into the first act, but if at least one of the BIG ones is there, you'll immediately get your audience's attention and interest.

As you can see, there's a lot to accomplish in one act. Typically, the first act is very, very busy, and the tendency at times is to get a bit talky as everyone introduces everyone else and describes their problems. Excessive talkiness needs to be avoided, however—more on that later.

Act II
In Act II, you should:

1. Resolve the cliffhanger you posed at the end of the first act. If this involved some mildly dangerous situation your protagonist faced,

it needs to be easily resolved. There's no need to get too carried away, because you'll want to increase the intensity of the cliffhangers as you go along.

2. Reveal some more about your "guest" characters. One of the standard ways to handle this, particularly on cop/detective/action shows, is to have the protagonist question the character, whether as a suspect, witness, relative, or whatever. During the questioning the person may be cooperative and polite, or may blow up at a certain question and throw a punch at the protagonist. Either way, we've definitely learned something about this person.

There are other, less "talky" options you can take to dole out character information. You might show the grizzled, grandfatherly character try to get rid of a stray cat that keeps hanging around the door, but finally give it a saucer of milk. Or, a quick glimpse of a teacher working in her office, as a night janitor comes by and says he needs to shut the lights off soon. In other words, you can *show* us something about the character rather than having them say, "People think I'm kinda gruff, but actually I'm very kind to helpless creatures" or "I'm a very dedicated teacher, and very often work quite late." Remember that television is a visual medium. The more you can accomplish visually, the better. For one thing, it'll help you avoid the stiff, awkwardly obvious expositional dialogue we've all come to know and hate when watching shows that are not particularly well written.

3. Complicate your plot(s). Make life difficult for your protagonist. Give him tough choices to make. Have her bungle what should have been an easy surveillance. Throw in some red herring clues that lead your hero on a dangerous wild goose chase. Have the young unwed mother not only turn down Jonathan's offer of assistance, but toss him out of the house as well.

Act II is when your protagonist tries out her first plan on the antagonist, and it doesn't work out at all well.

At the same time, you should use at least one scene to advance your B and C plots. (You should always have a B plot. A C plot is optional, and should be very simple and undemanding.) In some cases the B plot can be tied in at some point with the A plot, while in other instances it will stand on its own, and is many times used as a humorous sort of footnote to end the show. In any case, keep the subplot scenes short and to-the-point.

4. End with a cliffhanger or brick wall. The end of the second act arrives at the half-hour, right when new half-hour shows are starting

on some other station (unlike TV movies, where the breaks don't coincide with half-hour time blocks). This is arguably the most crucial act break because the commercial break is longer and the chances of losing viewers significantly greater. If you have not managed to enthrall your audience with a strong story and an act break that makes them *need* to stick around and find out what's going to happen, they're gone. What are examples of good endings for a second act? Well, perhaps the perfect answer to the mystery is spoiled when the suspect is murdered, or the protagonist is dropped by a well-aimed sniper bullet, or the recovering alcoholic is thrown in jail for drunk driving. In other words, just when things look like they might work out, the rug is pulled out.

Act III
In the third act you'll have to:

1. Resolve (or resume) the second act cliffhanger. The hero who was gunned down is now in the hospital, and the doctor's telling his partner that the poor guy may not ever walk again. Or saying (pardon the cliché) that the bullet would have killed him if it had been just *one inch* higher, but it went straight through and he'll be okay.

That second act ending should function as a springboard for the initial third-act action, and from there your scenes need to increase in tension as they move toward the end. Returning to our three-act "man-up-a-tree" analogy (put your hero up a tree, throw stones at him, then get him down), the third act is where stones are being fired at a machine-gun clip. Things go wrong, tough decisions are made, the cornered rat fights back with unexpected ferocity.

2. Complicate the plot. Increase the odds against your protagonist, and keep upping the stakes. With each scene, one thing piles on another to create a seemingly insurmountable barrier to success.

A good trick here is to increase the tempo of the scenes by making them shorter, more dependent on quick sentences and fast action. Set a pace that accelerates to breakneck speed by the time you smash headlong into the third act ending, where virtually everything has blown up in your hero's face.

3. End the act in turmoil: In "The Equalizer," McCall's client is abducted right out from under his nose, while he's left bleeding and unconscious; the lives of innocent people may be in jeopardy because Jessica's guess about the killer's identity was incorrect; on "Miami Vice," Rico's wire is discovered by a gang of vicious thugs, and no one knows where he is.

Obviously, the Eight o'Clock shows will have gentler third-act breaks than these, but the idea is the same: everything that *can* go wrong, *does* go wrong. Only the special talents, skills, strength, cunning, or supernatural powers of our hero, strained to the limit, will be sufficient to somehow wrest a victory from what looks like certain defeat.

Act IV

And now, in the words of legendary tap-dancer Bill Robinson, it's time to "Take it home!" All of the care and hard work you put into structuring your first three acts of conflict should pay off nicely in a fourth act that practically writes itself.

It's true. In most cases the fourth act is far and away the easiest to write, assuming you've laid a proper foundation from the beginning. The ending of your story is never obvious, but always inevitable. It is unpredictable, but, given your carefully drawn blueprint, inescapable.

The fourth act of a one-hour script is, in essence, the third act of your story. You've finished complicating things, and now it's up to the characters to unravel the mess you've made for them. Refer back to the chapter on structuring a feature screenplay, and you'll see that often this final act is almost one continuous scene, whether it be a thunderous gun battle, a roaring car chase, or a gathering of suspects listening as the killer among them is identified.

The important point to remember about the fourth act is this: once the protagonist embarks on his course of action, there is no turning back. The stakes are so high that his alternatives are narrowed down to one, in what has become (whether literally or figuratively) a "Do or Die" situation.

So, in the fourth act you must:

1. Resume the action. Remember, you left your heroine in a hell of a mess at the end of the third act. You need to find a logical, believable way to get her back on her feet, ready for action.

2. Resolve the plot(s). First and most importantly, of course, you need to arrive at a satisfying ending to your A plot. This ending should provide some catharsis: the bad guy gets his, and then some. It should also be an ending that relies completely on facts you've already revealed in one way or another. The ultimate cheat is to fool the reader or viewer by withholding a vital bit of information and using it in the last few seconds to explain a seemingly inexplicable ending. Certainly it's

okay, and in fact desirable, to "twist" your ending a bit. That's what keeps a show interesting and unpredictable, and also what will make your script stand out from the ordinary. What you have to avoid is coming up with a surprise ending just for the sake of a shock, and then lamely trying to explain it away with evidence or facts that seem to fall out of the sky.

You'll also use the fourth act to wrap up your B plot. If you've found a way to tie it in with the resolution of your A plot, terrific. If not, a quick scene at the very end of the show should take care of it. A lot of times this scene is used as a bit of comedy relief after the intense drama and/or action of the final scene in plot A.

• A SAMPLE BREAKDOWN

Here's a sample breakdown of an hour-long show, using a hypothetical episode of "Magnum, P.I."

Act I

Meet Booth Walker, an obviously insane man who shoots alarm clocks with a Derringer. Magnum meets with Goldbloom, Booth's publisher, and is commissioned to track down the out-of-control writer and keep him out of trouble, until his feature assignment is finished. Magnum starts with a list of hotels, and each one he tries puts him face-to-face with an irate manager who swears to kill Booth if he ever stays there again. He tries several bars, and after leaving one a couple of thugs follow him out and beat him savagely, finally dumping him in a Dumpster.

Act II

Higgins continues his earlier efforts to upgrade the Masters estate with computerized security systems. Magnum finds that Higgins has been spending more time playing "Star Zappers" than testing the system. Maggie Walker, Booth's ex-wife, pays Magnum a visit. She received a paranoid telegram from Booth, and fears for his safety. She found Magnum through Goldbloom. Magnum will get T.C. to fly them to the cottage she knows about, one where Booth frequently goes. Upon their arrival they find a dead man in the cabin. It's Hammerin' Harry, a cocaine syndicate hit man. From the hillside, Booth watches the cabin through the crosshairs of a hunting rifle. Magnum and Maggie report the body to the cops. Booth makes contact with Maggie, but when she and Magnum go to meet him there's an ambush. A carload of heavies pins them down as Booth comes screaming out of a building, and falls to the ground. The car leaves, and Maggie huddles over Booth, sobbing.

Act III

Booth was playing possum. Back at Magnum's place Booth tells them the cocaine dealers on the island are worried because of his feature article, the definitive exposé on the cocaine trade. Magnum decides they need to hide the highly unpleasant Booth at his place for awhile, and Booth meets Higgins. In moments, Booth has repaired a glitch in the computer system. Higgins is an enormous fan of Booth's. Booth can stay at the estate and finish his article. Magnum and Maggie get to know each other during a moonlight stroll. She tries to explain Booth's weirdness—his sister was killed, having driven off a cliff while under the influence of cocaine. They get back to Robin's Nest, only to find the place has been broken into and Booth is gone—and it's clear he didn't leave of his own free will.

Act IV

Magnum figures the bad guys took Booth to force him to give them the article. He figures they would have taken him back to the cabin, and goes there. Sure enough, Booth and the hoods are there—and the hoods are led by Goldbloom, the publisher. Magnum and T.C. decide to make their move. They don't think Booth will be alive long enough for the police to get there, even though they send Maggie to call them. Magnum and T.C. catch the hoods completely by surprise, and untie Booth. Just when everything is under control, in comes another hood who'd been on lookout, and he's got Maggie in a headlock. He'll waste her if they don't drop their guns. Booth is forced to tell where the article is—it's on a floppy disc, hidden in a stack of old 45's (records). Goldbloom gloats momentarily about the hell Booth had always put him through, and how great it's going to be to finally get rid of him. Suddenly, Booth screams, flinging his arm up, and his tiny Derringer pops into his hand. He fires it, superficially wounding Goldbloom, and Magnum dives for Goldbloom. There's a struggle, shots are fired, but T.C. and Magnum triumph. Goldbloom escapes with the floppy disc. Once again, Booth is down. Later, in the hospital, Magnum deduces that Booth had planned all of this, just so he could get Goldbloom. Booth blamed Goldbloom for his sister's death, and wanted him dead. In fact, he intended on dying himself, committing both an indirect murder and an indirect suicide. After all, when the cocaine kingpins find out that Goldbloom has just sold them a floppy disc containing nothing but "Star Zappers," they'll waste no time in getting rid of him.

• WHAT'S THE FORMAT FOR AN HOUR-LONG SCRIPT?

The format for an hour-long show is almost identical to that of a feature script. All action and dialogue is single-spaced, with a double-space used to separate the two. As with features, camera directions and shot descriptions are kept to a bare minimum. Include camera directions ("PAN the museum left to right"; "ANGLE from above the foxhole") *only* if it is absolutely essential to your story. Excessive miscellaneous directions and notes only serve to get in the way of the story. Furthermore, the chances are that even the shots you felt were so imperative that they *had* to be described will still be altered by the director, anyway. Therefore, it's best to leave them out whenever possible.

The following is an example of a page from an hour-long series script, written for a hypothetical episode of "Magnum, P.I."

MAGNUM enters, carrying a small grocery bag.

> BOOTH
>
> How's your friend?

> MAGNUM
>
> T.C.'s okay. The bullet made a clean exit. He'll have a sore leg for a while. How're <u>you</u> doing, Booth?

> BOOTH
>
> Frankly, I'm worried about my future.

He gestures to the soap opera on the TV screen.

> BOOTH
>
> Take a look at those people. Each one more beautiful than the next. If people like these are allowed to breed freely, it's inevitable that we carriers of distorted, inferior gene pools will soon perish in one fierce Darwinian flash. Didja bring me something?

MAGNUM looks around to see if the coast is clear, then reaches into the grocery bag and pulls out a six-pack of beer.

> BOOTH
>
> Once again, you've saved my life.

He uncaps one, and takes a long swallow.

> BOOTH
>
> I don't know where I'd have been without your timeliness. I owe you a great deal.

> MAGNUM
>
> You can stow all that baloney, Booth. I've finally figured this whole thing out.

• SOME GENERAL TIPS

1. Begin with a BANG! Make your first scene a real attention-grabber, practically forcing people to turn the page (or stay tuned, as the case may be). Take a look at any one-hour show on the air right now, particularly the good ones, and you'll find they all start off at a sprint. Newspaper journalists are taught to zap their readers with an intriguing first sentence; magazine writers sweat buckets over a killer lead paragraph; and scriptwriters have to grab their audiences by the collar and heave them into the plot with their first scene.

This is why you'll so often see an episode of "Miami Vice" begin with a fantastically violent robbery, or a "Murder, She Wrote" start out with a snarling family argument. The importance of involving your readers and viewers right from the starting gate cannot be overemphasized. This is particularly true if you're writing a spec script you hope to send around as a sample, because busy story executives and producers will rarely read an entire spec script and will almost certainly toss yours in the return envelope if the first scene fails to grab them.

2. Treat your hero with care. A common mistake made by beginning scriptwriters is usually brought on by a sincere desire to do something new. For instance, an aspiring writer notices that Magnum has never spent an entire episode helplessly tied up, unable to signal his friends. Following this line of reasoning, the writer continues: Magnum's friends, knowing his habits so well and using some brilliant de-

ductive reasoning, are able to locate him. Then, in spite of the fact that Magnum's captors use him as a defenseless hostage, they are able to free him and capture all the bad guys.

Nope. It'll never fly. Just take a look at the title of the show, and you'll get a big hint why. The main character of any show must in some way play the *key role* in resolving the story. He can and should be in some very tight spots, but *he* is the one who should triumph, and not just because the cavalry happens to arrive in the nick of time . . . unless, of course, the cavalry was summoned by some clever method the hero employed unbeknownst to his captors.

Along these same lines, never bring in a "guest star" whose part in the story turns out to be bigger or more important than the hero's. The show is about the hero, not guest stars, and everything should revolve around him or her.

3. Avoid "talky" exposition. Murder mysteries are notorious for ignoring this dictate, but every show is guilty once in a while. We've all seen it; the crazed killer holding a gun on our hero feels compelled to spend two minutes expounding upon all the details of his crimes. Or the detective, apparently succumbing to the need to show off how brilliant he was, gives a play-by-play account of the murder to someone who already knows all the facts. For example:

> **HERO**
> You know the thing I found amazing? That after Joey returned the gun to his dad's apartment, he never called Ruth to let her know he'd be coming home.

> **SIDEKICK**
> Yes, I remember how that puzzled you. Almost as much as I was puzzled by Joey's limp.

> **HERO**
> You mean the way it changed from his left foot to his right foot? Well, as you recall, I noticed that right away.

> **SIDEKICK**
> That's right, I'd forgotten that you said, "Hey, look at his limp. It's different."

This kind of gripping exposition still makes it onto the airwaves occasionally—just be sure *your* script doesn't make the same mistake.

And now, let's turn to a couple of very noteworthy experts in the field of one-hour episodic scriptwriting: Steven Bochco and Robert Van Scoyk.

STEVEN BOCHCO

As creator and writer of both "Hill Street Blues" and "L.A. Law," Steven Bochco has been responsible for some of the finest hours of dramatic television ever to grace the airwaves. He has also written for "The Name of the Game," "Columbo," "McMillan and Wife," and "Delvecchio," among others.

This interview was conducted during the time Bochco was Executive Producer of "Hill Street Blues," a show with twenty Emmy awards to its credit at that time.

When did you know you wanted to become a TV writer?

Not until I did it. I was a playwright in college, and I knew I wanted to come out here and work. I wasn't thinking so much in terms of television, as I was of film.

Were you confident you would be able to make a living at it?

Yes. It never occurred to me that I wouldn't make a living at it. And I always did. While in college, I was a recipient of an MCA Writing Fellowship, which got me out to Universal Studios. Then the summer before my senior year, I administered a writers' program that Universal ran in those days in which they brought out a few writers who had won the fellowship in the course of the previous year. And they were given two weeks' carte blanche run of the studio. It was a wonderful type of apprentice program, and I ran it. And at the end of that summer, I was going back to finish school at Carnegie-Mellon, and Universal invited me to return when I graduated.

So I was in the last year of college knowing I had a job to return to. I was lucky. Profoundly lucky. I graduated in 1966, and I got in my car—I didn't even hang around for the ceremonies—came out and went to work the next day. And I was at Universal for twelve years.

When you arrived to work at Universal, were you immediately assigned to a show?

No, originally I started doing small writing chores. I think I was making $150 a week, or whatever it was. I remember one of the earliest writing things I did was to write added scenes to the first seven or eight episodes of a new series called "Ironside," produced by Frank Price.

What shows did you work on over the next twelve years?

The first show I worked on was "The Name of the Game," then "Columbo." Then we produced a terrible series that only lasted a half-season called "Griff." Then I worked on "McMillan and Wife." Then I produced a show called "Delvecchio" with Judd Hirsh. That's when I met Michael Kozoll—he came on as story editor. Then I did a show with Steve Cannell that we created called "Richie Brockelman, Private Eye," which was a fun show.

How did the idea for "Hill Street" originate?

NBC wanted a cop show pilot. Michael Kozoll was here at MTM doing other things, and I was here, having just finished a show that had failed called "Paris" with James Earl Jones. Mainly at MTM's request, as a means to gainfully employ both of us simultaneously, they asked if I would mind doing a pilot with Michael. And I said, "Heck no." Michael and I were good friends and we had worked together in the past.

NBC wanted a cop show but we had other ideas about what we wanted to do. The idea that we wanted to do most, and which we pitched to them, was called "Hotel."

The prototype of the current series on ABC?

Virtually the same. We wanted to do a show with exactly that title, and NBC had no interest in it. They wanted to do this cop show that Fred Silverman was fantasizing about, based on *Fort Apache, The Bronx.* [aside] You know how they all talk in comparisons. [laughter] Michael and I very reluctantly went away to think about it.

The message from Silverman contained one element that really was interesting. He said that perhaps we might be able to concentrate on the personal lives of these cops. So we talked about it and talked about it, and we finally agreed to do it. And we said to NBC we would do it on two conditions: that we'd have complete creative autonomy, which to our surprise, they said OK. And, I said,

"You've got to, in effect, help us get a different standard under which to operate with Broadcast Standards or we can't do the show that we're envisioning."

And I can remember having a meeting with Broadcast Standards for an hour, sitting there and yelling at these guys about something that didn't exist yet. It was bizarre. Yelling. Really yelling. And the show was still all hypothetical. But I felt a real need to serve notice that in dealing with us, they would have to be prepared to see things and accept things that they were not used to accepting. And I've been at war with them ever since.

That must be a drain on your energy . . .
It's a massive drain on our energies.

And who ends up winning usually?
To the ultimate advantage of both sides, I think we end up winning probably 98 percent.

How do you go about outlining and plotting a season of "Hill Street"?
We don't.

I beg your pardon?
We do an hour at a time. Oh, generally, we'll conceptualize three hours, and that's about as far as we ever go. What we have discovered over the years is that, as uncomfortable as it is to be doing it almost on a week-to-week basis, so much happens in the process that we simply can't anticipate, or plot, or structure that far down the line.

First of all, plotting far in advance is exhausting. You'd need months to do that, uninterrupted. And we don't have that kind of time. For instance, we ended our 83-84 production season in April. We went off and took mini-vacations for a couple, three weeks. Then you come back, and it's already May, and you have to start shooting in July. So you have two months to start conceptualizing an entire season. You just can't do it.

Plus we have some new characters this season that we had to think through the cast. So as you get into the season, if you're a script ahead, it's a luxury.

That's surprising to hear. We talked with David Paulsen at "Dallas" last year, and he said that in February they know what they are going to do for all twenty-two hours.

I know. God bless 'em. I'm envious. I wish we could do it that way. But we don't seem to be able to. We have seventeen regulars. Multiple story lines. This is certainly not to denigrate other shows and how hard they all work, but given what we had to deal with, it's just not possible to plot that far in advance.

So you come back in May with your staff and say, OK, let's try to get the first three down . . .

Oh, yeah, we spend the bulk of our time locked in this office just putting together stories, then sending people out to write.

What about freelancers—do you use them at all?

Occasionally. You have to because you want to find people who can do your show. You know that 95 percent of the time you will not succeed, but you've got to invest that time and effort or you've got no chance at all. So this year, since we've lost two of our writers from last year, we've been putting out some more freelance assignments. Not a whole lot—like three, four, tops, out of twenty-two. Because when you're doing a serial show, how do you plug a freelance writer into that flow? You don't. So what you do for the three or four "singles" that you try to do during a season—episodes that are not tied to the other episodes—those are the ones that you put out. This year, so far, we've put out three, and I don't anticipate us putting out anymore.

That's a lot of work for you guys . . .

Yeah. But it pays off. This is a good show. And what it has is a kind of density and a richness and a community which I don't think you can maintain if the bulk of your writing is being done by outside people.

How do you determine which freelancers you will talk with?

We don't chat with freelancers. Frankly, that's a waste of time. People come in and can be very seductive, but it doesn't mean they can do your show. And by the same token, someone may come in who's terrible in a meeting—very impacted—and they may be the absolute right person to write your show. So we read material. Every year. And we still don't dent it. It piles up, and we get angry letters from agents saying, "Pursuant to our submission of February 9, blah, blah, blah." They don't realize that once we're in the soup, it gets tougher to stay abreast with the reading.

What do you like to see when you read?

Talent. Any type of material that's going to exhibit a tone or a sound and a sense of character and a sense of humor that in some way is indicative of what we can use. And I must say, you can spot it. You really can. It's tough to break it down into elements. But really good writing jumps off the page. Just jumps off the page.

And I have to tell you something—there are a lot of good writers who can't write "Hill Street," because it's an odd animal. Strange characters, and it's got an awful lot going on, and it's very dense. It has a sound, and a smell and a feel to it. A lot of writers just can't get it. These writers do other things wonderfully well, but we've found very few writers who really have the kind of "tilt" that make them able to do this sort of thing well.

Do you prefer to read something from freelancers with original characters, or from a series in which the characters are already established?

I don't have any feelings one way or another. I just want really good writing which jumps off the page. For example, Tony Yerkovich, who Mike and I found the first season. We hired him off of a "Starsky and Hutch." (snapping his fingers) His stuff just came off the page.

There's been criticism during your four-year history that you tend to put character over plot, and that your plots don't tie together neatly at the end of the hour, so that people who aren't familiar with the characters are often lost and confused as to what is going on. What's your reaction to that?

It's absolutely true. If you don't watch the show every single week, it's very possible that you're going to get lost. That's part and parcel of our format. We have so many characters and so many story lines that it requires some real attention to stay with it.

Our basic premise is that things don't resolve in life. Neatly. Cleanly. 48-minute chunks. In fact, some things don't resolve at all, particularly as you get older and things get more complicated. In "Hill Street," these are not cops who are out there solving crimes. It's not a show about good and evil, good guys-bad guys. It's about keeping a lid on a garbage can as best you can. It's a holding action. It's a war of attrition. It forces you into certain kinds of storytelling.

If I gave you a season's worth of scripts and you sat down and read them all, I think you'd be amazed at how structured the writing is, and how very carefully plotted it is. There's nothing random in any of it. That's not to say that we succeed all the time in what we try to do, or that we couldn't do it better. But our material has structure. Television, if nothing else, is a stringently structured medium. And anyone writing for television who doesn't come to grips with that won't be able to work in the medium.

In a serial, you have the opportunity to have your characters change and grow. I imagine you analyze that pretty carefully . . .

Massively. As a matter of fact, one of the real raps on us last year is that the show became sort of dark and more soap-opery. Furillo's problem with his marriage and all that stuff. His booze, etc. And my feeling was that it was really evolutional in the sense that you have a guy who is quintessentially middle-management. Turning forty. Married. Going through a mid-life crisis that touches on every aspect of his world. And if you're going to allow a character to really grow and change, you've got to see him through that. Without necessarily knowing exactly where it's going to take you, you've got to let that happen.

I have a hunch that whenever we stop doing the show—five years, six years, whatever—I think people will look back to the fourth season as a real pivotal season in terms of character growth, on a lot of levels. We did a lot of different things with characters.

You know, in life, people change in very small increments. They don't make those big massive leaps that people love to make in "television land." Most of us tend to make the same mistakes over and over again. And what we do is we trick ourselves into thinking they are different mistakes . . . by disguising the circumstances of the error. But the truth is that we screw up the same way almost always. And what that means is that when we change, we change in the smallest increments over a pretty long period of time. We try to honor that reality in the show.

When you accepted the assignment from NBC to do the show, was there something in the back of your head that you wanted to accomplish through "Hill Street"?

No. No. Absolutely not. Michael [Kozoll] and I both felt that the show would fail. [pause] Actually, that's not quite true about our aspirations for the show. I think Michael and I wanted to do something that hadn't been done before. In other words, we knew what we didn't want to do. We knew we had no interest in doing a typical cop show. We wanted to accomplish something that was atypical. Not only of cop shows, but of the hour form itself. The number of characters. The look and sound and density. With the exception of "St. Elsewhere," I don't think there is another show on television that puts as much information on a frame of film as we do.

Do you see any general mistakes that beginning writers make when trying to break into the business?

That's difficult to say, because the level of skill and talent varies so much from individual to individual. A guy like Michael Kozoll— the first script he'll ever write in his life is going to be better than the 1000th script that somebody else is going to write. Because he's gifted. The simple truth is, most writers aren't good enough to do this work. You've got to be really, really talented to write for television and be successful at it. You must believe that your writing is important. You've got to love what you write.

Do perseverance and discipline count for anything in your success?

You bet. There are lots of writers that are better than I. I have writers on my own staff that are infinitely better than I am. My goal in life is to have everybody who works for me be better at what they do than what I am. And I get to take all the credit.

I have been lucky. And I've been fortunate to take advantage of my luck. But I'll tell you what—I've been in this business for eighteen years nonstop. I've never been out of work in this business, but I've done some of the worst stuff you can possibly imagine. On shows I didn't believe in. On shows I didn't have an interest in. I served a very long, and at times, a very painful apprenticeship. I don't think that most people have the patience that I have to serve that type of apprenticeship that I have. Notwithstanding my good fortune in having had that opportunity.

I don't mean to be falsely modest. I think I am a good writer, and I think I'm good at nurturing other writers. I think that's part of my job.

ROBERT VAN SCOYK on PLANNING A MURDER . . .

Robert Van Scoyk, Executive Story Editor of "Murder, She Wrote," started in local radio in Dayton, Ohio. Then he went to New York and became a page boy at NBC. "While I was there," he says, "television was just getting started—in its infancy as far as weekly drama series. They had several Milton Berle-type shows—"Toast of the Town," etc., but they didn't have much in the way of episodic television. It was very young and primitive at the time."

When you worked in local radio and TV, was that as a writer?

Yes.

So you moved to New York as a page boy in hopes of breaking in . . .

But not into television. In those days network radio drama was a big thing, and I thought, "Gee, I'd like to write for radio." Radio, of course, died out while television grew, so I just went with the flow.

"Murder, She Wrote" has been going strong for several seasons now, and it's still one of the most popular shows on the air. What do you feel is the appeal of a mystery—why are they such a perennial favorite with the American public?

I think people like the element of suspense and danger, without actually putting themselves in suspense or danger. They also like a puzzle—but one that's not going to be too taxing. If it's too much of a puzzle, too difficult and demands too much of them, they'll either turn the set off, or if it's a book, they'll stop reading.

They're looking for some characters they like, too. In fact, as far as television is concerned, the success of the mystery genre depends on the star of the show. Likability and credibility of the star is what keeps viewers coming back.

If they don't like the star, they won't watch the mystery.

Which certainly explains the success, say, of the Agatha Christie mysteries . . .

Oh yes, all very likable characters. People like Jane Marple and the others. And you know, all of Agatha Christie's characters did not succeed as well. She experimented with some others—Tommy Tuppence, and a few others, before she got Miss Marple and Hercule Poirot.

You mentioned that people will put down books or turn off the set if the puzzle in a mystery becomes too enigmatic.

If it's too esoteric, or if they simply know it's going to be too difficult. If you're not a big anagram fan, for example, and you pick up a book that, ten pages in, introduces you to an elaborate mystery—the solution of which depends on unraveling a complex anagram—well, you're not likely to continue. Unless you can solve the kind of puzzle the mystery poses, you won't be interested in it.

Here's an interesting point about our show. A lot of our viewers don't watch it for the puzzle. They don't even try to solve it. They like to sit back and watch Jessica solve the case. They don't want to be taxed too much.

And yet when I sit there with my family and watch the show, we spend the whole time shouting back and forth, "He did it, she did it, no wait, he did it!"

Some people do that. Others are watching alone, or maybe with others, and depending on their frame of mind they may just watch it as a story that unfolds just like any other story. Others will watch for our clues—and they're always there somewhere, we always provide them . . .

And that's a very important point. There's apparently quite a delicate balance here, in that you have to come up with a

puzzle that's challenging enough to be a mystery, and yet . . .

Challenging, sometimes. Some shows are easier than others. In fact, on some shows we don't know why everybody doesn't know who did it! Even when the writer told us the story for the first time, as the first words came from his mouth, we knew who did it. Peter Fischer can watch an old mystery on television and tell you within minutes who committed the murder.

A lot of times that probably has something to do with the various writer's tricks that are used to present clues.

Sometimes, yes. Sometimes you can spot all of the intentional misdirection that's put in, and you say, "Ah hah, they did that because they didn't want you to know this . . ."

Along those lines, in structuring "Murder, She Wrote," planning the misdirection and red herring clues, etc.—what rules do you follow?

It's basically the structure of all television dramas, really. The first act is used to set up the characters, or suspects, in our case. We usually have our murder at the end of the first act—if for no other reason than to get the murder out of the way so we can go about the business of having Jessica do her thing. And her thing is solving the murder, so the show really begins after the murder.

We don't stick with exactly the same format each time, though. We enjoy occasionally going out of format. We did a show last season about a jury trial, and at first there were no suspects— just a man being tried for murdering some woman's husband. Supposedly they had lured him someplace to kill him. The defense claimed that the husband had arrived there and was killed in self-defense by the man. Now Jessica was the foreman of the jury, and even though the case appears a deadlock at first, the jury eventually finds the man innocent. And Jessica knows the man was innocent because he was actually off killing his wife at the time!

But in your standard structure, how do you set up your characters, your motives, without giving things away too early?

We usually "leak" our characters, let you meet them a little bit at a time. We also show some conflict right in the beginning, usually some misdirection. Certainly we don't get into everybody's motives until after the fact, or we'd have a first act that would be longer than the rest of the show.

Okay, moving on to the second act . . .

The second act is investigatory, mainly, with a revelation at the end of the act that is somewhat startling, or puts Jessica in danger, or puts someone she knows in jeopardy, or the wrong person is accused. It may appear that the case is wrapped up, although of course it's not.

And the third act?

Generally, by the end of the third act Jessica knows who the killer is, but hasn't proved anything yet. Often it will appear that someone she knows is innocent is suddenly found to be guilty, and she has to wonder if maybe she's been wrong . . .

And we, as experienced TV viewers, look at the clock and say, "Wait a second, there's still fifteen minutes left!" [laughter]

Right!

Do you find the four-act structure of television to be especially constraining or restrictive in writing a mystery?

No, it's something we're all very used to. It basically just means that there is a false climax every ten or twelve minutes. Some kind of cliffhanger or act ending that will keep people watching through the commercial break. Other than that, I don't find it to be too restrictive. Shakespeare had many act endings . . .

And hardly any television experience at all!

Right, hardly any!

Parceling out your clues is an important part of mystery writing. And of course you have to avoid cheating, you can't commit the ultimate sin in mystery writing—hiding a vitally important fact throughout, only to spring it in the fi-

nal moments. Is there a method you prefer in leaving clues?

Well, if it can be done visually, that's fine. If not, then we obviously have to do it in dialogue. But either way it's done so that the audience has a fair crack at it—if they're watching or listening, they will have seen it or heard it. We usually replay it at the end, so everybody has a chance to say, "Oh, yes, I remember that! Of course!"

Is it fair to say that in these shows you can pretty much manipulate the final act to prove that anyone could have done it?

There's an unfinished Dickens mystery that was made into a Broadway musical. And each night the audience would select an ending, they would pick the murderer. And of course there were different songs and dialogue to go with whatever ending the audience had decided on. So yes, it's possible, but we try to make the ending on "Murder, She Wrote" a bit more intrinsic than that. We're out to entertain, not trick people.

"Murder, She Wrote" is an Eight o'Clock show. Does that put you under any rules or restrictions as far as the subject matter of your mysteries is concerned?

We have no frontal nudity or startling profanity. A few "hells" and "damns," and that's it.

[Laughter] But the murders themselves . . .

The murders themselves are never gory. We don't dwell on lifeless bodies.

I've also noticed that a lot of times the victim was a rather unpleasant person when alive.

That's true many times, but of course it depends on the particular story. As a rule we like to avoid new, obscure ways of killing somebody. We don't want to suggest any that haven't been thought of before that someone might want to go out and try! We stick pretty close to shooting, stabbing, strangling, poison . . .

All the things we're already trying!

Yes, the things everybody already knows, loves, and that they've grown up with. [laughter]

A problem in writing mysteries, at least from my own expe-
rience, is the final exposition. After all, you want to put off
the final revelation of the murderer's identity until the last
second, but that can involve a lot of details that need to be
cleaned up in the final portion of the show.

Yes, sometimes more than others. If you handle your other acts
correctly, the motive and method and everything else will already
be there, and you can do it all very quickly. That way your exposition at the end really just fills in the gaps you purposely left in act
one. Like when you see a man in a robe and slippers walk down-
stairs, go into the library and close the door, and in the morning his
servant opens the door to the library and finds him dead—well, you
fill in everything that happened in between.

Do you ever find yourself "cheating" a little bit—leaving
some things out of the story completely, and kind of sneak-
ing them in at the end?

Sometimes, but there is always *THE CLUE* that Jessica Fletcher
sees, hears, or remembers—that we call "penny-dropping"—the
moment that the penny drops for Jessica and she realizes who the
killer is. The little light comes on over her head, she says, "Of
course!" That big clue is never left out, and there are also a lot of little clues along the way. Sometimes, though, the details are not given
in entirety, but that's not really cheating the audience . . . what
they're guessing at is "who done it," and we never cheat on that
point.

Now this clue may be something tangible, like a suspicious-
looking hook on the bottom of a boat that shouldn't be there. Or, it
might be something that someone says—or they misrepresent
themselves. One episode that demonstrates this is when a man pro-
fessed to be an avid bird-watcher, and claimed to be looking in some
trees for the nest of a particular bird—a bird which Jessica re-
searched and found to be a ground-nesting bird.

I remember a verbal clue in another episode when a char-
acter playing a sheriff made a remark that seemed quite
incongruous given the situation, and I thought at the time
that you guys had been pretty obvious with that one!

Yes, that was a character played by John Astin. We figured we'd get away with that one because that character had appeared twice before on our show, so he was kind of established as a running character. In both the previous shows, of course, he hadn't been the murderer, so everyone figured he was a regular.

Speaking of characters, let's talk about Jessica for a moment. How do you keep her involved in one murder after another without making her appear to be a walking Kiss of Death?

We try to overlook that aspect of it. People still invite her places, in spite of the fact that wherever she shows up death is sure to follow! [laughter]

In a series of mystery books like Miss Marple, where a book came out once or twice a year, that wasn't much of a problem. In a series, you've got one a week. It sort of hangs out there nakedly that this character is overly involved in murder, especially since she's not a detective, she's an author!

Well, we try to get her involved in some way through somebody she knows—we've had a series of nieces and nephews, old students from her school teaching days, former neighbors, you name it. Someone she'd had some association with, to keep her on the scene. Otherwise, she would simply say, "Call the police," and get the hell out of there!

A good example of "nailing her to the scene" would be the episode where the bus breaks down in a storm.

Right, in that one she's on the bus, it breaks down and all the passengers are stuck in a little coffee house while they wait out the storm. One of these people is a murderer, and so of course it's in Jessica's best interest to figure out who the murderer is before he or she decides to strike again.

What are the common mistakes made in writing a mystery?

Look to your right there. [Ed. Note: a formidable stack of scripts was on the desk] Those are scripts sent to me by people who watch the show, not by agents. Unsolicited scripts. We get them from viewers, from would-be writers, and working writers. And most of them make a common mistake . . .

Let me interrupt a second. All of those get read?

Well, yes, they all eventually get read. I feel an obligation to at least look at them. It's very unlikely that we would use any, but I guess it's sort of like the lottery—if you don't buy a ticket, it's certain you won't win. So I feel these writers all deserve at least a look because they at least tried. But it's unlikely that any story would hit our particular needs at the time it arrives. When a writer calls and says, "I have a story idea," I'll say, "What's the general area of the idea?" If the writer says, "It's about a family or a group trapped in a bus somewhere and they're snowed in," I can say, "Well, we've done one like that," or "We're doing one like that this year." That way they don't have to waste their time and energy.

But these people [who have submitted spec scripts over the transom] have already written sixty-page scripts—so when I look at them, all I look for is style. Can they actually write for our show? And frankly, most of the ones I get are not professional scripts. Which brings us back to the mistakes . . . They waste pages on introductions—"Jessica, have you met Miss Brown? Miss Brown, Miss Fletcher. And this is the Reverend Smith, and over there is Connie and Jeffrey," and on and on. Now see, the way we actually handle a group introduction like that is to say, "Everybody here knows Jessica Fletcher," and we go on with the show.

Another mistake. Many writers, even experienced ones, seem to forget we're not being shot on a feature film budget. We can't have someone driving up a mountain road, looking out at a castle, and seeing somebody on the castle terrace pushing somebody off. We don't have a castle, we don't have a mountain road, we don't have all that, and we're not gonna get it!

It's mostly interior work?

No, we do a lot of exterior, but we can't go outside of a thirty mile range from the studio or it becomes a distance location and it costs a lot more money.

So even though the show takes place in Maine, you've never done any shooting out there?

Never. Mendocino, California, is our Cabot Cove, Maine. Same location as was used in *The Russians Are Coming, The Russians Are Coming.* Two of our shows are shot there, and of course we have

Jessica's home, the sheriff's office, and the doctor's office on our stages at Universal.

OK, we've touched on two common mistakes made by beginning writers. Any others?

They make Jessica a little old lady. Jessica Fletcher is a sophisticated woman, she's traveled many places and seen many things. She's not easily shocked, although she can certainly be embarrassed. In other words, the mistake is that beginners simply misread her character. Jessica does not participate in bake-offs or things like that, but people are continually casting her in the role of a dotty old grandmother.

From a plot standpoint, the main thing I've noticed in these scripts is that a murderer is announced in the final pages, without any groundwork being laid throughout the story. The murderer seems to be simply "made-up" and arbitrarily decided upon. Certainly the solution should come as a surprise, if possible—but there has to be some preparation. The viewer has to say, "I should have known!"

When I think of a story, I simultaneously think of my ending. Then I work backwards and plan out how Jessica can guess this murderer's identity. Many writers, I think, start out by having fifteen people who could have committed the murder, and figure out the story from there.

How can beginning writers become more proficient at writing mysteries?

I think most people learn to write mysteries by reading them. You can't see many closed mysteries on television—"closed" mysteries are the kind where you don't know the murderer. "Open" mysteries are like "Columbo," where you know who the bad guy is and you're just watching the hero figure it out and trap him. Most television shows are open mysteries. "Perry Mason" is a closed mystery, "Matlock" is sometimes closed. We always do a closed mystery.

Lots of books, however, are closed mysteries. Although an interesting sidenote is that a lot of mystery novelists have not been able to write for our show. I think they find the form to be difficult—writing a novel is such a leisurely thing, meaning you have so much time to describe settings, do internal monologues, talk about your character's past. Of course, the pace of a TV show is much faster, and I guess they find that limiting.

Also, it's a lot easier to hide a killer's identity in a book. Heck, if you never say his or her name, it's a secret to the end! On television, of course, all murderers are easy to spot, because they all wear black gloves! [laughter]

Any advice for aspiring writers out there? I mean other than to become a page boy at NBC?

Keep plugging away. We use new writers, at least new to us if not necessarily new to the world. We used three or four last year that were new to us.

How did they come to your attention?

Through their agents. We really have to deal with writers through their agents, that's the only way we can even listen to their ideas over the phone. It's for their protection as well as ours. But once we're contacted by an agent, and we listen to the writer's ideas—we're open to using anyone that can write well, or more specifically, write our show well.

CHAPTER 9

How to Write Situation Comedies

HALF-HOUR SITUATION COMEDIES, or sitcoms, represent one of the best avenues for a new writer trying to break in to television scriptwriting. This is not to say that it's easy. Like anything else that has a high payoff (at present, about $10,000 per script) the competition is fierce, and those who have already made it guard their positions zealously. However, the sheer volume of material eaten up by weekly exposure to a nation of viewers necessitates the use of outside writers.

Very interesting, you say. But how do *you* become one of those freelancers these shows continually turn to?

You need a calling card. You need a sample script (referred to as a "spec" script because you write it on speculation), one so good and so funny it will compel a story editor or producer to call you in to a pitch session to present story ideas for his show. This script needs to be the very best piece of material you've ever written, without one weak story point, one forced joke, one characterization flaw, or even one typo. It needs to be as perfect as you can make it.

• SO HOW DO I START?

Pick a show you like *very much*. Make sure it's a show that's considered a "quality" sitcom: a "Cheers," or "Family Ties," or "Golden Girls." Avoid shows that target an audience of kids, and definitely stay away from those few that seem to be aimed at semi-intelligent house pets. (Thankfully, the majority of these kinds of shows usually don't last long enough to qualify for spec script consideration, anyway.)

Now, study that show. This doesn't mean you simply learn the characters' full names and where they live. You have to really *know* the show's rhythms, its comedic style, its patterns. Who gets the sophisticated humor, who gets the ribald lines, who handles the physical gags? Who gets the *most* laughs? What type of subject matter does the show tend to deal with? Are the stories generally straightforward, or complex? Does the show use a brief introductory scene—a teaser? Does it end with a brief scene after the main story has been resolved—a tag?

To really *know* a sitcom, there are physical guidelines and limitations you need to be aware of. A sitcom is shot in one of two ways: three-camera videotape, or one-camera film. To see the difference compare the look and texture of an episode of "M*A*S*H" to a "Night Court" segment. Film tends to offer a certain variation in lighting and a graininess that adds to the realism—which is why most one-hour shows are shot on film. Videotape invariably gives a flat, evenly lighted look to a show.

Why should you care how a show is shot? Because it could have an impact on how you plot your script.

The overwhelming majority of sitcoms are shot on videotape, with three cameras, on a sound stage, and in front of a studio audience. Normally this precludes including any outside locations in your script (once in a while a show will fake an outside location on a sound stage, but it usually looks phony). For the most part, you'll want to set your scenes at interior locations you've seen on the show before.

Let's take "Cheers" as an example. You've got the bar, Sam's office, the back room with a pool table, and one changeable set that's usually used as an apartment interior. There have been episodes in which Sam takes a girl out on a boat, or the characters are in fancy restaurants, or whatever. The point is, those were exceptions to the rule, probably quite costly exceptions, and were debated long and hard by the entire production team before being considered important enough to produce. Your sample script must engender no such debate. Stay with the sets and locations you see each and every week.

Also, keep the cast of your spec script within the circle of regulars as much as possible. Keep the introduction of "guest" characters to an absolute minimum, and avoid them entirely if you can. You're trying to show how well you can write for an existing show, not how clever you are at original characterization. A common mistake beginners make is to write a script featuring Alex's new friend, who's a very funny guy, gets all the laughs, and finds himself in all kinds of trouble from which he manages to extricate himself, thanks to his quick wit and clever repartee. Unfortunately, no matter how hilarious this script is, what it shows is that you were unable to write a script for an existing show, using existing characters.

Finally, remember that sitcoms are shot quickly and on a tight budget (thus the three-camera tape method, which is far cheaper and faster than film). So, no wild special effects, no expensive props, no stunts requiring the destruction of an existing set—no *anything* that's out of the ordinary from a production standpoint.

• WHAT'S THE STRUCTURE OF A SITCOM?

Before the jokes must come the story, and structuring your sitcom requires the basics of storytelling: a beginning, middle, and end. The trick is to fit them into the two-act framework.

It's essential in a sitcom that your character gets involved in a problem immediately. The term "situation comedy" wasn't arrived at by chance. It suggests that your story and humor needs to spring directly from a given situation in which your main character finds himself, whether it be over his head, beneath his dignity, out of his hands, or another fine mess he's gotten himself into. The fun comes in seeing this character somehow bungle his way out of that mess, at the same time that he realizes he's learned something from this experience.

Let's see how a story develops by first examining what should happen in Act I.

Act I

The very first thing to do is kick the story into gear. The audience is watching to find out what that wacky pair of gals will get into next, and you need to grab their interest right away. Before your first scene ends, which means by page 3 or so assuming there's no teaser, the conflict or problem should be out in the open and ready for action.

In many cases, you'll also use this first scene to set up your B plot. Almost without exception, sitcoms have an A or main plot, and a B or subplot. For example, on the "Newhart" show, a scene might open with Larry, Darryl, and Darryl demonstrating the song they've chosen to perform in the upcoming Three-Man Team Tuba Competition (B plot) when Dick comes in and demands some quiet so he can finish up on the novel he's been trying to complete for ten years (A plot). The A plot carries more significance, and at least twice as much screen time will be devoted to seeing it through. The B plot is mostly there for variety's sake, giving us some relief from the main plot, and allowing for a different type of interplay and humor among the supporting cast. If not in the first scene, certainly by the second scene your B plot should be underway.

Each successive scene in Act I proceeds in a series of story "beats" . . . occurrences, actions, or decisions that serve to complicate the story and force reactions from the characters. The consequences of these reactions then have further consequences of their own, and so on, until things are in a true and seemingly hopeless uproar.

• SHOULD THIS UPROAR OCCUR BY THE END OF THE FIRST ACT?

No. This is a common mistake, and one that spells disaster for your second act. Your story should continue to build *through* the act break, reaching its point-of-no-return roughly halfway through the second act. The reason is quite simple: if you jam all your complications into the first act and peak there, what do you do for the next twenty pages? You lose all pace and momentum, and your story comes to a screeching halt, as does the interest of your reader/viewer.

The act break is the midpoint of your story, and is really just another story beat that happens to have a lot more significance than any of the beats preceding it. It's the turning point that sends the plot in a new and hopefully unique and funny direction, the surprise twist you build in to keep your audience loyal to you through two minutes of fast food commercials. So, continuing our "Newhart" storyline, the act break might come when, after convincing everyone in the lodge to leave for the weekend and let him finish the final chapter in his book, the chapter that has taken five years just to *outline*, but the one he now feels welling up inside him, Dick finds himself staring at blank paper and realizing that he simply can't do it.

Act II

The first scene in Act II is obviously dictated by the cliffhanger left for us at the end of Act I. As in every script, there are lots of choices available—the key is to find the avenue that affords the most complications and the biggest laughs. We might open with a tight shot of Dick yanking a piece of paper out of the typewriter, balling it up, and taking aim at a trash can. When we pull back, we see the trash can is completely buried by similar wads of paper. There's no way he can even *see* it, much less hit it. He watches the paper ball tumble down the stack, stares at it a moment . . . and then scoops his typewriter up and heaves it along the same path.

As you can see, we've taken the idea of his novel being revealed as nothing more than a pipedream (end of Act I) and reinforced it, rubbed his nose in it, with our first scene in Act II. The next scene must build upon that idea, and begin to incorporate the glimmerings of a solution. It doesn't have to be a correct solution, or an effective solution, just a funny solution, given his character's personality. Would he just knuckle down and pound out any old trash just to finish, knowing full well it will be rejected? Would he secretly toss in the towel, while maintaining a facade of great progress and accomplishment when his wife and friends come back? Or, would he clean up the mess, and admit to himself, *and* his wife and friends, that he just isn't a novelist, that he oughta be happy with his role as a successful how-to writer, and that's all? Or, would he clean up, sit back down, and finally get that last damn chapter done just the way he'd always felt it would look?

The choice you make when writing your script is dictated by several factors: 1) Is it true to the character? 2) Is it true to the tone of the show? 3) Is it funny?

As Act II progresses, you'll be developing your B plot, in a much less detailed fashion, of course. In most cases the B plot is little more than a sequence of gags that follows a very straightforward storyline, and resolves itself with little complication.

Your A plot, on the other hand, must resolve itself in a very specific manner.

• A LESSON LEARNED

Since the beginning of sitcoms, main characters have been "learning their lesson" from the situations in which they've found themselves embroiled. Lucy learned not to sneak into Ricky's band, just because she was jealous of his glamorous lifestyle. For the sake of the show, of course, she forgot the lesson by the following week. She snuck into Ricky's band on a pretty regular basis. Ralph Kramden learned to quit coming up with get-rich-quick schemes (again, at least for the period of one week). More recently, Sam finds that he was wrong in trying to lie to Carla; Alex decides that maybe some things *are* more important than money; Judge Harry Stone discovers he has the capacity to make the hard decisions a good judge must make in spite of personal feelings.

A note here: in a spec script, make sure your A plot features the main character as the one who learns a lesson. In an ensemble comedy, there's a little more latitude, but even ensemble shows have their "anchor" character (Sam, in "Cheers"; Barney, in "Barney Miller"; Alex, in "Family Ties"; and another Alex in "Taxi"). Your script should have the key characters figure prominently in the action. Don't make the mistake of having your script be the one where some obscure secondary character suddenly comes into his own. That kind of decision is not yours to make, and the producers are not interested in reading that story. They want to see how well you handle character and dialogue, and how well you can hang a story together, and, of course, if you can write funny.

• IS THERE A METHOD TO WRITING JOKES?

There are many people who consider the ability to write comedy something you're born with—you either got it or you ain't. We concur . . . up to a point. You're either born with a sense of humor or it's learned at a very early age. But it's quite possible to learn how to train that sense of humor, and learn how to construct a joke that works in a sitcom script.

There's danger in the tendency to intellectualize comedy. It's impossible to tell someone what's funny and what isn't. After all, what's funny to one person goes right over the head or under the brow of somebody else. Instead, let's generalize a bit about the kind of humor that traditionally works well in sitcoms, and give you some guidelines to follow. It's up to you to make a laugh riot ensue.

First of all, break out your Mr. Fix-It Woodburning Set and engrave this on your desk: *All humor must flow from, and be true to, the show's characters.* Whether it be a reaction to whatever situation confronts them, or certain character flaws and/or idiosyncrasies, the comedy comes from them. They do not do stand-up routines, or tell long, involved jokes that have nothing to do with the story (unless of course they're Bill Cosby, in which case they do whatever they want). Instead, they react to each other, and to the particular crisis that confronts them in this episode.

The whole idea of a *situation* comedy is that you plunk your funny folks down into a situation that's either completely foreign to them, or one they cause to go awry and eventually erupt, becoming something far above their heads and out of their hands. Now, speaking very generally, there are two ways you'll get laughs at this point: verbal humor, and physical humor.

• VERBAL HUMOR

Watch one episode of "M*A*S*H" and you'll receive a Master's course in verbal humor. They relied on it constantly, and achieved it with a consistency as good as, and arguably better than, any other sitcom to date.

Verbal humor, or more simply, "funny lines," should seem to come naturally, given the personality of the character. This holds true no matter how much sweat and blood you put into getting that *one word* just right to make the joke play. When the character says it, it has to sound exactly like something that character would just say naturally.

Let's take "Cheers" as an example. Here's a show that offers some of the finest, most intelligent humor on the air, and one of the main reasons is the very distinct, different personalities and deliveries of each of the cast members. There would be no mistaking a Carla line for a Diane line, or a Woody line for a Norm line. When written correctly, the jokes you write for these characters will sound precisely like something they would say. In fact, when you write those lines you should be able to actually *hear* the characters delivering them. If you can't, something's wrong with the line.

Avoid forcing a joke just for the sake of a joke. Admittedly, many sitcoms that make the airways are a bit guilty of this, but remember that your spec script can't be "as good as" anything on the air, it has to be better. So, be sure your gags are intrinsic to the story, or at least timed correctly and written well enough that they don't come off sounding like a limping attempt at humor that just doesn't quite make it. Don't settle for a joke just because you can't come up with a better one. Either work harder to find a funnier joke, or eliminate it altogether. It's better to have no joke at all than a bad one.

Avoid long speeches. A good exercise that'll help you learn the rhythm of a sitcom is to simply listen to it, paying no heed to the visuals. Tape record the show, and transcribe it if you like. You'll find that the sentences are succinct, and the jokes punched out with as much economy of words as possible. Nothing kills a verbal gag faster than talking it to death. Another way to get a good idea of the pacing of a sitcom is to obtain a sample script from the show you're writing for. They'll usually send you one if you write a nice, polite letter and provide an envelope with plenty of postage.

• PHYSICAL HUMOR

For some, writing physical humor can be the most difficult part of writing comedy. For others, it almost comes without thinking, as a natural extension of the character's behavior. Whether you are one of these or somewhere in-between, the physical humor you write will follow pretty much the same guidelines as the verbal humor. It has to spring directly from the character, and his unique method of dealing with, or not dealing with, the situation. For this, you must of course be very familiar with your characters, not only so you'll remain consistent with his or her traits, but so you'll know what kinds of things that actor is capable of pulling off. There are not a lot of Buster Keatons or Harold Lloyds out there in sitcom land—but then again, both Mark Linn-Baker and Bronson Pinchot of "Perfect Strangers" are capable of amazing physical agility (see the interview with Bill Bickley at the end of this chapter).

As you can see, your cast dictates the type of humor you'll rely on most. "Golden Girls" uses very little physical humor, while "Perfect Strangers" or "Night Court" uses it quite a bit. I should hasten to note that physical humor doesn't necessarily mean falling down, pie-in-the-face slapstick. It could be a look, or a long sigh, or a quick and graceful dance step. Anything other than a snappy line qualifies as a physical gag, and needs to be included in the action portion of your script whenever appropriate.

• A SAMPLE BREAKDOWN

Using an episode of "Perfect Strangers," here is a sample breakdown demonstrating the two act structure:

Act I

Balki agrees to take care of a young woman's baby boy for the weekend. He didn't consult with Larry, but ends up getting tricked into agreeing to the idea.

Balki takes care of the baby, and a disgruntled Larry won't help. Balki does the baby's laundry, washing its Pampers and creating quite a mess. Larry accuses Balki of taking his responsibilities too lightly, and ends up pitching in.

The baby is crying all night, and the boys try all sorts of hilarious methods, none successful, to get the baby to sleep.

Act II

The next morning the boys take the baby for a trip to the park, but on the way back discover the baby they have now is a *girl!* They've taken home the wrong baby! They go back to the park to look for him.

They return to the apartment, unsuccessful in their search. Worse yet, the boy's mother is coming back any minute for her baby.

When the mother arrives, they go into a classic stall. Fortunately, the mother of the little girl shows up, and they make the exchange without the baby boy's mother finding out.

In the end, Balki and Larry discuss what it was like having a baby around, and how much there is to learn about being a father.

• WHAT'S THE FORMAT FOR A SITCOM?

If the show is shot on film, the format is identical to that of a feature film. Single-spaced dialogue, separated by a double-space from the single-spaced description of the action, with the dialogue centered and the action description justified left.

On the other hand, a videotaped sitcom's script format is unique. As with a feature script, you'll single-space action description and justify it to the left—but it's all typed in capital letters. Also, these descriptions are kept as sparse and spare as humanly possible. Pretend you never learned all those terrific adjectives you've got standing by, and just tell what goes on in as few words as possible.

Dialogue is double-spaced, and written in upper- and lower-case. This was originally done to facilitate the use of the teleprompter, which rolls pages of the script out so an actor can read them during a performance. That's not done very much anymore, but the format remains as a standard.

Naturally, this nearly doubles your page calculation—instead of a page per minute, you'll estimate about thirty seconds per page. Since a half-hour show is on the air roughly twenty-six minutes, your script should be anywhere between thirty-eight to forty-two pages long.

A sitcom is performed in two acts, sometimes with a teaser, sometimes a tag, and occasionally both. As explained earlier, a "teaser" is a short scene at the beginning of the show that may or may not have anything to do with the plot to follow ("Cheers" and "Kate and Allie" both use teasers), while a "tag" is an editable, funny little tail that also has little or nothing to do with the plot of the episode, and comes on after Act II is resolved and there's been a commercial break. The reason the tag must be inconsequential to the plot is it will be cut once the show is put into syndication, in order to allow for more commercial time. Tags don't seem to be used as frequently as they used to be.

Both tags and teasers are only about one and one-half pages long. Each of the two acts in your script should run between eighteen to twenty-one pages for videotape, roughly fourteen pages for film.

The following is an example of a scene from a hypothetical episode of "Family Ties," demonstrating the videotape format.

INT. MALLORY'S ROOM

MALLORY COMBS HER HAIR IN THE MIRROR, AS ALEX STANDS BEHIND HER.

> MALLORY
> No kidding, Alex? He really cheated?

> ALEX
> He really did. I'm sorry, Mallory.

> MALLORY
> He cheated? Just so he could win a date with me?

SHE SMILES.

> ALEX
> The man is completely without character.

> MALLORY
>
> I think it's kind of romantic.

ALEX IS STUNNED.

> ALEX
>
> Romantic?

> MALLORY
>
> To think that he was so madly infatuated with me that he was
>
> willing to cheat to win that bet.

> ALEX
>
> Hey, let's not forget, the man had twenty bucks at stake.

> MALLORY
>
> Alex, you just don't understand romance. You can't put a price
>
> tag on love.

> ALEX
>
> (EXASPERATED) Of course you can! And twenty bucks is a
>
> very fair price!

MALLORY TURNS AWAY FROM HIM.

> MALLORY
>
> Get lost, Alex.

ALEX STANDS.

> ALEX
>
> Love may be blind, Mallory, but I'm not. My duty as a brother is
>
> clear. I got you into this, and now I'll get you out.

> DISSOLVE TO:

Once you've combined all that we've talked about—format, story, pacing, and humor—you will have a spec script you can be proud of.

• AND IF THEY LIKE MY SCRIPT, THEY BUY IT?

No. Or, more correctly, very, very rarely. We've heard of that happening exactly one time. What usually happens is they'll give your agent a call (or you, if you don't have an agent and you were somehow able to get the spec script to them), and will ask to have you in for a pitch session. It should be noted that your spec script is a calling card to *any* similar series on the air. In other words, it's perfectly okay, and indeed common practice, to send a spec "Golden Girls" script to "Cheers," "Family Ties," or what have you. In fact, very often the people who work on a show don't want to see a script done for their show. They feel too close to the subject to be objective, and they probably are. That's why you pick a well-known, successful show to be your spec script—everyone's familiar with the characters, and the script can be shopped around. Once you have an appointment, you have to put about half-a-dozen ideas together, go in, and "pitch" them verbally. Chapter 16 of this book deals with the specifics and techniques of successful pitching, so we won't go into them here. Suffice it to say that you should know your stories very, very well, and they had better be the best ideas you're able to come up with. Think long and hard about each idea as you work it out; obtain a "bible" (a listing of past stories done on the show) so you don't duplicate any ideas already aired; be prepared to junk one idea and move on to the next if you seem to be getting a negative reaction; and be flexible! Don't fight for your ideas—if the producer or story editor doesn't like it, it's no sale, so don't belabor the issue. Just knock 'em dead with the next one!

Now let's talk with a seasoned pro in the field of sitcom writing. William Bickley offers some sound advice based on years of experience, not only in writing, but in story editing, producing, and creating successful sitcoms as well.

WILLIAM BICKLEY

William Bickley and his long-time partner Michael Warren are the Supervising Producers of "Perfect Strangers."

I've noticed not only on "Perfect Strangers" but on many other shows you've been part of, there is a significant amount of physical comedy written into the story. How would an outside writer come in to you and pitch physical gags—do they have to rely a lot on your imagination?

Well, it's not hard to imagine physical comedy on a show where the actors are so good at physical comedy. We don't even really seek out stories that have physical comedy in them, that's not one of our priorities. Our priority is to find a story that the viewer can identify with, something that might be right out of their own experience. Off that, we simply plug our characters into that story, and say, "Now how would these guys deal with this particular problem?" The key is to stay as faithful as possible to our characters, and how they would respond to these situations.

Now, on our show, as I say, we don't look specifically for physical comedy. We know we have actors who are capable of incredible physical gags—Mark Linn-Baker has a lot of experience as a mime, and Bronson Pinchot is a tremendous physical comedian, so we know we have that available to us. But we don't go into a story saying, "Where's the physical comedy?" We know that if it's there, we'll find it.

But I can see that as a writer coming in to pitch to you, I might say, "The two guys fall asleep on the couch after a hard workout at the health club, and when they wake up for their dates they are really sore!" And you'd look at me and say, "And . . . ?" Yet a recent episode featured that exact scene, and it must have gone on for about five minutes— and it was hysterical.

But that idea, that they were so sore they couldn't move, was the last thing we came up with for that story. It started simply as, "What if Balki joined a health club?" Now in terms of any foreseeable physical comedy, we thought it would be funny to see the two guys in the health club. In the development of the story we thought they needed something at stake, so we had them meet women at the health club and make a date. The very last thing that came up was that they would experience the kind of soreness that's incapacitating, and try to hide it.

In that kind of situation, do you rely a lot on the actors for input?

When we write a script, we'll include some physical comedy—but a lot of it comes from the actors during rehearsals. Every time we go see a rehearsal of a show, several times a week, we always see what we wrote plus what they've come up with. Which is a lot, with these two guys!

For instance, in one of our first episodes we wrote a brief opening to a scene where we just say that Larry is helping Balki tie his tie in preparation for Balki's first date. Well, the actors turned it into a physical bit that we could never have written on paper. The actors take what we've written, apply their craft, and what we come out with is a lot more physical comedy than we may have originally intended.

Okay, let's take a closer look at the kind of stories you like. You mentioned you like them to be reality based . . .

But keep in mind that I can't prove that by some of the episodes we've done! The rule gets violated sometimes. However, I know that Michael and I don't particularly believe that there's such a thing as an idea so new that no one else has ever done it. All we really care about is that it has those ingredients I mentioned—that it could actually happen to someone. It might be unusual, but it still might happen, and our characters can then respond in a manner true to their personalities.

For instance, we did a show where Balki gets his driver's license. Now, a show where one of the characters gets his driver's license must have been done a hundred times on television. But it's the common quality of the experience that makes it worth doing that many times.

So you don't really care if the story has been done before.

Not as long as it's something we want to see our people do. We have confidence that our characters can do a story that's been done, and it will still be interesting.

So the initial conception of the series' characters is crucial.

Characters in a TV series start out as skeletons and take on flesh as the series goes on and on. Even in the first few episodes, the characters grow and change so much that they're quite different— not contradictory, but different, than they were in the beginning. As you write about them, they grow, and as the actors find out about them, they grow and take on more and more facets. Theoretically, characters should continue to grow throughout the series, always in a manner consistent with the way they've behaved in the past. So, you would eventually be able to say that the characters were created by everyone who's ever written for the show, and by the actors that played them.

And once the characters stop growing?

That's when the show gets stale.

Do you use outside writers on your show?

We use outside writers. Not as often as staff writers, of course, for two reasons. One is that many writers in the Guild who are available to freelance episodes are not very good, and the second and biggest reason is that a show changes from week to week. Not drastically, perhaps, but it changes. And it's the writers who are seeing every dress rehearsal of the show and every filming and every rough cut, and who attend every reading of the script, that know how the series is changing. Obviously they have a better grasp than someone who has seen the show on television, where they're seeing an episode that was shot four or five months previously.

Outside writers are at a clear disadvantage when they come in to pitch or sit down to write a script—but that's OK. We take that into consideration; it's the reason outside scripts are so extensively rewritten. But when time is of the essence the most normal thing to do is go to the writers who will write the fastest, the best, and be closest to the bull's-eye on the first draft, because sometimes you don't have time for a full-fledged second draft. So, you go to your strengths.

However, we're not closed off to outside writers. We've used outside writers, and we intend to use them in the future.

Do you have them in to pitch a half-dozen ideas, or do you assign stories already conceived in-house?

We work in any number of ways. One way is to have a writer we know and like come in and pitch some ideas, one of which we might like. We might not like any of them, but we'll develop an idea we've had in-house that hasn't been written yet. Or, we might not have anything at all, and that writer moves on until such time as we would have something for him or her.

Or there might be a writer who we specifically want to do a script for us, and we'll call them in for the express purpose of doing that particular story. In that case, the writer may have some ideas of his own, but we are bringing him in with the intention of having him do a script.

How do you decide who you're going to see?

In the early stages of a new series it's very difficult to use writers who don't have a track record, because it makes the network nervous. That's unfortunate, because an uncredited writer might be far, far, far better than one with a hundred credits. But any producer's going out on a limb when he gives an uncredited writer an assignment on a new show, because if it turns out badly, then the network and the executive producer are going to jump on the producer's neck.

As a show ages, solidifies, becomes more established—then those restrictions lift.

So strategically it's much better for new writers to be aiming at shows that have been on for a while?

It's more likely the writer will get a chance on a show that's been on for a while. It's also more likely that the show will have developed to the point where a writer can learn a show by watching it on the air—it's no longer in the early stages of development. The show is set clearly. So, the writer has the ability, simply by watching television, to get an idea of the characters and the kinds of stories to do.

A new show is in such a state of transition that it's very difficult for a writer to know what it's about.

The prescribed way for an unknown and uncredited writer to get a pitch session is to send in a spec script. Now I (Cox) had an experience lately where a producer called me and said, "Your spec script is very funny, but we're not interested in doing stories like this." That seemed like a strange comment to me.

Well, it's kind of an ignorant comment. I'll tell you what Michael and I look for in a spec script, and I think it's true of most producers who have their wits about them. We never look at a spec script with the idea that we'll find a script that we can just send in and shoot. It's just a sample. Can the writer write? That's why it doesn't matter whether it's a script for our show or some other show. Inevitably, writers are not going to come up with a story that you either haven't done or haven't already considered. Spec scripts are a way for a writer to get noticed.

Do you look more for the ability of the writer to handle a story, or to write humorously?

I'm not particularly interested in a spec script as to whether the story works, except if I see the writer take the story in an absurd direction, or turn a story in a way that is not good storytelling. Then I'm worried that the writer might do the same thing to the character, or might have some other fault with his writing. It's a bad sign. I don't really care if it's a dynamite story, because I'm looking for how a writer writes dialogue, whether a writer writes intelligently, and if he can actually capture a given character consistently.

In fact, for me anyway, scenes would serve the purpose just as well, and the writer wouldn't have to beat his head against the wall trying to find some story that hasn't been done on the series, or is so unique it'll grab someone's interest. I'm not reading it as a novel, I'm trying to see if the writer can write character. I never read all of a spec script anyway—I read enough to tell me whether a writer can write. We take care of the story.

So, in summary?

Aim for established shows, write an intelligent spec script with good dialogue, and do anything that keeps you writing.

CHAPTER 10

How to Write For Daytime Serials (Soaps)

A SCIENTIFIC POLL HAS PROBABLY never been taken, but it's our bet that daytime serials (termed "soaps," thanks to their origin as shows sponsored by companies selling detergents to housewives) can boast a larger number of fans who swear "I never watch those things" than any other type of show. Soaps rank as one of the most enduring and relentlessly popular forms of entertainment, dating back to the days of radio drama and "Helen Trent," evolving along the way to the steamy drama of shows such as "General Hospital" or "Santa Barbara." They are watched by housewives, househusbands, lawyers, firefighters, schoolteachers, schoolchildren, college students, retired colonels, and office workers on lunch breaks. In short, just about everyone has seen a soap at one time or another.

True-blue soap opera viewers are nothing less than addicts, manipulating their daily lives around that all-important midday half-hour or hour when it's "Time for my soap." Note the proprietary "My." Soaps aren't just for passive viewing; they inspire *involvement*. People who watch soaps keep a daily tab on their favorite characters; they write fan letters—to the *characters*, not the actors—offering counsel and advice; they will literally shout warnings at the television screen; and they will make life miserable for a show's producers and head writer if a beloved character is suddenly killed off.

For the writer, the soaps offer several unique challenges. If ever there has been an entertainment form where teamwork is the essential factor, soaps are surely it.

• WHO WRITES THE SOAPS?

The sheer volume of scripted material eaten up by any given soap demands the talents of many writers working at breakneck pace all day long, and all year long. Remember, there are no repeats in soaps (in fact, taped episodes only have a shelf life of a month or so before they're erased and the tape reused), so five days a week, fifty-two weeks a year, something fresh, interesting, and brand new must take place on that television screen. To make this kind of output possible, a well-organized team system is utilized that keeps those scripts coming with assembly-line dependability and speed. While each show has its own way of doing things, there is a general chain of command that applies to all, beginning with the Executive Producer and the show's sponsor.

These two entities, along with a show's producer or producers, will meet for a story conference with the show's head writer. Together, they will work out a general, long-range projection for the show. This will contain the basic direction the series will take that year, with major story lines mapped out in such a way as to target various goals for each of the main characters.

At that point, the head writer breaks that projection down into weekly, and finally daily, outlines. These are known, appropriately enough, as "breakdowns," and they take into account such things as the "Friday hook," which will keep viewers eager for the next week's first episode. They will also pay due consideration to the show's production budget, the number of sets available, the need to work new characters in and eliminate others, the amount of time available for shooting each episode, and all of the thousands of other production details that always seem to pop up and spoil the fun of simple, unbridled creativity.

The daily breakdown is a very detailed outline, even to the point of specifying which characters have speaking parts and which don't (an important budgetary consideration, since Screen Actors Guild rates are based in part on the amount of lines an actor speaks). Character motivation is clearly noted, as is any action necessary to the scene's completion. A breakdown of a single scene might look something like this:

CUT TO: APARTMENT
Robert has entered in spite of Laurie's pleas. She pulls on his arm, trying to keep him from storming into the bedroom. He won't be stopped, and finds Mark inside. He's wearing Robert's robe. Robert stands for a moment, his anger suddenly drained. He turns, and his eyes are filled with tears.

Scene-for-scene, a summary like this is done for each episode of the week. Once finished, this breakdown will go to an associate writer, who will be assigned a show and given a deadline, usually about a week.

An associate writer has an office at the studio, or, more commonly, works at home. When the mail arrives with his assignment the clock starts, and he gets right to work reading the breakdowns. He reads breakdowns not only of his episode, but also of the ones before and immediately after his, to get as clear an understanding as possible of the intentions and directions his show must follow. And then, to work.

Once his assignment is turned in, it's probably the last he'll see of it until it hits the airwaves. Soaps are produced at such a frenzied pace that usually all rewriting is handled by in-house staff writers and the head writer. The associate writer will have already received his next assignment, and it's off to the races again.

• THE STRUCTURE OF A SOAP

Because the plotlines of a soap are planned out over a number of scripts, no single script will be structured with a traditional beginning, middle, and end. Instead, each script serves the function of moving the story along toward its planned conclusion, which may be due to occur three days, three weeks, or three months from the date of the show you're writing. This is one reason why many "nighttime" writers (of sitcoms or hour-long shows) have been unable to find success in daytime serials; they find it frustrating and unnatural to conclude their scripts in mid-story, so to speak.

The soap opera writer must concentrate on a much larger picture when writing her assigned script. She needs to keep the general thrust of the storyline in mind, fulfilling her script's function in the overall master plan, all the while making sure her scenes are filled with enough conflict and character development that viewer interest will be maintained. She is always aiming toward that ultimate resolution, but she rarely will see it through to completion.

Rather than overall structure, then, the soap writer must be concerned about other factors, such as pace, rhythm, and style. Each scene needs a special energy and drive of its own, turning a passive viewer into an *involved* one who will yell angrily at one character's nefarious deeds, or fall in love right along with another character. For that kind of energy, a great deal depends on a writer's ability to handle dialogue efficiently, effectively, and with credibility. Let's take a look at the sample scene breakdown we used earlier as an example, and try two different approaches to turning it into a script.

CUT TO:
THE APARTMENT. LAURIE IS FUMBLING DESPERATELY WITH THE CHAIN ON THE DOOR, BUT CAN'T SLIDE IT INTO PLACE IN TIME TO KEEP ROBERT FROM SHOVING HIS WAY IN.

LAURIE
(PULLING ON ROBERT'S ARM AS HE STORMS BY HER) Robert! Robert, don't go in there! I asked you not to come!

ROBERT
(SHAKING HER LOOSE, HE CONTINUES TOWARD THE BEDROOM) I'm through listening to you! You've been nothing but trouble since the day I met you. Now, where is he?

LAURIE
Robert, don't ... (SHE COLLAPSES ON THE COUCH, SOBBING)

ROBERT
Oh, so he is here, eh? Where, in the bedroom? Sure, that's it! (HE FLINGS OPEN THE BEDROOM DOOR, AND SEES MARK INSIDE, WEARING ONLY A ROBE) You! And that's ... that's my robe! Take it off! (HE TURNS TOWARD LAURIE, AND STARTS TO CRY). Laurie ... How could you do this to me ... (HOLD ON A C.U. OF HIS TEAR-STREAKED FACE).

Before your gorge rises to a point of no return, we'll take another shot at this scene, changing only the dialogue.

CUT TO:
THE APARTMENT. LAURIE IS FUMBLING DESPERATELY WITH THE CHAIN ON THE DOOR, BUT CAN'T SLIDE IT INTO PLACE IN TIME TO KEEP ROBERT FROM SHOVING HIS WAY IN.

> LAURIE
> (PULLING ON ROBERT'S ARM AS HE STORMS BY HER) Robert, no! I swear I'll kill you this time!

> ROBERT
> (SHAKING HER LOOSE, HE CONTINUES TOWARD THE BEDROOM) This is still my house.

> LAURIE
> All right. Fine. Then, assuming you can remember where your own bedroom is . . . Go ahead. (SHE COLLAPSES ON THE COUCH, SOBBING)

> ROBERT
> (HE FLINGS OPEN THE BEDROOM DOOR, AND SEES MARK INSIDE, WEARING ONLY A ROBE) Nice touch, Laurie. (TO MARK) Take the robe off, Mark. I think it's supposed to be my Christmas present. (HE TURNS TOWARD LAURIE, AND STARTS TO CRY). You'll be happy to know I've brought you a little Christmas present too, Laurie. (HOLD ON C.U. OF HIS TEAR-STREAKED FACE).

As you can see, we've managed to inject a bit of subtext in the dialogue, while also making it more credible and less melodramatic. Additionally, it's shorter; and, as in any script for a visual medium, it's best to show, not tell, whenever possible. What we've also done is end the scene with a cliffhanger. Admittedly, it's not a real chair-gripper, but it does leave us up in the air, wondering what's in store for Laurie. What kind of Christmas present has Robert brought? Flowers? A matching robe? A gun?

Because dialogue is of such vital importance in soap writing, you need to be very, very familiar with the speech patterns and rhythms of the show's main characters. Most soap producers suggest that an aspiring writer track a show for at least a month before even attempting to write a word of a sample script. We recommend you also study Chapter 4 of this book, where we give a detailed treatment on the subject of writing believable dialogue.

• THE FORMAT

As you may have noticed from the sample scenes in this chapter, the format for a soap opera script differs from that of any of the other types of scripts we've come across so far. But the real hitch is that the format can vary from show to show! Some programs use the standard soap format described below, while others prefer a radio script format, which looks something like this:

LAURIE: Robert, no!

ROBERT: It's still my house, Laurie.

This format cuts the average length of a one-hour soap in half, down to about thirty-five pages or so. The running time for a soap script is generally a bit more than one minute per page, ignoring the commercial breaks. In other words, figure a one-hour show to be 60 minutes long (even though commercials will shorten it by 8-10 minutes or so) and a script for a one-hour show to run about seventy pages. A half-hour soap will be roughly thirty-five pages long.

As the sample scenes show, the main thing differentiating soap format from feature format is that all directions for actors are capitalized, single-spaced, and enclosed in parentheses within the same margins as the dialogue. A soap script is practically devoid of camera directions, other than CUT TO, DISSOLVE TO, and other simple transitional instructions.

The best thing to do is to try to obtain some back scripts of whatever show you're intending to write for, and learn their format. Pay close attention to the credits given before and after the program, so you can learn the name of the production company you need to contact. Then, call the offices of that company and speak with one of the secretaries. Explain that you're interested in writing for daytime serials, and would like to obtain some back scripts. Offer to send a postage-paid envelope. This extra effort to match your script's format to the show's accepted format will give your submission a mark of professionalism, and that's the first step toward success.

• HOW DO I BECOME AN ASSOCIATE WRITER?

Because soap writing offers steady, dependable employment, week in and week out, the supply of willing writers generally exceeds the demand. Take a look at the astounding credits list of our interviewee at the end of this chapter, Robert Shaw, and you'll see that soap writers are tradesmen of the first order, churning out a quality product fifty weeks a year, with two weeks paid vacation. Just like a regular job!

This is, in other words, one of the toughest markets to crack, since a new writer isn't trying to sell a script or pitch specific ideas, but rather be taken on as an associate writer. Occasionally, however, the veteran writers do burn out, or quit, or move on to something else, and suddenly an opening exists. At this point an agent who deals with soap writers would be very helpful, since he would certainly get first notice of any such opportunity. Barring that, any connection with the insiders of the industry will increase your chances of getting a head writer to take a look at your sample script. Such insiders would include secretaries, receptionists, or people in the business office.

Of course, the majority of aspiring soap writers have no such connections and must rely on their own initiative and ingenuity to convince the head writer to give them a trial run as an associate. (Associates are taken on a probationary basis at first, before being given a more lengthy contract.) Many writers working in soaps have established a track record in other forms of scriptwriting, which lends them a certain degree of credibility when approaching a head writer for a job. Also, there are occasional apprentice programs started up by soap sponsors (Procter & Gamble, who owns a number of soaps, began one a few years back). You might try phoning the production offices of the show you're interested in, and inquiring if they have such a program available.

As in any "big break," when trying to break in to soap writing there is an element of being in the right place at the right time that can't be overrated. However, luck is often the by-product of perseverance, and as we've said before, the only people who are currently working in the business are the ones who didn't give up.

Let's turn to a man whose list of credits in the daytime serial field are highly impressive indeed. His name is Robert Shaw, and his comments provide a fascinating look at the inner workings of the world of soaps.

ROBERT J. SHAW

Less than a year after he graduated from the University of Wisconsin, Bob Shaw became the only writer for "Mr. District Attorney," which stayed on NBC radio fourteen years, fifty-two weeks a year, and was never out of the top ten. Shaw wrote all of the 728 scripts. When Robert Montgomery joined NBC to inaugurate "Robert Montgomery Presents," Shaw became his only contracted writer, and wrote approximately forty original hours for that series. He wrote the first 'Hawaiian Eye" episode for Warner Bros., and approximately fifty more. He helped prepare "Peyton Place" as the first serial in prime time, and wrote approximately sixty of the initial episodes. He next became Story Editor for "Medical Center" at MGM-TV, wrote some twenty episodes, and then moved on to become Story Editor for "Dallas."

During the same period he wrote *The Users* as a Movie-of-the-Week for Aaron Spelling, and other movies for TV for David Wolper and Factor-Newland Productions. He then became Associate Head Writer for "General Hospital." Of Procter & Gamble TV Productions' eight serials, Bob has been head writer of four, and has written under contract for six. In addition, he was the only writer on "Love of Life" for five years, and has written other daytime serials for all three television networks. He was nominated for an Emmy for a special daytime drama, "Once in Her Life," produced for CBS Daytime 90.

How did you get started writing for soap operas?

I should explain to you that I never intended to be a television writer or even a radio writer, for the obvious reason that there weren't schools for it in my day. I went to law school and I hated law so much that the Dean of my law school gave me a letter of reference to the editor of the *New York Times*. I grabbed it and went to New York. I didn't end up with the *Times*, I ended up in the publicity department of NBC, writing press handouts.

There was a woman there named Ann Hummert who produced fourteen soap operas a day—these were 15-minute shows. I listened to about ten of them and I thought, "God, I can do those," and I went down to the basement and I got practically everything she'd ever written and I studied it for a while and I wrote one just like those. I took it over there, and it sold. It was called "Front Page Farrell," and it starred an unknown actor named Richard Widmark. So I just drifted into it.

Then I thought up a half-hour nighttime show called "Mr. District Attorney," and that stayed on forever. I've never been exclusively a soap writer; I've gone back and forth. After four or five years on the same soap, you see, you simply cannot think of another idea, especially if the soap has been on twenty-five years. I'll tell you a story about that. I did a show for a long time, called "Search for Tomorrow," and there was a very fine actress on it named Mary Stuart. Mary is one of the best in the business, and she has played the lead in "Search" for all twenty-five years. When we go to New York, one of the obligatory things is to take Mary to lunch so she can find out what's coming up for her. One time we finished dessert and she said, "Well, are there any exciting plans?" I said, "As a matter of fact, Mary, I don't want you to get in a stir, but in the next few months you're going to have a mastectomy. Don't worry, it'll come out fine, it's done all the time, and there's no danger." She said, "Oh, that's very interesting . . . it'll be my third."

So you bounce around, and I've usually gone from a soap to a nighttime show, then back again, but I really do like soaps.

What are the advantages and disadvantages of writing soaps?

It's steady work, fifty-two weeks a year. The only adverse thing is that there are no residuals. Oh, there are Australian rights—that amounts to about a buck-and-a-half a year . . . but, on the other hand, you get a check every Friday.

Let's talk about the soaps themselves. When I was a kid I would see them once in a while, when I was home sick from school, and they seemed to move at a glacial pace. But recently I started watching some of them again and it seems that now the pace is similar to that of nighttime shows.

It is. The distinctions are blurred. I was hired at Fox to develop

Grace Metalius' book, *Peyton Place*, into a nighttime show. We decided to do two episodes a week, which really made it a serial—in many ways it was the first nighttime soap opera. I did "Dallas" for three years, and that's a soap opera. I cannot for the life of me see any difference in the plots between "Dallas" and "General Hospital."

I admit, though, that the pace was painfully slow in the old days. I had a show, "Love of Life," where I literally had a woman in labor for seven weeks. Thirty-five shows, and she was still in O.B. waiting to deliver the child.

He was ready to graduate from college by the time he was born.
Right! And, you know, we didn't think a thing of it.

Are there any other changes that you've observed in the soaps over the years?
Oh yes. To cover the insidious subject first, we're much freer. There are very few moral restrictions in soap operas, except for good taste. I can't think of a single subject we couldn't tackle, if we did it well, with some taste. Whereas, at nighttime, there still are.

Now, years ago at soaps, my God! When I first started writing soaps we couldn't have a married couple in a double bed. Now we got 'em getting laid in elevators. Between the fourth and fifth floors. And that doesn't bother anybody.

We had something going for us on "Peyton Place," for example, because people thought it would be just filled with dirty stuff, because the book was. Actually, it was practically the cleanest show I've ever worked on. In the first three years Mia Farrow and Ryan O'Neal, who played the young lovers, never kissed, much less did anything else. We made great use of the word "almost" . . . "I almost kissed Mia last night . . ." We had churches condemning us before we got on the air. We were so scared when the first show came out that a bunch of us went to Hawaii that week. We were so afraid that the network would be calling us, saying, "Get off the air and stay off!" But it was number one for three years.

We actually are not all that lascivious in daytime, but the suggestion is there, and the viewer can easily supply the rest for himself. We seldom have an out-and-out sexual scene, but we have a lot of the beginnings of them. We usually go to black when he's pushing her down toward the bed.

That's another thing that's confused our lives, because now when we go to black, to a commercial, we have no idea who the sponsors are—all the commercials are computerized out of New York. And somebody who makes a lot of money at his job has to make sure the commercial doesn't conflict with the last part of the scene. I had it happen on "Love of Life." The story had a guy on the operating table, ready to die, and the doctor says, "Scalpel," and rips the guy open, and we go to black. The next scene is a doctor holding up a baby—it's a commercial for Pampers. So help me God, it looked like my actor had given birth.

The soaps have changed—has the audience for them changed too?

Yes, I think our audience has gotten younger. "General Hospital" is a good example—I don't know whether Jackie Smith, Daytime Vice-President of ABC in New York, would agree with me, but the important audience to me is the eighteen-to-twenty-five group. I know that's the group Procter & Gamble wants. They feel, with justification, that your grandmother and mine have been using a certain kind of soap all of their lives and nothing is going to make them change. But younger people—and our audience includes a large number of them—are very receptive to advertising, and have an open mind about which products they're going to buy.

If you look at the commercials in those soaps, they are all, eventually, sexy. The guy has ring-around-the-collar, then this woman buys Wisk, and he comes home and says, "No more ring-around-the-collar!" and grabs her, and she's going to get it right there in the hall!

The age of our viewers is reflected in the mail, and as I said, most of it is young, the eighteen to twenty-five group. We also hear from people that work at night, and from people in the veterans' hospitals, from college students—and we pay attention to the mail.

We even get a knot of people waiting outside the studio, either for Rick Springfield or John Stamos (from "General Hospital"). It's very ego deflating; they look in my car when I drive up and say, "Oh, he's nobody!" and they take their autograph books and shove them back in their pockets.

It's probably one of the few areas of television where actors have that kind of following, similar to the following that a movie star had in the old days.

Yes, and there's a difference in the way people regard the daytime and nighttime actors. When people write to Larry Hagman on "Dallas," for example, they say, "Dear Mr. Hagman." When they write to a soap opera, they write to the name of the character: "Dear Luke"—that's Tony Geary. They write as if they are writing to a dear friend, they write details of their lives that you wouldn't send through the mail. And advice: "Dear Luke, don't marry Holly, because I know a girl just like her."

I know women, older women, who really think the actors make up their own lines. Eileen Fulton played a villainess for "As the World Turns," and a woman walked right up to her in the middle of Saks Fifth Avenue, tapped her on the shoulder, and hit her right in the face with her purse. There's identification for you.

Let me add one thing about the differences between the old days and now. I think there used to be a stigma about daytime. I don't think that's true any longer. We had Elizabeth Taylor on "General Hospital"—and she wrote and asked to be on. Sammy Davis, Jr., Milton Berle—Carol Burnett did a week on "All My Children." So it's no longer consider slumming by any means. New York's better than L.A. in that respect, because we can get an actor out of a New York studio by four or five o'clock, which allows him to support himself during the day on a soap opera and still do Broadway theatre if he wants to. And we're very lenient—if he has a two weeks' tryout in New Haven, we'll write him out for that length of time.

What's the split, as far as location of the production of soaps, between here and there?

It's getting more equal. It used to be that predominantly it was New York. Now my guess is that it's closer to fifty-fifty. Initially all television came from New York. CBS bought up the old Ed Sullivan Theatre and all those other places: there's one out in Brooklyn where you can't tape a soap opera on the days it rains, because the roof leaks. They were stuck with all that real estate, so they kept the shows there.

Also, of course, we're going in much more for location shooting, which is more easily done here than in New York. We're doing more exciting things: we've had floods and cyclones, and earth-quakes . . . production values are bigger than they used to be.

Are the networks actively looking for new soaps?

The slots are pretty much filled. Procter & Gamble buys a new soap maybe every ten years. It isn't like nighttime, where if you don't make it in the first three weeks you're out. "Texas" is a perfect example. They let it go two years before they took it off the air, and it never got a rating above 2.4. But they are very patient, so it doesn't allow a lot of room for new programming. "General Hospital," for example, is twenty-four years old.

When something works, they like to stick with it. There was a very famous lady in soap opera named Irna Philips, who created six Procter & Gamble shows. She lived in Chicago and when she sneezed, people flew in from all coasts. I was sitting with Bob Short (of P&G) at the Pump Room one night and I asked him, "Why does this lady get so much attention?" He said, "Because we figure after twenty-five years she has sold two billion dollars worth of soap." That's answer enough.

So, no, the networks are not actively searching for new soaps. On the other hand, there's always an exception to the rule. If I had a brilliant, fresh, new, innovative idea for a soap, I could sell it. I just can't sell more of what they've already got.

Can you explain the structure of soap writing—not an individual script, but the writing staff.

It has become complex. It's a committee system, with a Chairman of the Board. You start with whoever owns it, and then you hire a head writer. There are two systems. In one, Procter & Gamble would give a head writer $20,000 a week, and that person's obligation was to deliver five scripts a week. Obviously, you can't write all five yourself, so that means you don't keep anywhere near the twenty because you hire writers in turn, and pay them.

The other system, which "General Hospital" happens to use, is that everybody is hired by the network, and by the Executive Producer. That starts with a head writer, whose function is to prepare and sell and defend and alter a year or more of what we call the bible. That's the storyline covering a considerable length of time. Sometimes it's broken down into periods of six months and three months.

Then she goes out and hires three kinds of writers. First, writers who do nothing but outlines. They take her basic bible and break it down into daily episodes, and then each day is broken down into scenes, and each scene is broken down into segments. When I get an outline from one of these writers, it runs about twenty-five typewritten pages.

That in turn is sent to one of maybe five writers, and they follow it almost exactly. By the way, the head writer and the outline writers meet two, three times a week, sometimes well into the night, devising these outlines. They do this in a chorus, all around a table, helping each other, revising. When they're in agreement, the Executive Producer okays it, and the scriptwriter takes it from there.

Even though the scriptwriter is working from a detailed outline, we want him to be imaginative. If we indicate that the scene opens with Leslie and Rick in the kitchen, and then Joe comes in, we'd like the writer to say something about what Leslie is doing in the kitchen, and to make it come alive—to have her say, "Damn, the potatoes are burnt!" or whatever. They have to put the human touch in, and that in my opinion is the difference between the good and the bad scriptwriter.

Now, to continue on structure, the scriptwriter sends that script back, and in nine out of ten cases he does no further work on it. But it is edited by the head writer, or she may hire an assistant who does the editing. And then it's gone over by another group of people off in another wing, to see that it all correlates. If Rick says, "When I did that appendectomy last month," they check to make sure it wasn't a tonsillectomy, because if it's wrong, you'll get twenty letters saying, "It was tonsils!" The viewers are sharp, and they'll catch you.

But, with the exception of a few changes the director might make, that's about the way it runs. As I hope I've made obvious, the head writer is the key to the whole thing. He can be, and is, given a lot of leeway on scripts, and he can revise and change story lines.

That includes being involved in adding new characters and getting rid of others?

Sure. When an actor picks up his script and reads, "I haven't been feeling well lately," the head writer will get a phone call saying, "Don't do this to me. My kid needs braces, please!" Gertrude

Berg is famous for it—she put half her cast on a bus, had the bus go over a bridge, and killed 'em all in one fell swoop. She once got angry with a lead actress, and gave her the line, "Excuse me, I have to go to the bathroom," and that poor woman never came back. She's still in there! Another actress she didn't like was given one line every day. She'd poke her head halfway through the kitchen door and say, "Excuse me, my leg is in the oven." That was it.

The head writer, while he or she is highly paid and has many responsibilities, is usually the first one whose head is chopped off. They never think to examine the whole committee, it's the head writer's fault when things go badly.

It seems to me that in a soap opera format it's even more important than it is on a weekly series to know the characters—how they sound and exactly what they'd do. It seems very important that the staff writers are all in sync.

It is. One of the head writers' jobs is to assign certain outlines to certain writers. We find that Writer A will do a much better job with a certain character than will Writer B. You see, they don't necessarily write in sequence. They get a copy of the bible, too, so they know what's going on.

In the old days of early television, I used to write all five scripts. Those were half-hour scripts and I could write five in two days, easily, and take three days off. But no longer. Now they've become productions. Soap operas got that name not only because they sold soap, but because the average scene was played out in the kitchen. Now "General Hospital" has a whole city underground; they're going to freeze Port Charles, and now we've got a new character we're bringing in, a police commissioner, and he has a secret room with so many gadgets you wouldn't believe it: teleprinters, computers, and so forth. This all takes time to write.

How far ahead are you usually writing, versus what's on the air?

About six weeks.

Let's touch on some of the qualities of a person who wants to be, or already is, a soap writer. One of them, you've already implied, is that he or she can't be too much of a prima don-

na, because the outline is coming from someone else; the writer can't say, "I am the creator." So that's one quality.

That's the important one.

Being able to write quickly seems like another.

That's right. To show you how little things affect your life, a while back all the writers on "General Hospital" got a memo saying that they were going to have to tape an extra show for ten consecutive Saturdays, because the Olympics coverage was going to commandeer our studio.

I think the principal thing a writer must understand about daytime shows, in addition to the fact that their obvious purpose is to entertain, is that their main function is to move products off the grocery shelves. I think the kid who is dabbling in television until he can write the Great American Novel is making a great mistake, because the two don't mix. We're very commercial. I happen to like it. I think it's fun to take hold of a show and try to pull it up to Number One, and see it gets there. But believe me, we're not John Updikes.

Now, I'm not deprecating what we do. Most writers that I respect in soap opera do as well as they can, they do their very best work, they won't hand in junk. But it's a genre in and of itself, and it's commercial. I think it was Cardinal Newman who said, "If you're going to be a writer, be a man of the marketplace."

Going back to the requisite writing skills, how about dialogue writing?

Remember that in soap operas you have to depend on the type of dialogue you hear every day, dealing with everyday things. The outline is extensive, but it by no means contains sixty pages of dialogue—that has to come out of your head. Learning to know how people talk is so important. We are not writing for publication, we are writing for the ear, and I'm not at all certain, by the way, that you can be taught to write good dialogue. I think it's a little like playing piano by ear, you can do it or you can't. You can learn to improve, though. If you listen carefully to the way people speak you'll realize that most of them use contractions, they don't use complete sentences, and so forth. That's the way you've got to write, or it's going to come out stilted, it's going to come out like Lord Chesterfield's letters to his son.

Since realistic dialogue is so important, if you have a particular theme coming up, do you spend time with cops or doctors, or whoever else is portrayed?

Oh yes. And we have paid research people. "General Hospital" has at the moment a doctor and a nurse who we can call anytime to ask questions. On "Medical Center" we had a doctor on staff, and that helped me immensely. I would tell him, "I've got to have a sixteen-year-old in bed, and he's got to look fine from the neck up so he isn't grotesque, but he's got to be totally paralyzed and in danger of dying, and we've got to operate on him, and Chad Everett's got to save his life, and at the end the kid has to walk out of the hospital." The doctor would call me back two hours later and tell me what disease the kid had, the surgical procedure to be used, and so on.

Any further pointers for would-be soaps writers?

The other thing I'd like to mention is so obvious I hate to bring it up, but you'd be astonished how many people come in and ask for jobs, or ask to try out for jobs, and say, "I'd like to write for 'Search for Tomorrow' but I've never watched it." Our first advice always is to go home and watch the show for a couple of weeks.

Procter & Gamble has a set system. If you want to join them as a writer, they ask you to watch the soap for a while and then do two or three scripts based on your own outline, what you think should come next. Of course those scripts will never be on the air, but they will give them an idea of your skill.

How much turnover is there? Do people burn out?

Yes, that's only human nature. I can do "Search for Tomorrow" for five years and think, "If I have to write one more line for that woman, I will go out of my mind." So you leave one show and go on to another one. The characters will be different, and that can be stimulating, although of course the stories won't be all that different. Let's face it, we've all done the same story twenty-five times, with refinements and twists to fit the particular show we're talking about. There are, as you probably know, only a few basic plots. The triangle always works, the Lady and the Tiger always works. It's a terrible thing to admit, but I think every writer to some extent follows the dictum, "When in doubt, steal!"

Anything else to add about writing for the soaps?

Well, if I were going to characterize writing for daytime, I'd say it's more fun, you work with very pleasant people—it becomes like a little family, really. I know writers on "General Hospital" as well as I know my own mother, and they know me. We can talk in short-hand—and that's quite different from being a freelance peddler, where you walk in to a Story Editor and say, "Good day, Sir, I'd like you to read my script, please" and then on that basis you pitch. Anybody who has a job on a soap is lucky, because he's secure. I would urge anybody interested in soaps to try to get into it. It pays well—it's probably the highest-paid job in television.

Really?

Sure, if I do a Movie-of-the-Week for Aaron Spelling—which I'd love to do—that's going to take six months. So how many can you do in a year? A good head writer on a soap makes between $6,000 and $7,500 a week, fifty-two weeks a year. A good writer makes $3,000 a week, fifty-two weeks a year.

Plus, you're not spending time pitching, having stuff rejected, starting over . . .

And you don't go to meetings and get bawled out, and your time is your own, which is important to a lot of creative people. Let me finish with one of the most wonderful Hollywood stories I know. It may be apocryphal, but it's about Julius Epstein, who was hired to deliver a treatment to Jack Warner by the end of six weeks. He worked on the lot and on the third day Jack called him and said, "Julie, Monday you came in at 10:05 and you went to lunch at 11:45, and you returned at 2:24, and you left the lot at 4:15"—and he went on and on and told him, "Julie, when a writer works for Warner Brothers, he works from nine to six." Julie said, "Oh, I'm sorry, Jack. I didn't know that." Jack said, "Well, that's the rule." So Julie came in every morning at nine, and he made designs with paper clips and wrote to his mother, and at the end of six weeks, he turned in his film treatment. Jack went to Palm Springs and read it and called him and said, "Julie, I don't understand this! Your treatment is terrible!" And Julie said, "I don't understand it either—I was here every morning at nine!"

CHAPTER 11

How to Write for Animation

MANY OF US CAN RECALL THE DAYS when Saturday morning meant one thing: cartoons. In fact, hours and hours of cartoons, with all their glorious color, broad slapstick humor, and riotous action. Well, Saturday mornings and weekday mornings too, for that matter, are still chock-full of cartoons. And those cartoons, by the very nature of the changes they've gone through, are relying more and more on the skills of the animation scriptwriter.

In the early days of animation, a "Story Man" would take a simple concept, such as a fly getting into Woody Woodpecker's kitchen, and expand it into a succession of gags ranging from humorous to raucous to downright violent. There really was no need for a writer per se; any dialogue needed would be called for by the Story Man.

However, for a variety of reasons cartoons have changed their approach. Consumer watchdogs long ago put a halt to the kind of gratuitous violence that was a mainstay of shows such as "Tom and Jerry" and "Woody Woodpecker." Cartoons are no longer just a series of gags; rather, they have evolved into stories requiring a beginning, middle, and end, with character development, believable dialogue, and all the other elements you associate with good storytelling.

Because of this metamorphosis, skilled writers who are able to handle the unique demands of animation are in constant demand. In fact, some "live-action" producers, such as Aaron Spelling, have taken to hiring animation writers for their shows, feeling that such writers have mastered the ability to be efficient and funny in writing action and thinking visually. This has not, however, turned animation writing into a mere "training ground" for writers trying to break into live-action shows. Many writers make animation scriptwriting their career, finding it to be very challenging, stimulating, and financially rewarding.

• WHAT IS THE STRUCTURE OF AN ANIMATION SCRIPT?

Animation shows are either 11 or 22 minutes long, depending on a variety of factors such as the age level of the viewing audience and the episode length that best suits a particular story. Regardless of length, however, the basic structure of an animation plot will follow the same general rules.

All of the experienced animation writers we've talked to tell us they approach an animation story in the same manner as they would a feature script, insofar as conflict, complications, and resolution are concerned. There are, however, a few things they do quite differently.

To begin with, all cartoon shows must have a thematic moral. It can be a simple concept, such as "being greedy is bad," or it can be more abstract, depending upon the target age-group of the show. All cartoon shows are targeted at specific age-groups. They are: 2-6, 6-9, 9-12 and up. The earlier in the morning the show airs, the younger its target age-group. A quick look at a television schedule will verify this; early in the morning you'll find shows such as "Wuzzles" or "Kissyfur," while later in the morning shows such as "Alvin and the Chipmunks" and "Punky Brewster" will be on. These shows differ dramatically in the complexity of their "moral" themes, and the good writer understands how to address those differences.

Similarly, your plot should also reflect the comprehension levels of your target audience. Simple, easy-to-follow plots are necessary for the younger age-groups. An example might be a story in which one of The Smurfs has lost his favorite ring, and everyone has to team up to find it. Older audiences, on the other hand, are ready for the ghost stories and mysteries that require more attention to plot exposition and detail.

Whatever your target age-group, it's crucial that an animation story be well underway by the end of the first page. That's a tall order, but one that must be filled, because the cartoon audience is intolerant of slow-developing stories. They want action, and they want it *now*! Your very first few lines will have to set up the story and get the conflict right out where we can see it.

Additionally, your first page should begin with a gag. Remember, humor is the lifeblood of animation, and there needs to be something funny on each and every page. It's very important that the writer command the kids' attention right away, and the way to do that is with something funny. This can be a simple sight gag, such as Farmer Smurf (of "The Smurfs") falling face-first into a pile of Smurfberries, or, for the older kids, a verbal gag, as Alvin (of "Alvin and the Chipmunks") shares the words to his latest rock song with his obviously unappreciative brothers.

After that initial gag, establish your conflict. Using the above examples, Farmer Smurf realizes that he has simply got to find somewhere or some way to store his surplus Smurfberries, or soon the entire town will be buried in them. Alvin's brothers make fun of his new song, so he challenges them to beat his entry in the big rock video contest coming up.

As you can see, in both cases our plot is off and running, and we've managed it in one page or less by using simple plots that require little exposition or set-up.

From this point on, the animation story should be handled in much the same way as any three-act story. The next few pages establishes the conflict more clearly, complicates matters a bit, and possibly introduces a B plot if the show has an older audience. In the case of Farmer Smurf, he might find that every possible storage place in town is filled to the brim with Smurfberries, and even Greedy Smurf's enthusiastic efforts to eat and/or cook every last one of them are to no avail. Theodore and Simon will make attempts at rock videos of their own, only to find it's not quite as easy as they thought.

Roughly a fourth of the way through the script—and this goes for 11-minute as well as 22-minute scripts—a decision must be made or an event must occur which kicks the plot into high gear. The main character in our story decides on the best way to achieve his goal, and the scriptwriter's job is to make that goal as difficult as possible to reach. So, in spite of Papa Smurf's advice to never venture into the forest alone, Farmer Smurf is convinced that he must go there to try to find the rare Smurfberry Caterpillar, whose mysterious disappearance from the fields is the reason for the Smurfberry glut. In our other story, Alvin decides to stack the deck in his favor by secretly sabotaging the efforts of his brothers.

Now the second act of your story swings into motion. Keep in mind that throughout each act, and in fact on every page, you'll use visual gags to advance the plot. Very rarely will dialogue be used as an expository vehicle, except when absolutely necessary. In fact, a good guideline might be to imagine seeing your script on television with the sound turned off. Would you still be able to follow the plot? Granted, you'd miss some of the gags, particularly on the "older" shows, but you should still have no trouble understanding the basic storyline.

As you progress to the midpoint of your story, you'll be hitting a commercial break on the 22-minute scripts. And as you've learned by now, commercial breaks mean cliffhangers. Even in the 11-minute scripts, where no commercial break is required, you still should write to that midpoint climax. In our sample stories, Farmer Smurf is captured by the evil wizard Gargamel, who's been hoarding all the Smurfberry Caterpillars as part of a plan to allow the Smurfberries to completely overgrow the village. Meanwhile, Alvin's efforts to wreck his brothers' videos backfires, causing his own video to be ruined as well. Now the contest is just one day away, and nobody has an entry.

As the second act continues, more and more obstacles and barriers are thrown up between our main characters and their goals. By the end of the second act (roughly three-quarters of the way through the script), our characters are in the worst possible fix. The idea is to get the viewers wondering, "How are they ever going to get out of this one?" Your task as writer is to make sure there is a solid, logical, but by no means obvious way out of the predicament. Escaping that predicament will take up the major portion of the third act, with the rest being devoted to the achievement of whatever goal was set. So, Farmer Smurf is rescued when Papa Smurf is able to find a spell that will cause the Smurfberry Caterpillars to devour Gargamel's entire house. Alvin, Simon, and Theodore convince Dave to let them do extra chores in order to earn enough money to shoot another video, only this time they'll work together and utilize their own special talents to make the best video possible. Our stories end on an upbeat note, of course, just as all animation stories should. Farmer Smurf returns the caterpillars to the Smurfberry orchards, and order is restored to the farm. Farmer Smurf has learned a valuable lesson about wandering off by himself. Alvin, Simon, and Theodore win the rock video award by working together, and learn the value of cooperation and teamwork.

As you see, we've used simple, straightforward plotlines that allow for plenty of visual action and variety, with an underlying thematic thread that runs throughout and pays off in the end. Certainly the sample stories here would require a lot more fleshing out before they'd be ready for scripting, but you get the idea: Keep it simple, well structured, visual and *funny*.

• SOME GENERAL TIPS

1. Be imaginative. In animation, you have the whole wide, wonderful world open to you. There are no sets too expensive or exotic for you to use; the laws of physics are yours to command (within the confines of the show's parameters, of course); and no stunt is too difficult for your characters to pull off. In animation you can blow up cars, blow up buildings, and have tornadoes level whole cities, as long as nobody gets hurt.

About the only restriction regarding settings in animation writing has to do with action around water. The fast-moving and varied reflections of running water are difficult to pull off from an artistic standpoint, so it would be best to avoid it in your spec script. Underwater action, on the other hand, is no trouble at all, since all that is needed is a few bubbles once in awhile.

2. Use dialogue sparingly. One or two lines of dialogue at a time is plenty when writing for animation. Remember, the dialogue does move the story along, but it isn't the single most vital element. In fact, if you watch cartoon shows (which we of course recommend, if you're planning on writing for this field), you'll see that most dialogue consists of reactions and exclamations, rather than anything very substantive. Kids do not want to be talked at—they want *action*.

3. Think visually. We can't emphasize this enough. When you first sit down to work out a storyline, try running it on your own mental video screen. Examine its potential for sight gags. Try to imagine moving your story along without any dialogue at all. When writing the

script, do your best to keep things moving, even if characters *are* just talking for a moment. Instead of having them talk to each other in a stagnant position, give them something to do. Keep your scene active at all times, and you'll stand a better chance of keeping your audience riveted to the screen.

4. Avoid violence. Ever since groups such as Action for Children's Television worked to remove violence from cartoons, writers have had to go to great pains to eliminate all violent acts from their scripts. As Kayte Kuch and Sheryl Scarborough, our interviewees at the end of this chapter, point out, even the action shows such as "Rambo" or "G.I. Joe" never depict anyone actually getting hurt. Tanks, planes, and buildings are blown all over the map every couple of seconds, but the people are always shown escaping to safety prior to the explosion. Therefore, of course, you must never show one character punching another, pushing somebody down, or throwing something at another.

5. Avoid "Imitatable Acts." This is a major bugaboo of even the most experienced animation writer, because the interpretation of what could be a dangerous, imitatable act is so broad. The idea is that kids are liable, or even likely, to imitate what they see on television. If Punky Brewster were to attempt to learn tightrope walking by practicing on a clothesline, and a little girl watching the show decided to give that same stunt a try at home—well, you can imagine the repercussions.

This rule is one of the most frustrating restrictions an animation writer must deal with, because it can so severely limit any action a character might undertake. It can also make it tough to put a character into any kind of jeopardy, since that character shouldn't have been doing anything dangerous to begin with. But, a rule's a rule, and this one's here to stay, so as an animation writer you must learn to function effectively within its limits.

6. End each scene with a gag or a suspenseful moment. Each scene should lead naturally to the next, but it should also button up very nicely on its own. It's important to the overall pacing of a cartoon that the acceleration of action and story is continuous and steady, and the most effective way to accomplish that is to make each scene begin and end with a "punch."

7. Reinforce your theme. The clever animation writer continually hints at the little moral lesson he's trying to impart, without ever resorting to preaching. Then, at the end of the show, the theme is

brought out into the open and stated in plain, simple terms, just in case anyone missed it along the way. In this respect, the animation script is very similar to most of today's sitcoms, which typically have a warm little moment at the end of the story.

Try to derive your themes from character flaws or mistaken intentions intrinsic to the characters themselves, rather than from some outside source that arrives from nowhere. Kids have very little control over their lives, so they like to see their cartoon heroes get themselves into a mess and then get themselves out of it. Uncontrollable, unpredictable dangers that arrive from who knows where are uninteresting at best, and downright frightening at worst.

8. Think "funny." Keep humor in mind every line of every page, and inject it into your script whenever possible. Like all good humor, it should spring from of the characteristics of the main characters, and from the unique situation your script has thrown them into. Also, remember that, just as in adult shows, cartoon protagonists and antagonists have distinctive personalities and speech patterns, and any verbal humor must remain true to those traits.

• WHAT'S THE FORMAT FOR AN ANIMATION SCRIPT?

Basically, the format is the same as that for a feature script, with one big exception: each page equals only thirty seconds, instead of a minute, of actual running time. This is because when you are writing animation, you must describe *absolutely everything* that takes place on the screen. When writing a script for a cartoon, you are, quite literally, the director, too.

Let's take an example, one given to us by Gene Ayres, a prolific veteran of many animation shows and a former staff writer for Hanna-Barbera.

Suppose you were writing a live-action show, and you wanted to set up a bank robbery. In the script you might just write:

EXT. BANK—DAY

An old PICKUP TRUCK drives up to the bank entrance and stops.

TWO MEN carrying shotguns jump out and run into the bank.

Now, the director would then choose the shots and the angles. In animation writing you would probably never call for a bank hold-up, but for the sake of comparison, let's see how that same sequence might look:

EST. SHOT—THE TOWN

There are several buildings on the corner of the street. One of them has a very prominent sign saying, "Bank."

LOW ANGLE on the street. THE TRUCK approaches camera.

CLOSE SIDE ANGLE as the TRUCK passes camera.

ANGLE THE BANK

We can see that the building has two swinging glass front doors, as the TRUCK pulls INTO FRAME.

CLOSE ANGLE ON TRUCK—DRIVER'S SIDE

We get a good look at the DRIVER through his window. He pulls on a mask.

MEDIUM ANGLE ON TRUCK—DRIVER'S SIDE

The DRIVER gets out, carrying a shotgun.

OVERHEAD ANGLE ON TRUCK

The passenger door to the truck opens, and the HENCHMAN gets out, also carrying a shotgun.

TWO-SHOT—ANGLE FROM BELOW

The DRIVER and the HENCHMAN walk toward and over camera.

ANGLE DRIVER AND HENCHMAN—FROM BEHIND

As they enter the bank doors.

The reason for this much description is quite simple: the artist will only draw what you tell her to draw. If something isn't mentioned in the script, it won't be in the storyboard. That kind of detailed description is what makes the animation script twice as long as its feature format would seem at first to indicate. As an example, the following is a sample page from a produced episode of "Punky Brewster":

CHERIE-MOUSE
(high-squeaky voice)

It must be his cold, Punky. He heard "mice" instead of "nice."

GLOMER AND PUNKY

Glomer leans closer and picks up his now tiny friend, holding her in his hand.

PUNKY-MOUSE
(high-squeaky voice)

You've got to change us back.

GLOMER
(nasally)

Okay, okay . . . changing you back before you saying . . .

Suddenly they react to . . .

DOBERMAN (VO)

(BIG GROWL)

PUNKY'S POV

The doberman is chasing Margaux-mouse, Cherie-mouse and Allen-mouse across the parking lot.

KIDS
(ad-lib screams)

ANGLE — PARKING BERM

*The kids-mice skitter (on hind legs) over it. The CAMERA TRACKS with them as they run around empty food boxes and cans. They stop when they come to an abandoned automobile hub, wheel and tire and look around.

MARGAUX-MOUSE
(high-squeaky voice)
(overly dramatic)

This is horrible. Margaux Kramer . . . dog food!

CHERIE-MOUSE
(high-squeaky voice)
Quick. Into the wheel.

The kids-mice struggle to climb up the tire and disappear through the axle hole in the wheel just as the dog leaps INTO SHOT.

DRAMATIC UP-ANGLE — DOBERMAN — THROUGH AUTO WHEEL

We just see his glinty eyes, flashing white teeth and red vicious mouth as he digs at the wheel.

• HOW DO I BREAK IN TO ANIMATION WRITING?

Once again, you'll need to prove your writing ability with an outstanding spec script. Watch cartoons, pick a show you like and feel you could write for; do a script based on an original story idea of your own.

Animation producers and story editors are much more accessible than their live-action counterparts, and tend to be more helpful in lending a hand to aspiring writers. They'll usually be happy to send you a couple of sample scripts and a "bible" (a brief summary of the show's characters, and a rundown of all the stories that have been done). It's best to obtain both before attempting your spec script, to avoid duplicating a story already done.

Once your spec script is done, you can either write or call the story editors on the show you've chosen, let them know you've written a sample script, and inquire as to their willingness to take a look at it. You can find their names listed on the credits, or call the production company and ask the secretary for the names of the story editors. Both *Daily Variety* and *The Hollywood Reporter* trade papers run a weekly list of production companies and current projects (see Chapter 20). You don't need an agent in order to submit scripts to animation shows, although many producers will send you a standard release form to sign and enclose with your submission. (A note about release forms. They are virtually the same regardless of whether you're submitting a feature, sitcom, animation, or any other type of script. They are for the protection of the production company, and simply stated, ask your permission to take a look at your script, free from the threat of a lawsuit should something similar be developed later independent of you and your script. It isn't, however, a license to steal. With enough convincing evidence, even a writer who has signed a release form can bring legal action against a production company if he feels he's been ripped off. However, most production companies won't look at an "unagented" submission without first having a signed release form in hand, if only to protect them from "nuisance" suits.) At that point, if your script is good enough you'll be asked in to pitch other ideas, or, if you're really lucky, they may buy your sample script. This happens with much greater frequency in the animation market than in live-action, where spec scripts are virtually never bought.

• A FINAL NOTE ABOUT ANIMATION

Animation writers are not members of the Writers Guild, as are sitcom writers, feature writers, and even the folks who write questions for game shows. This is a legacy of the early days when writers were considered unnecessary or at best incidental, and the Story Men were members of I.A.T.S.E., the International Alliance of Theatrical Stage Employees. Animation writers today are still members of that union, in which they are a small minority compared to the numbers of grips, stagehands, and set carpenters. There have been efforts to rectify this and incorporate these writers into the Writers Guild, but those efforts have thus far been stymied.

Because of this, animation writers are not eligible for some of the benefits normally associated with television scriptwriting; most notably, they receive no residuals. They are paid a flat fee (currently, the minimum is about $1900 for an 11-minute script; $3200 for 22 minutes) for each script they write. Naturally, experienced writers are paid more than that, frequently triple the minimum or more, and staff writers can earn a wage competitive with their live-action counterparts.

How does all this affect the writer? Occasionally, animation writers may feel that their craft is unappreciated, their skills unrecognized. In point of fact, however, the animation writer very often has to be more resourceful and skillful in execution than a live-action writer would have to be, if only because of the restrictions unique to animation.

The following interview with veteran animation writers Kayte Kuch and Sheryl Scarborough provides a unique insight into the difficulties and rewards to be found in this challenging field.

KAYTE KUCH AND SHERYL SCARBOROUGH

Kayte Kuch and Sheryl Scarborough believe strongly in the need for animation writing to receive the kind of recognition as both a craft and art that it has long deserved. Previously story editors on the animated "Punky Brewster," and staff writers for the Ruby-Spears Production Company, they are currently at Marvel Productions as story editors on "Little Clowns," a children's show for NBC.

You mentioned to us before this interview that you were eager to upgrade the "status" of animation writing as a craft. Do you feel that animation has a bad image?

K: Most of our peers writing outside of animation sometimes look down on writing for children. They don't see it as requiring the same craftsmanship and skills, storytelling skills, as writing other types of scripts.

S: They think it's easy to write for children. And actually, in discussing some of the things we wanted to talk with you about today, both Kayte and I agreed that writing for children is in reality more difficult than writing for adults. We're adults, so it's easy to write for adults. But writing for children means you have to think like children, without talking down to them.

Would you say that a condescending tone is the main pitfall you find in scripts written by writers new to the field, writers trying to break in?

S: Yes. People who come in who have never written for children before think that all you have to do is repeat the alphabet, and say, "Don't touch that, don't play with fire, don't talk to strangers." And of course that's not all there is to it.

All right, given that, what is there to it? What's unique about writing animation?

S: There's a good side and bad side. On the good side, the scriptwriter and the story editor function pretty much as the director on every single one of their scripts. An animation script runs roughly two pages per minute, even though the format is in the minute-per-page feature style. And the reason for that is you must describe *everything*. If you want a tree in a front yard, and that tree is important because the character is going to fly into it or something, you have to describe what kind of tree that is. An artist is not going to guess what kind of tree you want, so you have to describe everything about it.

If there are shelves in the room with items that will eventually be used, you have to describe them in detail. If you want a treasure chest, and it has to have two handles, you have to set it up right out front. There's no way to cover you for that, if it's allowed to slide by.

A very detail-conscious kind of writing, as opposed to features, where you might say, "He goes outside and sees the tree."

K: We don't do cover shots. We break down each specific shot, even to the point of telling our storyboard artist, "We see this dramatic up-angle as the car comes careening over camera."

S: "With gravel spraying." See, if you don't say it, it won't get in there.

K: So if you have aspirations of being a director, or you want to know you'll be involved in what the show will finally look like, animation is a good medium for you. It's a visual medium, forcing you to think visually and write visually.

S: You even control the sound effects. You note each and every one of those as well.

It seems you literally do everything but sit down and draw the thing.

K: Exactly.

It's clear that you feel that the good side of animation writing is the amount of creative input and control you have as a writer. What you say is what you get, which most certainly isn't true in just about any other type of scriptwriting. What's the bad side?

S: There's another part to the good side, and that is that we don't have the budgetary constraints that a network series might have. In animation, you're expected to blow up buildings, you're expected to crash planes—the bigger the explosions, the better. So that's also good.

The bad side is there's more outside intervention than other types of shows. The networks have fairly strong broadcast standards that all shows must meet, and at times they really nitpick. There have been shows in the past that have had psychiatrists attached to them, who would decide whether children could understand this, and whether it would do damage to them.

We had a show that had a time travel theme. Now, this was on the heels of *Back to the Future*, the most successful movie of 1985 or whatever. And the psychologists were convinced that children could not grasp the concept of time travel! That's typical of the constraints we have to work under.

What should happen in the course of a show? Should the main character undergo a change, or learn something about him, her, or itself, as would a main character on a primetime show?

K: We *would* like our characters to go through some changes. We like to learn a little more about them each time.

S: It's not like a big lesson, where the neon lights blink on and off—it can be something as simple as the consequences of jumping to conclusions. But we don't beat them over the head with it.

K: We don't deal with morals. There are some shows that do, but we try not to. We look upon what we do as entertainment. We're not necessarily trying to teach children anything, we're just trying to entertain in what is hopefully a quality manner.

How much input do you have once the script passes through your hands as story editors?

K: After the writer hands the story in to us, and we do our story editing, and the script has gone through its process of approvals, it goes to the storyboard artist, who does a visual interpretation of the story. After they finish the storyboard we check it very closely to make sure it contains what we wanted.

S: They're interpreting the written word into a visual image, and sometimes those can be two different things.

Do you find that working together as a team is a more effective way to write animation?

K: We didn't set out to write together. Joe Ruby (of Ruby-

Spears) put us together, and we just found that it works. We're a lot alike in many ways, we think very much alike, our styles of writing are very similar—and yet we each bring something to the team. Some days one handles characterization while the other handles the action, and two days later it might switch around. It's not consistent that way, but for some reason we just mesh very well together. She can pick up where I leave off—sometimes even in the middle of sentences.

S: It can really get spooky sometimes.

Did both of you choose animation as a field of interest, or did it choose you?

K: Probably more of the latter. We have similar backgrounds. We both wanted to write, and happened to be in the right place at the right time.

And are your goals within the animation field?

K: We find a great deal of satisfaction in this field. We like what we're doing. We're not here because we can't do something else, it's fun here. On the other hand, we are looking forward to making the crossover into live-action when the time comes.

Do you feel limited by the subjects you're allowed to handle as animation writers, or perhaps by the way you're allowed to handle them?

S: It's a little of both. Steven Spielberg can do something like *E.T.*, where the kids behave like real kids. We can't always deal with kids that way. In fact, rarely can we deal with kids that way, due to the various factors we've already mentioned. So, we are limited, and it reflects back on us sometimes. People will watch *E.T.* and say, "Now those are real kids, why can't we see characters like that on Saturday morning?" And we'd love to, but we're usually forced to deal more with stereotypes.

Also, we have to constantly keep in mind that the network feels that any kid of any age can get up on Saturday morning and watch any show, and might possibly see something that . . .

K: Imitatable acts.

S: Exactly. Imitatable acts. And there *are* some important things to avoid.

What does a writer need to know about these imitatable acts? Any standard rules?

S: If you have kids riding skateboards or bicycles, they wear helmets. In the car, they have to wear seatbelts. And remember, all this has to be specifically written in by the writer, or the artist won't draw it.

Basically, imitatable acts are things that can be construed as dangerous. Things a child might see and try to do himself. Things like walking through a darkened cave or haunted house with a candle. Fire is basically out. You don't show a minor driving a car. You don't show a minor stealing something, even though he or she is doing it with the best intentions. In other words, a detective on a live-action show might lift something because it could help with the case and possibly save a life—but you don't show a minor doing that.

A real pet peeve of mine are the people who tell me about the amount of violence in cartoons today. When they say that, I just tell them they obviously haven't been watching any cartoons recently, because we're not *allowed* to have violence in them.

K: Even the syndicated, quote-unquote "violent" shows, such as "Rambo" and "G.I. Joe" are not violent. Nobody ever gets hurt. There's never even an implication that anyone got hurt.

S: Which kind of grates on us in another way, because it sort of glorifies war without showing the consequences. I mean, when you blow up a ship, someone's going to get hurt! But they're very careful to avoid even hinting that anyone was hurt.

So that's something a writer should be careful about . . .

K: We don't see mangled, dead bodies in cartoons . . .

[Laughter] I don't think it would be taken to that extreme, but what you're saying is that kids can't be shown pushing each other down, or hitting anyone . . .

S: Never.

K: Even when Rambo takes a bazooka and blows up a tank, there's a moment when everybody in the tank is able to jump free. And then, just in case it got by the kids, someone will say to Rambo, "Aren't you glad nobody was in that tank?"

The thing you *can* do is blow up robots. Robots are dead meat in the cartoon world. [Laughter] But that's the limit.

So much for what to avoid. Now, what should you try to include?

S: That's a good question. Kids in a situation, a jam, or whatever—and they use their own wits to get themselves out of it. They use whatever's on hand—and sure, maybe it's stretched a little bit—but they deal with it themselves. Ingenuity, creative imagination, and the idea that kids aren't helpless. That's the kind of thing we like to get across.

How does someone interested in writing animation go about breaking in?

K: In much the same manner as breaking into episodic. You have to write a spec script . . .

S: And you have to watch the show!

K: Right. And it obviously has to be a spec animation script. I don't care if you can write a "Hunter" or a "Family Ties," I want to see if you can write animation.

So a writer should watch enough episodes of something like "Punky Brewster" until they feel they know the show well. They then write a spec script, and send it to you, the story editors. Let's assume you don't like it for one reason or another. Can that spec script be used as a calling card for other cartoon shows?

K: Oh, sure. Keeping in mind, of course, that there are comedy shows, and there are adventure shows. You don't want to send a "Punky Brewster" script to the people who are doing "Lazer Tag," because that's a different kind of a show. Again, just like episodic television.

S: It would be a good idea for a new writer to get their hands on a couple scripts to see what the format looks like, to see how detailed the description is, and to just get a general feel for this type of writing.

How do they do that?

S: If someone called or wrote to us with a stamped, self-addressed envelope, we would see that they'd get a script.

All right. Once the writer has written what they consider to be a good representative script, what do they do? Do they call and ask to submit it?

S: We prefer a call as opposed to just blindly sending a script in. We have to have all scripts submitted with one of our release forms.

But it doesn't have to be submitted by an agent?

S: No. Actually, there are very few agents in the animation business. In fact, there was a time when there were absolutely no agents.

So a writer would call you, and send in the script . . .

K: Right. And we'd read it as soon as we got a chance, and if it's a good sample, and really shows the writer can handle this style of scriptwriting, we might have them in to pitch some ideas. We've also assigned ideas that have been on the back burner in-house for some time, waiting to be written.

Any last words on writing for animation?

K: It's respectable. [laughter] And it's a fun way to make a living. It's fun being a kid once in a while.

S: Right. And you can feel comfortable telling your Mom to watch.

CHAPTER 12

How to Write for Variety Shows

THIS WILL BE A RELATIVELY SHORT chapter because variety shows are, to put it mildly, scarce these days. For decades they were a staple of network television, from "The Ed Sullivan Show" to "Hollywood Palace" to many specials featuring people like Bob Hope, Andy Williams, Tony Bennett, and Dinah Shore. Typically they featured an opening monologue, several songs by the host or hostess, several musical numbers by the guest stars, and comedy sketches of a topical nature.

It's not clear why this program format has gone into such a steep decline, although even people who miss this type of show will have to admit that many of them were rather corny. Will they come back? There have been a number of attempts to revive them, notably by Dolly Parton. Also, there are still a few that thrive in syndication or on cable outlets, most of them featuring country-and-western music. And, as of this writing, Bob Hope is still dead-panning jokes on three or four network broadcasts per year.

Other than that, there are "specials," many of which are produced by our interviewee, Gary Smith, for his company, Smith-Hemion Productions. And there is "Saturday Night Live," which employs a staff of comedy writers.

Frankly, because the market is so small and because there are a handful of writers who have long experience at doing this type of show, this is perhaps the least promising of the markets that we address in this book. But in case this is a form to which you are passionately devoted, or in case it makes a sudden comeback after the date of publication, we wanted at least to touch on the basic facets of writing variety.

• THE COMPONENTS OF A VARIETY SHOW

Variety shows usually have several components in common: music, narrative, and comedy sketches. The parts that require the services of a writer are the narrative (including introductory comments, transitions, monologues, and concluding remarks) and comedy sketches. The host or hostess of such shows often have their own writers and use them solely, or in conjunction with others hired by the producer.

The best way to get experience in this type of writing is to write jokes for stand-up comedians, speeches for after-dinner speakers, and material for roasts. Many cities now have comedy clubs featuring up-and-coming comedians who welcome outside material (although usually what they can pay for it is limited), and tailoring jokes to them is good experience for writing sitcoms as well as variety shows. Be sure to keep copies of your material to use as samples if the opportunity to write for a variety show comes up. Since there are now so few people left with extensive experience in this type of writing, your background even on the local level will be valuable.

Sketches are, in effect, mini-sitcoms. They last anywhere from a minute to ten minutes, and they should have a beginning, middle, and end. If you watch "Saturday Night Live" you will see that often their sketches have beginnings and middles, but no ends. Examples of better crafting can be found on reruns of "SCTV" and the old "Carol Burnett Show." Sketches, by their very nature, are rooted in a situation more than in characterization. For one thing, there just isn't time in a sketch to try to have character growth. However, the nature of the character and his or her attitude toward the situation must be very clear if the sketch is to work.

If you want to get some experience writing sketches, link up with your local dramatic society or the drama department of your local college or university. Frequently these bodies will do an annual show for which they would welcome (alas, usually without pay) the contributions of a writer. Many larger companies also present comedy sketches as part of their annual meeting or as part of sales presentations, so you may wish to approach them to see if they are interested in hiring you. Again, these kinds of samples, assuming they are good, may be helpful later.

The technique for writing a sketch is not that different from the approach you use to write anything else. Your starting point may be a situation, either topical or universal, but then you will still have to decide who your central character is, what he or she wants, what stands in his or her way, and how it is resolved. For example, if you decide to write a sketch about that universally hated phenomenon, the telephone answering machine, you'd decide who has the machine, what sorts of problems come up as a result of the machine, and how the central character finally solves the dilemma. As far as dialogue and physical comedy are concerned, most of the tips included in the chapter on writing sitcoms will also stand you in good stead when writing sketches.

• FINDING WORK

Because the market is rather small, there are few agents specializing in placing writers in this field. A better way to proceed is to keep your eyes open for any variety shows that you encounter on the air (whether network shows, cable, or in syndication). Watch the end of the credits for the name of the production company and then contact them directly, initially with a letter of inquiry. Chapter 20 of this book provides the names and addresses of publications that list all current production companies. Let them know that you have appropriate samples and would like to submit them. These producers are not nearly as inundated with sample material as are producers of sitcoms and one-hour shows, so they may well be more receptive. If you are proposing a special—that is a thematic show of the type described in detail in our interview with Gary Smith—you will have to give an overall description of the program. However, beware of building an entire concept around just one performer (for example, a special based on the notion that Bruce Willis attends his twentieth high school reunion and, in his alter ego of Bruno, is also the one providing the music for it) because if that one performer isn't available the whole idea is dead.

Now we turn you over to a gentleman who, with partner Dwight Hemion, has taken the variety show out of the tired vaudeville category and elevated it into a new program form: Gary Smith.

GARY SMITH

Gary Smith started as a staff designer in New York, came to California to be Art Director for the Judy Garland series, and at the age of twenty-seven was made producer of that series. Together with Dwight Hemion, he produced many highly acclaimed television variety specials, including "Uptown," Shirley MacLaine's "Every Little Movement," Ann Margret's "Hollywood Movie Movement," and "Baryshnikov on Broadway."

Where does an idea for a special come from?

There's no formula, but I can give you some examples. Paul McCartney decided to do a television special. There are artists like that; when they decide to do a TV special, it's going to be sold. Neil Diamond was that way, too. Other artists that are not quite as heavyweight need to have a production company involved in order to make the sale, whether it's Smith-Hemion or one of a number of others. The idea for the "Baryshnikov on Broadway" show came from IBM; they were the perfect sponsors for that kind of program and they came to us. That's the star special. The other kind of special is the concept special, where there isn't necessarily one star carrying it all. Specials like that may be "America Salutes Richard Rodgers," a Radio City Music Hall special called "Rockette," and one called "Uptown," a history of Harlem's Apollo theater. For those we usually go to a network or an advertiser and pitch it and try to get a commitment.

It sounds as though a concept special calls upon the writer to be a storyteller, almost the way he or she would be doing in a drama.

The concept special is interesting because you are starting, in a sense, from scratch. You are creating an idea and the idea comes first, so therefore the idea is going to be the product of a writer, a producer, a director, etc. A case in point was the "Uptown" show. It started with a book somebody brought in, called *Uptown, A History of Harlem's Apollo Theater.* The task of the writer at that point was to organize the multitude of ideas that came about once we decided the concept was going to be the history of black entertainment, as told through the Apollo Theater—breaking it down into music, dance, comedy, with some kind of chronological order, and so on.

What kind of storyline evolved for the "Uptown" show?

In the case of the Apollo show, what was interesting was that the theater, which was so important to the history of black entertainment, was owned by a white man—a very community-conscious, Damon Runyon type of character. I felt that somebody should play him in the show—that would be the glue that holds the show together. So Jack Albertson played Frank Shiffman. The scenes with him were always in his office, which was over the marquee, and we learned about the Apollo theater through him. He was like the Stage Manager of "Our Town."

You mentioned that the other kind of special is the star special. Does the writer have a lesser role to play in those?

No, the star special is also incredibly challenging and very difficult. The writer still gets extremely involved because now you have to come up with ideas related to that performer. We try to hinge it on all the "truths" that exist with that particular performer. We try to have the star specials be very personal, especially the artist's first one. It's a lot of fun doing somebody's first special; you're dealing with the things that made them become a performer and their anxieties and their dreams, and those are wonderful things to touch on . . . wonderful things for a writer! It's awfully interesting, I would think, for a writer to sit down with the performer for six hours or so and just talk to that person and find out where he's coming from, literally and spiritually and emotionally. The writer becomes a little bit of a biographer in variety—then the question is, how do you deal with that in entertaining terms?

OK, how?

Well, to give you an example, Ben Vereen was a fountain of information; it all just poured out. What you're looking for is one little idea that you can grab onto, one hook. With Vereen we found it when he said, "We used to have a big tree stump outside our house, maybe two feet in diameter, and we used to call it the dancing tree. We tapped on it like a drum, we danced on it, it became our stage when we were kids." What a wonderful image! And of course the audience knew him from a series called "Roots," and this tree had roots, literally, and also related to his roots as a performer—so it all fell into place. It's a warm, natural truth. At least that kind of approach turns *me* on. I know that I'll stay up nights sometimes because I'll not be satisfied with what we're doing with somebody— when we haven't found the key idea.

So you look not for a gimmick, but for something central to that person?

Absolutely. It's not phony, it's meaningful to that person. But I don't want to make it sound all that easy. The writer still has a lot of work to do—you have to know what to do with the performer's "truths"—how to theatricalize their story, when to change it. You can't always use the literal experience, but you can use the spirit of the thing. In the Cheryl Ladd special we had a cafe where she hangs out and dreams about being a star; that's not to say she's really had a place just like that. The creation of Ma's Cafe, the booking of a group of boys that she could interact with, having another actress, Ellie, play the dreamer, having her come back, using slow motion in the cafe, having a mechanical bucking horse—all those things were elements Dwight and I and the writers used in order to theatricalize her experience.

It's also possible to come up with star specials that aren't autobiographical, isn't it?

Sure. One time we were approached to do a special for Julie Andrews, and for some reason I had the idea of doing "Julie on Sesame Street"—I liked the thought of taking the children's show and putting it into a nighttime, adult form. We made some phone calls and they were amenable to letting us use the sets and the characters. Again, isn't that a nice thing to turn over to a writer? You have Ernie, you have Big Bird, you have Julie and the guests, you can do dance numbers using the theme of numbers, and so on. That one grew easily. It was a case of bringing together John Stone, a writer-producer for "Sesame Street" and one of our writers.

What kind of form is used to outline a variety show?

We'll sit and talk for weeks about different ideas. We'll cata-
logue the many different ideas that come up for a given project.
Certain ideas will wear well; they're still good after that week, or
they have grown into something good. At that point I'll do a rundown—a list of elements of that show, in order. If we really get
stuck, maybe we'll just put down "Julie, intro and first number," and
figure out later exactly what it should be. But you have to force
yourself to put it into a rundown, you need that structure for things
to start happening.

Is that list—the rundown—a standard format?

Yes—some people also use index cards. On these cards you
put different ideas relating to your central concept. For example,
songs, dance numbers, comedy sketches, and so forth. You start
playing with them. I find that when you start putting these ideas in
juxtaposition to other ideas, they create new ideas. It's very much
like the old Stanley Kubrick image, relating to editing. He said that if
you see a shot of a man's feet, walking along the street, you attach no
special significance to that, beyond what it is: a man walking along a
street. But if the next shot is an open manhole, and then you go back
to the same shot of the walking man—suddenly it's a whole new
thing. There's suspense and there's danger—will he fall in? There's a
whole story, simply because of the sequencing. You can apply that
principle in many ways. But even more than what he meant, what
I've found very interesting is that sequencing breeds new ideas—
you may end up not even using the original ideas.

That sounds like a process you could use in all kinds of writing.

Sure. Don't just accept the idea for itself. Put it down, put
something near it—before it, after it, next to it—and see where that
takes you.

When somebody has an idea for a special, what's the best form in which to present it?

Usually you have a three or four page presentation that can include a rundown, a storyline, a story outline, a script excerpt; in variety, it takes all different forms. Basically it's a little sales pitch that

gives somebody a clear picture of what you want to do, and shows the uniqueness of it, the entertainment value of it.

And typically the writer would have to interest a production company, which would then take the idea to a network—the idea by itself isn't enough, is it?

Ideas are kind of easy, if you really put your mind to it. It's the packaging and the execution of the idea that becomes important—not only creatively, but the business side of it, too. Putting together all the elements that'll make it work. The networks like to deal with people who have shown they can do that.

Am I correct in assuming that if the presentation comes from an unknown, it should be more detailed and include some sort of samples?

It's very difficult to write relevant samples for a variety show. If you want to write a spec script for "M*A*S*H" you know the characters, you know the tone of the show, the level of taste, the kind of humor, and so on. Somebody can look at your script and say, "Yes, this person can write for 'M*A*S*H.' " But if you do a spec script for a variety show, right away you have to pick who's going to be on it—I'll give you an example. I received a nicely written treatment tailor-made for Frank Sinatra. The problem is that Frank Sinatra doesn't do that many TV specials. So the writer has put all his eggs in one basket. You could write a spec script for a concept show, but again it's a very long shot. We'd have to be excited by it, we'd have to be able to cast it—because the networks won't buy a concept show unless it includes big stars—and then we'd have to sell it to the network.

But if somebody did choose to do something for you or another producer, on spec, what sort of samples would it make sense to include?

I'd rather read original material for original characters, rather than a monologue tailored for Johnny Carson or Jonathan Winters, for example. I'd rather see revue-type material, maybe something like the material done by Second City. That way I can evaluate the premise and its execution. In other words, a scene with a beginning, middle and end, so I can see the pacing, the taste, the kind of humor. In humor, the jokes have to be good, but there has to be more to it than just jokes. It's probably best if the samples relate to the ideas you're proposing.

Are you gun-shy about considering unsolicited material that may coincidentally resemble something you already have planned?

I've been sent things by strangers, with the most elaborate warnings: "Writer protected! Writers Guild Patented!" all over the front page. You feel like you're opening something that came from the White House. And you open it and you read the most mundane, ordinary, obvious thing. And you want to say, "This person really felt this idea should have eight rubber stamps on it?" It's the most vague, neutral idea, it's been done before and it'll be done again. So aspects of it are bound to resemble something you'll be doing. This makes the lawyers nervous; I try not to worry about it.

Have you done a show based on something that came to you from a newcomer?

It's rare. But I can tell you about one incident—a girl who was a back-up singer for Ann Margret, a songwriter named Gail Heideman. Via Roger Smith, Ann Margret's husband and manager, she sent me a cassette of her songs, and one was called, "Hollywood Movie Girls." I thought that would be an interesting subject for an Ann Margret special. Gail wasn't qualified to write the show, but her song was the basis of the idea. The song itself only made up three minutes of the 90-minute show, but I hired her as a consultant.

It sounds as though variety might be even more difficult to break into than the other areas of TV writing.

The variety special seems to attract the best class of writers. The writers we tend to use a lot get big money. People like Buz Kohan, Marty Farrell, Harry Crane, Rod Warren, Danny Simon—top, top people who have done the sitcoms and everything else. It's a very small group of people.

A lot of new comedy writers start out writing material for young comedians. Is that a good way to get experience?

I think working for ten dollars to give jokes to the David Letterman of today is a very constructive and valid way to hear your stuff done—to know when it's screwed up, to know when it works. The writers do it because they need the experience, the comedians do it because they need the material, or when a guy like Letterman makes it he remembers who helped him along the way.

Are there any other outlets you'd recommend?

There's one unusual, neglected area: helping people write material for their night club acts. It's pure variety. It's just what we've been talking about: in their act, people always want to deal with their background, where they came from, so you're dealing with that biographical material in the monologue. You want it to be witty, it relates to music—you have to do intros to certain songs. It's a simple format, one-to-one. It's a practical approach because a lot of the performers are always open to changing their acts. They don't have huge budgets, but they do have certain funds for that.

You'd have to study these performers, just as you'd study a series before writing a spec script.

You have to learn not just their style, but also how far to push the humor. Sometimes material can be funny, but it makes the performer go too far for a laugh; it makes the performer look like he's trying too hard. But you'd go see their current acts when possible, you'd buy their albums, come up with witty intros, and so on.

And doing material for a star might give you an opening to present an idea for a special to the star; presumably if you get a star interested in your idea, that improves your chances of then interesting a producer.

No doubt about it, it's the difference between night and day. It's almost imperative. But doing club material for people like Edye Gorme, Leslie Uggams, Rich Little, gives you good experience and contacts. I guarantee you, if you get material to somebody like Rich Little on a spec basis, they'll look at it. If they use it, they pay. That means you have to have a little faith, and maybe somewhere along the line you might have some material stolen, but you have to take chances when you're starting out. And I think with this approach you'll find a receptive talent pool interested in your work.

CHAPTER 13

How to Create a New Series

Are you interested in creating a new hit series that runs for years and years, makes you an esteemed writer/producer, and makes you rich? Welcome to the club—so does just about everybody working in television, as well as those not yet working in television but planning on it. Getting a series on the air is akin to winning the lottery: the rewards are just as big, but the odds are just as long.

• WHY YOU SHOULDN'T TRY TO CREATE A SERIES NOW

What's this? A chapter that shows you how to create a new series but first tries to talk you out of it? Yes, that's pretty much what we have in mind. The reason is that this is the most difficult endeavor in television. The networks look to established production companies for proposals for new series. In turn, the established production companies look to established writers and producers for proposals for new series. In this arena, the new writer is at a tremendous disadvantage.

If series television is the field in which you are most interested, your best bet is to try to break in as a freelance writer of sitcoms or hour-long shows. After you've had some success as a freelancer, you'll inevitably be invited to join the writing staff of a show. If you do that job well, you'll progress from staff writer to story editor, and on to producer. At that point people will be coming to you for ideas for new series. Before that point, you'll have trouble getting people to take you seriously.

If you believe that you have a series idea that's the best thing since sliced bread, you won't care about the fact that you're facing an uphill battle—you want to get your series idea considered. If that's the case, the rest of this chapter is for you.

• WHAT KIND OF SHOWS ARE THE NETWORKS LOOKING FOR?

The kinds of shows that networks are looking for vary from year to year—sometimes from month to month. Just before "The Cosby Show" became a tremendous hit, the conventional wisdom was that sitcoms were on the way out. Then came Cosby, and suddenly everybody was looking for family sitcoms. After we saw a rash of Cosby-clones the networks decided that was enough of that, and the market shifted to other types of comedies. If you've been watching television for a while, you'll have seen all sorts of shows come into vogue and then fade: cop shows, detective shows, courtroom shows, ensemble sitcoms, family sitcoms, action-adventure series, and so on. The only genre that seems to have died is the Western (amazingly, in the 50s and 60s Westerns constituted the dominant form of prime-time television), but we wouldn't bet that even that form might not come back someday.

As an outsider, your best plan is to concentrate on ideas that are different from the shows that are currently the hottest. The reason is that when a show is a hit the network machinery immediately goes into motion to generate copies. These clones then hit the air and some of them are successful. At this point you, the viewer, become aware that this is the most popular form, but you're coming into the process too late. By this time networks are already looking for the next big thing. As we suggested before, when discussing what type of feature film to write, you should go with projects that mean something to you, rather than projects that you develop just because you think they'll be commercial (naturally, the best idea is one that means something to you *and* seems commercial).

So, in short, the networks are looking for all kinds of programs at all times. Even when the trend is for one type, if you come up with something else that's fresh and exciting, they may be interested. Furthermore, the usual answer when you ask someone at the network what he is looking for is, "I don't know . . . but I'll know it when I see it."

Whom Do You Approach With Your Series Idea?

Although networks are the ultimate buyers of new series, you do not approach them directly. Incidentally, now there are new buyers on the horizon: pay-TV channels like Home Box Office and Showtime, as well as syndicators like the Fox Network. You also do not approach them directly. Instead, you approach production companies and studios that supply these other entities with programs. A network is not only interested in the idea, but the execution of that idea. They want to do business with companies that will do a good job of casting and producing the show, that will bring it in on time, that will be adept at staying within their budget, and so forth. Therefore they deal with Paramount Studios, with Universal, with Embassy, with Taft Entertainment, and many others that have a track record. Individual producers make their homes at these companies and draw upon the experience and reputation.

To see who is producing shows, you can watch the credits at the end of the shows on the air. At any given time, however, there are many entities that do not have a show on but that are interested in developing shows and presenting them. If you read one of the trade papers (*Daily Variety* or *The Hollywood Reporter*) you'll remain current on which companies are developing series, which ones are getting shows on the air, and so forth. This type of awareness is very important.

How Do You Approach These Companies?

As with almost every other kind of submission you might want to make, usually you need an agent in order to submit ideas for new series. Agents, knowing that this is the most difficult sale of all for a new writer, are leery of making these submissions. But again, if the idea is great enough and you can convince an agent to take a look at your proposal, there's a chance she may want to represent you and submit it.

Don't submit your entire proposal to the agent to begin with. Instead, write a query letter that summarizes the project and conveys your sense of enthusiasm for it, and ask whether the agent is willing to look at the complete proposal. See Chapter 17 for tips on how to write effective query letters to agents. If the agent reads the material and feels she can sell it, she will either submit your proposal to producers, or will set up pitch meetings during which you'll make a verbal presentation directly to the producer. See Chapter 16 for detailed suggestions on how to pitch your ideas effectively.

If you strike out with agents or want to try bypassing them, you can write directly to producers at production companies. Indicate in your letter that you are willing to sign a release form. Frankly, most won't read material not submitted through an agent, but a few will.

Later in this chapter we'll give you a full description of what you need to include in a proposal for a new series, but for now we'll take you through the complete process of submitting a proposal and having it accepted.

What Happens When a Producer Likes Your Idea?

When a producer likes your series proposal and believes he may be able to sell it, usually he will option it. This means that during the option period (typically three months, six months, or a year) he will have the exclusive right to take it to the networks or other possible outlets. For this option usually you will receive little or no money. When a feature film is optioned, the money is greater. The reason is that a film producer can take your feature script to dozens of possible financing entities, whereas a TV producer has only three main buyers to approach. If those three say no, it's the end of the road. Therefore, the TV producer doesn't want to spend a lot of money up front.

As part of the option agreement, your agent should negotiate what your role will be if the production company sells your idea to the network and get a pilot commitment (that is, if the network agrees to film or tape one episode as a sample of the series) and also what your role will be if the show makes it onto the network schedule. Of course your agent will try to have it written into the contract that you will be hired to write the pilot script, but usually this will be subject to network approval (more on this in a moment).

Part of the negotiating strategies we have worked out with our agents is *not* to put primary emphasis on upfront money, but instead to put the maximum pressure on getting a very solid deal, stipulating that we would be story editors or co-producers, that our salaries would be in the mid-high range, that we would write the first draft of the pilot for a set fee, and that we'd have the right to write a certain number of episodes during the first season.

Who Pitches the Idea to the Network?

If the producer feels that you are an asset at a pitch meeting, they'll take you in with them and have you make part of the presentation. Before you go in, they'll rehearse the pitch with you so everybody knows what will be going on. If you break into a rash or faint when called upon to make a speech, they may go in by themselves the first time or may ask you to be present but not take on a major part of the presentation. Usually you leave behind a copy of the proposal.

Will You Be Allowed to Write the Pilot?

Maybe you will be allowed to write the pilot, maybe not. Pilot writing is considered a special art and each network has a list of pilot writers with whom they like to work. Cracking this market is difficult. The network's first impulse will be, frankly, not to let you write the pilot if you don't already have a list of credits.

The biggest factor on your side will be the degree to which the production company with which you go in is willing to fight for you to be the pilot writer. If they are absolutely adamant on this point, and if they are people who are respected at the network, they will prevail. Oftentimes such a company will indicate that they will team you with a writer/producer who, in effect, will act as an insurance policy for the project. The idea is that if your script goes off course, this more experienced person will work with you to get it back on course. Additionally, the production company may argue that you should be given a shot at writing at least a first draft, because if that comes in and is awful it will be possible to bring in a more experienced writer without losing more than $25,000 or $30,000, which is a fairly puny sum in the context of the overall costs of producing a pilot.

If the production company doesn't have this type of confidence in your ability to write the pilot they will pay you a fee and you will still receive a credit that will be "created by (you)" or, more likely, "created by (you) and (the writer of the pilot)" since the pilot writer probably will make contributions to the concept of the series. It's wise to fight tooth and nail to be allowed to write the pilot—and also to know when to give up if it's just not in the cards.

Now let's go back to the core of the whole discussion: the series idea itself.

• HOW DO YOU KNOW WHETHER YOUR IDEA WOULD MAKE A GOOD SERIES?

First, realize that your idea should not be just a retread of what's already on. The major producers can do just that—duplicate a successful show and get that clone on the air. But from a freelancer, they're looking for something different and new, something they haven't already thought of themselves.

You also have to determine whether the idea can sustain a large number of episodes. There are some ideas that would be wonderful for two or three shows, but not three years' worth of episodes. Remember that the production companies will make money only when the series has been on for a while and can be syndicated, and that networks are looking for shows that will attract audiences for a good long time. If your idea doesn't lend itself to being stretched over twenty-two episodes a year for several years, either convert it to a Movie-of-the-Week or a feature, or drop it.

As far as the writing goes, you should know where the conflict is going to come from, and also you want to have a very appealing central character. Basically, you have to apply to your series idea the same criteria you apply to anything you write: Is it entertaining? Does it offer something a bit new? Is it structured correctly? Are these characters that people will like or identify with in some way? And, perhaps most important, is this a series you would really enjoy seeing?

Finally, you must be prepared to answer the question of how this series is different from the ones already on the air. It can't be *too* different or it will frighten producers and networks, but it should have some fresh feel. If it's a detective show, what sets it apart from "Magnum, P.I." and "Simon and Simon" and all the others? If it's another family sitcom, what makes it different from "Cosby" and the others? There must be at least a minor way that you can easily distinguish your idea from what's already on the air.

One note to people interested in creating sitcoms: don't get hung up on notions about workplaces or arenas in which "a lot of crazy characters come in" and do zany things. The heart of any series, even ones like "Night Court" in which a lot of crazy characters *do* come in, is its central characters. They have to be strong and interesting and involved in every episode—in "Night Court" it is Harry and Dan and Bull and the others that are the key to the series, not the nutty accused people who come in and provide subplots.

What Goes Into a Series Proposal?
The recommended components of a series proposal are:

1. A one-page single-spaced overview of the series. This summary tells what the series is about, who the central characters are, what the setting is, and the types of stories that will be included. Writing this sheet is one of the hardest things to do, because you have to say so much in so little space. Not only do you have to convey the content of the series, but also the tone. If the series is going to be funny, the one-pager should be funny; if the series is going to be suspenseful, some of that quality should be relayed in the overview as well.

2. A one or two paragraph description of each major character in the series. The description should concern itself much more with personality than with appearance, although sometimes appearance can be important, as in the case of a detective show in which the leads are ex-wrestlers, for example. For the most part, though, the reader wants to know what kind of person this is, and how that person will interact with the others on the program.

3. At least four or five (and preferably six to eight) storylines. The summary of each story need only be a paragraph or two long, but it should include the story's beginning, middle, and end. It should make clear which of the show's characters is involved, and how. People looking at these storylines will be judging how effective the show will be at sustaining the interest of the audience. Therefore, these storylines must be absolutely the best, the most interesting, in the case of a comedy the most amusing, ones that you can come up with.

4. An optional but helpful element is a summary of an episode. Alternately or in addition, you may want to write a sample scene from an episode of the proposed series. By actually writing a scene (or two) you will show (not just describe) how these people talk, how they interact, the types of situations they get into, and so on. Some writers even choose to write an entire script on spec, although it's debatable whether this is helpful. Certainly it shows that you can write this show, but it may make the network people feel that they have been ex-

cluded from the development process. If you do write some sample scenes or an entire script, generally it's a good idea not to make your subject the "first" show—the one in which Laverne meets Shirley, the one in which Kate moves in with Allie, the one in which "Moonlighting's" David and Maddie set up their detective agency. The networks and producers are more interested in what a typical episode looks and sounds like, and these "first" or "kick-off" scripts are not typical.

• A SAMPLE SERIES PRESENTATION

What follows is a sample series presentation for a one-hour dramatic series, written by Jurgen Wolff and created by Wolff and Rob Kenneally. Notice that we broke the suggested rule of not focusing on the "first" episode. In this case, the situation of the show was rather unusual, and we felt that the fastest way to get producers to understand the basic concept of the show was to describe it via the plot summary. Also, in many cases one-hour shows are introduced via a two-hour Movie-of-the-Week, and we had a hidden agenda in hoping to plant the seed of that possibility in the minds of the people who read this proposal.

Following the sample series proposal, we present an interview with a gentleman who has been closely involved in the development of new series, Larry Lyttle.

BA's in Blue

proposal for a one-hour action series
written by Jurgen M. Wolff
created by Rob Kenneally and Jurgen M. Wolff

Take a group of college kids. Give them uniforms and guns. Put them out into the violent streets of the city, where guts and quick reactions are as vital as intelligence. What you'll get is the action, adventure, and drama of "BA's in Blue."

"BA's in Blue" is the story of a small group of the young people from across the country who get college scholarships from the Justice Department. The string: they have to take police training and function as street cops a day a week.

The group consists of TED THORPE, a handsome 20-year-old who thinks being a cop will teach him more about psychology than any class could; MICHAEL STUART, a young Black who doesn't particularly like cops but needs the scholarship; STEPHEN BROWN, a country boy who's full of ideals; and LAURIE HARRISON, a top athlete who's always looking for a new challenge. Overseeing them is SGT. AMOS BILLINGSLY, a crusty career police officer who believes good cops are born, not made in a college program.

Ted, Michael, Stephen, and Laurie soon learn that from now on they'll be living in conflict—with their fellow students who view cops with suspicion, and with the career officers who mistrust them.

The crimes this group gets involved with take them from the dirty alleys of dope dealers and hookers to gleaming corporate offices where industrial espionage can end in murder. Each episode of "BA's in Blue" focuses on one of the young people as they learn about life and love on the campus at the same time they make life-and-death decisions on the street.

CHARACTERS

SGT. AMOS BILLINGSLY is a career cop in his fifties, a well-liked and respected veteran of twenty-five years on the force. He's the ultimate police officer—so much that his wife left him because he was married more to the job than to her. Now he drinks a little too much and spends his free time around the cop bars. Billingsly doesn't like the new college program; he didn't even finish high school and he feels that being a cop is something you learn in your guts. He's worried that these young people won't have their hearts in their jobs and he throws as many obstacles as he can into their paths. If they feel ready to make life-and-death decisions, they'll have to prove it to Billingsly. Over the course of the series, this man will develop a grudging respect for the young part-time officers, but he'll never stop being the one looking over their shoulders.

TED THORPE is a handsome 20-year-old, a sophomore majoring in psychology. He resembles a young Robert Redford and could be a movie star if he wanted (in other words, he's a hunk), but he's got brains as well as brawn. He's not necessarily committed to staying a cop once he's finished the program; he thinks he may want to go into teaching or (a choice that makes Billingsly go red in the face whenever Ted mentions it) social work. Ted's from a middle-class family that's too poor to pay his way through college, but too well-off for him to qualify for a regular scholarship. He's got a good sense of humor and is the easiest guy in the world to get along with—until you cross him or one of his buddies on the team. He may be young, but he's not soft. He gives himself 100 percent to doing whatever he takes on—and now he's taken on the task of trying to be a top student and a tough cop.

STEPHEN BROWN is a Southern country boy, the first one in his family to go to college. He liked the farm and the country life, but he wants more for himself, so he jumped at the chance of a police scholarship. A good-looking kid, he's still idealistic about people, maybe because on the farm he wasn't around that many. His muscles and down-home way of talking make a lot of people underestimate him, but he's plenty bright. His first tour through a ghetto neighborhood shatters some of his illusions about how people live, and he's got a lot to learn yet about city life and how much one man can do to set things straight, but his sense of optimism and his personal code keep him going.

MICHAEL STUART, a black man originally from the ghetto, is the oldest member of the group. Now 25, he started college but had to drop out because of financial problems. A police recruiting officer sent to the ghetto to recruit minority police officers convinced Michael that the program was a way to finish his education. Michael's not crazy about the police and is even more torn than the others about his new role; being a student and a cop—and a Black—at the same time isn't easy. But he wants the degree and he thinks it's important for the new breed of cops to understand the streets as well as the classroom.

LAURIE HARRISON is a sharp and beautiful 20-year-old who thrives on adventure. A Navy brat, she's already seen most of the world by traveling with her parents as she grew up. The only child of a father who always wanted a son, Laurie loves proving that she can handle anything a man can, but it hasn't made her lose an ounce of her feminine charm or appeal. At college she's on the track team, and she gives the same kind of non-stop dedication to her role as a cop—her newest and most worthwhile challenge. She likes the fact that the police program mirrors the discipline of the military environment, and she's determined to prove to herself—and especially to her father—that she can handle it.

RECURRING ROLE

TERRENCE TURKEL ("Turk") is Ted's roommate at the dorm. Turk is a hyperactive brainy type, always full of crazy ideas about how he can gain women, money, and fame. He's a natural comedian, but also a good friend—somebody Ted can talk to honestly and count on in a pinch.

PILOT EPISODE

We open on the streets of Watts. Police sirens pierce the air as a group of squad cars and police vans screech to a halt in front of a rundown storefront with bars on the windows. Shots ring out from inside the building. The SWAT team pours out of one of the vans, smashes in the door, pumps cannisters of tear gas through the windows, then goes in. Watching all this is an oddly out-of-place group of college-age young people—their expressions show that this is the first time they've been exposed to this kind of violence in this kind of neighborhood. The cops hustle out two men in handcuffs. A crowd of local people is building up, they're jeering, a few throw bottles and cans—further violence is in the air. The cops hurry the prisoners into one van, the group of young people into another van, and speed away.

We cut to a mostly-empty college campus. The only activity seems to be in one building where a tough senior police officer is addressing a group of thirty young people—among them are the half dozen we saw in Watts. The officer is saying that what they saw in small groups this morning was a taste of what they'll be dealing with if they decide to take part in the Justice Department police scholarship program. We find out that the program will provide a full scholarship for a select group of students. The catch: they have to go through a police training course this summer and then—if they make it—have to serve as cops for a day a week. The hope is that they'll also decide to stay in police work after they graduate—"If you don't burn out, flunk out, flake out . . . or get killed . . . in the meantime," the cop says. He tells them they have a week to go home and think it over. If they come back they'd better be prepared to grow up fast—kids don't last long on the streets with a uniform on.

We go to the dorm where the applicants have been staying for this orientation. As they prepare to go home, we meet our core characters: TED THORPE, a handsome 20-year-old hunk who's a psychology major; LAURIE HARRISON, an athletic Navy brat who loves new challenges; MICHAEL STUART, a Black from the ghetto who needs this scholarship to finish his education; and STEPHEN BROWN, an idealistic brawny country boy straight off the farm. We follow these characters home:

Ted returns to his suburban middle-class family, which is too poor to pay his way through college but too well-off for him to qualify for a regular scholarship. His parents want him to get a good education, but they worry about the dangers he'll face, and they try to talk him out of signing up . . .

Laurie goes back to her home on a Navy base where her father is the Commander. He always wanted a son and is proud that his daughter has turned out to be the match of any man. He likens the police program to the military and encourages her to join. She wants to prove herself to him, but has to come to grips with the fact that the program may put her in the position of having to take someone's life . . .

Stephen goes back to the farm to see his parents and his four younger brothers and sisters. His parents encourage him to do what he thinks is best. He loves them and life on the farm, but he recognizes that the small farmer is a dying breed, and he'll never be able to make a living the way his father has . . .

Michael goes back to his ghetto neighborhood. His parents want him to join the program, knowing that the more black cops there are, the better things will be in areas like theirs. But Michael's older brother has been hassled by the police all his life and he considers Michael a traitor . . .

Back at the college, Ted, Michael, Laurie, and Stephen all return, but a few of the others we saw before do not. The police officer running the program welcomes the twenty recruits: "You are either the brave or the foolish," he says.

Their training begins the next morning at 5 AM and they are in for a 90-day program that will make boot camp look like kindergarten. The program has its share of detractors among the career cops, notably SGT. AMOS BILLINGSLY, and they've made sure that the training will weed out any weaklings. As they go through the physically and mentally grueling routine, each reveals more about their personalities and what keeps them going.

Ted and Stephen quickly become good buddies. Laurie becomes best friends with another woman, who washes out halfway through; after that, Laurie stays somewhat aloof—now only one of a handful of women, she wants to keep her relationship with the guys strictly professional. Michael also keeps his distance, afraid of being co-opted—he'll be a cop but he won't forget that he's black or that he comes from the ghetto.

The training is a crash course in all facets of police work: using handguns, shotguns, and special weapons; interrogation techniques; crowd control; riot duty; taking on drug users. And it's accompanied by an endless series of physical tests. Some just can't hack it, and the group shrinks further.

It looks like Laurie will be one of the next casualties—she's not making the marksmanship scores she needs. Ted offers to help. At first she's too proud to accept, but she relents and he and Stephen (who's a crack shot because he grew up hunting) coach her. Michael is helping the officer who runs the firing range, and because he admires Laurie's toughness he's rooting for her. She gets better, but not fast enough—she gets a failing score on a crucial weekly test. Ted asks Michael to "lose" her score for the week. Michael protests that it'll be his neck on the line—why should he do it? "Because she'll make a good, fair cop," Ted says. He tells Michael that they're just buying time—if she fails again next week, she'll accept that and be out of the program. Michael says he'll have to think about it. When the test results are announced, the training officer reprimands Michael for losing one of them. Laurie practices in every spare moment. The next week she passes the test, and the experience has brought our group together.

By the end of the 90 days, they're in better shape physically and mentally than they have ever been in their young lives. The dozen who are still in the program are the brightest and most motivated—but Billingsly and others still see them as amateurs who'll be distracted by their college lives and may endanger the regular officers in the field. Billingsly scoffs at the training simulations set up for them as Mickey Mouse "let's pretend" exercises.

They're out on a final simulation when suddenly it's no longer "let's pretend." The exercise has them surrounding one of a number of abandoned warehouses by the waterfront. Suddenly the air is alive with gunfire—the cops didn't know there was a PCP factory at a near-by warehouse, and the drug-makers don't realize that the cops are just on a training mission. Out of this confusion a small war has erupted and several cops go down, hit by gunfire. The trainees suddenly are in the real world of life and death—and they go into action.

One of the wounded cops is in the no-man's land between the warehouse and the police vehicles, and Michael and Stephen carry him back, escaping unhurt in the hail of gunfire. Laurie backs up the cops who lob tear gas into the warehouse. For some reason, the tear gas has no effect—the men in the warehouse aren't coming out. Ted's orders are to stay put, but he climbs onto the warehouse roof and gets a look in through a skylight: the drug-makers, routinely working with chemicals, had gas masks handy. Ted fires into one of the vats of chemicals and scrambles to get out of the way—just in time, as a small explosion leads to a larger one and then the whole warehouse goes sky-high. The men inside rush out, some injured and one on fire.

The cop in charge pulls Ted aside. "Didn't we teach you not to do a goddam John Wayne glory-seeking stunt like that?" he demands. "I forgot, Sir," Ted says. "Good," the senior cop says with a grin.

Our final image is of the graduation and we freeze frame on the look of pride, strength, and determination on the faces of Ted, Laurie, Michael, and Stephen. It will be another few years before they receive their college diplomas, but at this point they receive something that's come to be just as important to them: their police badges. They have made the grade.

STORY CONCEPTS

1. Stephen goes undercover to check out a pornography operation that is recruiting attractive young men and women. He hits the streets posing as a male hustler and soon finds himself in a sleazy underworld where money, drugs, and violence are used to control the "stars" of straight, gay, and sadomasochistic films.

2. Laurie investigates a report of the sexual abuse of children at a day-care center. Laurie's outrage deeply involves her in the case, but the charges hinge on the testimony of one little girl—is she having fantasies that could destroy the lives of innocent teachers . . . or are her stories the tip of the iceberg of sexual abuse of little children?

3. Ted's assignment is to act as a police liaison with a group staging peaceful protests against the nuclear research plant on campus. He's sympathetic to their cause—but then he finds out that a brilliant but eccentric member of the group has plans to use the peaceful protests as a diversion for violence that will culminate in the destruction of the plant. Ted has to keep the man's actions from discrediting the group, at the same time he has to prevent an explosion that would endanger the entire campus.

4. Sgt. Billingsly orders Michael to serve as a narc on the college campus. He reluctantly agrees and finds out that one of the dealers is no small-time student doper—he's part of an organized crime effort to make college campuses America's most lucrative drug market . . . and he knows that Michael is a cop.

LARRY LYTTLE

Larry Lyttle has been Vice President of Program Development from Warner Brothers Television where he was in charge of creating TV series, both comedy and drama. Prior to joining Warner Brothers in 1982, Lyttle served as Vice President of Comedy Development for Paramount TV. He began as a television packaging agent for ICM.

How do you know what the networks are looking for?

They always tell you that they are looking for something fresh and innovative, which doesn't help you much. So at the start of the year—and June is about the start of our year—I'll say to them, "What are you *not* looking for?" If they say, "We're not going to make a western," I know immediately I'm not going to develop a western, as much as I or one of the writers on the lot may want to do one.

We're in the market for good ideas . . . and they're tough to find. I go by instinct, and I've learned what I cannot sell. Then it becomes a question of execution.

If you told someone the idea for "The Cosby Show" and you read the "Cosby" scripts, it would sound real mundane. But then you get people executing it as Ed. Weinberger and Michael Leeson did in the pilot. Then you continue with Earl Pomerantz and Jay Sandrich, a wonderful director. And suddenly an idea that seems mundane comes alive under these people, and those in front of the camera—notably Bill Cosby and the wonderful actors that play his family.

Talent is the key. We're very big on putting together talent here. Alan Shayne, my boss, who is the president of the studio, spends a lot of time with casting and talent and making overall deals with people.

Would you say that network comedy has become more star-oriented than concept-oriented?

No, it's clearly concept-oriented at the outset. I'll give you a typical example. Two years ago a writer by the name of A. J. Carruthers came in and spoke to us, and he pitched us an idea we really liked. We then said that we had a deal with Bill Bixby, and we had a deal with Mariette Hartley, and this two-character comedy would be right on the mark for them.

Then we got Carruthers to sit down with Bixby and Hartley. The two actors had a personal friendship and had indicated a desire to work together if possible. And the initial conversation was the genesis of "Goodnight Beantown."

Ultimately, the execution of that show did not work, and I'm not pointing the finger at anyone.

So it's concept first, then star-power behind the concept. I don't think people are interested in seeing a great name unless the concept is appealing to them.

We seem to have seen the demise of the so-called gang comedy . . .

The ensemble comedy, as typified in "Taxi," "Barney Miller," "The Associates" which was rather short-lived, is really not there anymore. We're now looking for "family, adult" comedies. "Family" seems to be a buzz word. Maybe that's a result of the Cosby show.

However, you must remember that it's a very transitional world here. Ensemble comedy may not be in vogue now, but two years down the road someone is going to come up with one, the network is going to air it, it'll be successful, and they'll be back in vogue. At the moment, they're sort of in a nadir.

What about the "socially relevant" comedies of the '60s and '70s that frequently dealt with issues—shows like "All in the Family" or "Maude." Any shows like that on the horizon?

It's very difficult for the networks to go on record as saying they're not interested in "socially relevant" issues. But I don't think that "socially relevant" comedies have a marketplace today. Look at the comedies that are working: "Family Ties"—a familial setting; "The Cosby Show"—a familial setting; "Growing Pains"—a familial setting. You just don't see the issue-oriented shows that we had during the '60s and '70s.

Television as a medium reflects the sociology of the country. And if you look at the politics of the country today, we've evolved into something different from the socially conscious attitude we had in the previous decade.

Where do you get the comedy series ideas that you pitch to the network?

There are a number of ways that you can go. All of the major studios invest a substantial amount of money in writer-producers we have under exclusive contract.

With those people, they'll call me up on the phone and say, "I have an idea for an hour show or a half-hour show." And they'll come in and we'll discuss it, and after a series of meetings, we'll set up a network meeting to go in and pitch the idea. These are people whom the networks perceive to be "viable" in the sense that the networks know these people can execute the ideas they are pitching.

Another way to come up with ideas is through agents. Agents are a source of great talent. They represent many of the writer-producers we have under contract, but they also keep us abreast of the young people coming up. These are writers with some experience, because the "pilot game" is really not for inexperienced writers (i.e., those without credits).

Agents will call me up and say, "We represent so and so. He's been working on "Family Ties," and he has a very interesting idea for a pilot and we'd like you to meet him." So they send me something to read, and we'll get together to discuss the idea.

The last process is that you make talent deals. We'll tailor a series idea for an actor and pitch it to the network with the actor as part of the package.

Let's clarify packaging. When you get into the network to pitch a series idea, what elements do you have besides the writer-producer?

It depends. At times, we'll just go in with a Reinhold Weege who is a viable executive producer-writer. At other times, a writer-producer will present a project to me, and I'll say, "We don't have to, but it's going to help you and us, so why don't we bring in Bill Bixby."

Then if we have a real attractive package like a Reinhold Weege and a Bill Bixby, we can say to the network, "We're not going to just accept a pilot script OK. We've got a major writer and a major star, and it's either going to be a pilot commitment or a short-order series commitment for six shows, or we're going to take it to your competitor." So it's a play. That's where the nuances come in.

What is stipulated in the deals you have with writers on the Warner Bros. lot?

Most of the deals put the writer-producers under exclusive contract to Warner Brothers Television. Everything they do in television during the period of the deal—usually a year or two with an option period after that—is done with us. If a writer-producer that we have under contract pitches me an idea I don't like, I'll try to dissuade him from pitching the concept to the networks because I don't think we can sell it. Ultimately, I'll support him if he really wants to go in.

Do you ever give freelancers a chance to pitch series ideas? Let's take a writer who has had a few episodic assignments, but hasn't been on staff?

If that writer has spent some time writing a few scripts on

spec—and I don't mean an episode of "Family Ties" or "Cheers," but an original screenplay with his own characters—and he's had a little work experience behind him, and he says to me, "Look, I know I'm not really viable in the sense that the network people really know me. But I've done a couple of episodic assignments and I've written an original screenplay," you give the guy a shot.

Do the networks have a list of "Approved Writers"?

I think there's simply a list of writers whom the networks know. And naturally, if you've worked with a writer once or twice and you don't particularly like his material, you're not going to want to use him again.

But there's no approval list. It's all done on the basis of, "Yeah, we've worked with that person. We've given that person a couple of shots, and he just has not performed for us. We'd rather use someone else."

Everybody thinks there's an "A" list and a "B" list or a "no touch" list. That's baloney.

When you take a meeting with a freelancer to talk about series ideas, what do you like the writer to bring in?

Usually just the idea. This is a very verbal business. Most of the ideas are discussed—you talk about the idea, the characters.

When you come in, you don't pitch a pilot story. You say, "Here's the concept." Then you define the characters in the piece. And then if the writer has a treatment he wants to leave behind, that's fine.

Does it ever buy you anything to go ahead and write the full pilot script to show you can execute the idea?

Absolutely not. It's a waste of time. Well, let's put it this way— 95 percent of the time it's a waste of time. Especially with the networks. If a great pilot script comes in on spec, the networks aren't going to buy it, because developing a series is what they do for a living. When people on the outside start doing it, the network people say, "Whoa, they don't need my job."

On another level, the best thing you can get out of a spec pilot script is the network saying, "Yeah, we like the area, we like the concept, we like the character of Bill, we like the character of Joyce, but this is what we want to do . . ." So they start almost from scratch anyway, whether they should or not.

How often do you go into the networks and pitch series ideas?

In the height of the pitch season—June through October—as many as three times a week. In a given season, you pitch thirty or forty ideas.

Who goes in with you?

The writer-producer. Maybe someone who works for me. If it's a big deal, someone I work for may go in. That's it. You want to keep it tight.

Take me through that process of going to the networks for the first time with an idea through actually getting it on the fall schedule.

When we're satisfied that the idea is ready for presentation, we'll call up, set a meeting, and go over to the network. We discuss the idea, we discuss the characters of the piece. And generally they say, "Let us think about it." A few days later, they'll call us up and say, "OK, we want to do it."

The writer-producer and I will then meet in my office and we'll discuss what the pilot story will be. Narrative is everything. We sometimes spend as long as a month working on the storyline. When we're satisfied, we go back to the networks and pitch the pilot story. Oftentimes they don't like the storyline we've picked. But for the sake of our conversation, let's presume that the story is approved.

The writer then goes off and writes it. We go over the draft here, submit it to the network. They give us notes. We do a second draft. And they either make it or they don't. It's real simple.

Did something similar to what you just described happen with "Night Court"?

"Night Court" was a little different. It originated with some of the experiences I had when I was in college, and every January I visited some friends in Philadelphia and we used to play poker, get a little loaded, and then go over to night court at midnight and see all those ridiculous characters—pimps and hookers and junkies.

At two in the morning, we'd go by the bail bondsman's office and see all the degenerates, then go into a local joint and have a Philadelphia cheese-steak, then go home and go to sleep.

Flash forward to 1979. My favorite movie that year was "And Justice for All." A few years later, I'm driving down the freeway and I hear that Joe Wizan, who produced that film, has become the head of Fox. And all of a sudden the thought occurs to me—boom, boom, boom.

So I worked on the treatment for a couple of weeks—three or four pages. And I went over to Jeff Sagansky and Warren Littlefield at NBC, and they loved the idea. They said why don't you get Reinhold Weege, a writer-producer who had done "Barney Miller" for Danny Arnold. And I exposed it to Weege, and he thought it was a good idea. He made some changes in it which I think helped it. And he then went off and wrote it. He wrote a great story; they loved it. But they didn't want to make it the pilot story.

Why is that?

Because it was a Christmas story and the pilot wouldn't air around Christmas. We wrote another script, and they said, "We're going to make this." Interestingly enough, we just shot that original script last week and it'll air this Christmas.

What steps should a new writer take in order to sell a series concept?

People starting out in the business should not concentrate their energies trying to create a series. Write an episodic script on spec. If it's good, you'll get a chance to pitch ideas to a current series, and hopefully receive an assignment.

What I do is the upper level of the business, in a sense. I create new television shows. But as a new writer, it's just as if I were a young baseball player starting out. The chances of me starting out with the New York Yankees are slim. I'd have to play on their Single A, Double A, Triple A farm teams, and hopefully matriculate to the big leagues. If you use the analogy, "development" is the Big Leagues.

So if you want to end up eventually developing comedy television series, you have to start in Single A. Well, Single A's not bad. You write a spec script for "Cheers" and you find someone to represent you, and you get this script around. I can't tell you how rarely we get a good script. But when we get one, that writer gets work. Absolutely doesn't fail.

I'll read a script here that I like, and I'll call whoever's in charge of current programming, and I'll say, "I just read a script by a guy I don't know, but this is a terrific piece of writing. Take a look at it." If he concurs with my assessment, then we'll get the writer in to discuss storylines with the producers of a show such as "Night Court."

III

TURNING THE CRAFT INTO A BUSINESS

CHAPTER 14

How to Collaborate

WRITING IS, IN MANY RESPECTS, one of the loneliest professions on earth. Facing that blank page, day after day, trying to come up with something unique, something dramatic, or something hilarious, can occasionally make you feel like you're writing into a void, into some vast maw of nothingness where all your words are swallowed and no one will ever hear or see them. That's why many writers find comfort, assistance, and even a lifelong soulmate in a writing partner: someone to bounce ideas off of, work out dialogue with, or toss a joke to, and also someone to share the frustration of failure or the elation of success.

Comedy writers in particular seem to enjoy teaming up, and there's a very good reason. Humor is subjective by nature, and what's funny to some people goes nowhere with others. Furthermore, when writing comedy it's sometimes easy to convince yourself a line is "probably funny," just because it's two o'clock in the morning and you can't come up with anything better. A good partner won't let you settle for less than your best. In comedy, two heads really can be better than one.

On the other hand, there are some disadvantages to teaming up as well. Let's take a look at them, first.

• WHY SHOULDN'T I TEAM UP WITH A PARTNER?

Well, for one thing you have to split the money. Freelance assignments are few and far between for most of us, and when we're fortunate enough to get a high-priced gig like a television script assignment, we usually need the money too badly to be able to spare half. Should you be lucky enough to land a staff position as a team, you'll be paid—as a team—more than other staff writers who are on their own, but less than twice as much.

Financial problems are said to be the leading cause of marital disharmony, and that same bugaboo is there for the writing team. Splitting income also means splitting expenses, and we all know how some people just never seem to have any cash on them, and you always end up footing the bill on their solemn promise to pay you back. The question is, how often do they remember? And of course, it's sometimes very awkward to ask a friend for repayment, especially on a ticky-tacky amount. But those ticky-tacky amounts can add up quickly.

Scheduling problems can arise that start to throw an uneven workload on one of the partners. Suppose you're on a deadline, with an entire rewrite of the last act in your screenplay to finish over the weekend—and your partner can't make it for one reason or another? Even if the reason is valid, you're probably going to resent it.

What if your partner starts missing pitch meetings, leaving you on your own? Worse yet, what if your regular work sessions are taking second place to last-minute errands and minor crises that seem to arise on a daily basis? Getting two people's schedules together in these busy times is difficult at best, and if you're both working other jobs and trying to launch a writing career in your spare time, it can become a nightmare.

Scheduling can also become a factor when setting up meetings. It's quite common to play a couple days of "tag" with producers—they postpone, they cancel, they can't show at the last minute—and that can be tough to deal with, even if it's only *your* schedule you're juggling. The problem is doubled when you have a partner.

There are times when a writer feels dry, when nothing seems to come out the way he or she would like. Those are the times it's great to have a partner who can pitch in. But what if that starts happening too often? What if, after a while, you start to feel like *you're* the one doing all the work, while your partner just keeps coming up with lousy ideas or no ideas at all? How do you say something like that to someone who has become (or was in the first place) a close friend?

How do you divide the labor? Which one does all that typing, while the other gets to pace the room or recline on a couch? Who takes care of trips to the post office, the stationery store, the photocopy shop?

Finally, on a different but no less important level, what happens to the ego-massage you always get when you look at a completed project and know that it's truly yours? There is a joy in contemplating something you have created out of thin air, something someone else is willing to pay a lot of money for. Won't it lose something to see two names on the cover page:

"Written by: Me, and that other guy who maybe had a couple lines in there and still owes me ten bucks for photocopying this thing."

• ARE THERE AS MANY REASONS WHY I *SHOULD* TEAM UP?

Certainly there are many advantages to working with a partner. As mentioned before, comedy writers in particular find it to be an especially productive and effective way to come up with consistently good material, and many dramatic writers prefer a teamwork approach as well.

The most obvious advantage to working with a partner is the most important one—you get instant feedback, in much the same way as you'd go to a doctor for a second opinion, or get two estimates on a repair job. A partner can tell you right away whether the surefire line you've just come up with is more like a misfire, or if the scene you've just constructed really has no place in the progression of the story. Of course, he might also tell you that it's the funniest line or best scene written since the invention of ink. Whether or not you agree with him, as long as he's being honest he's functioning as a good working partner.

Many people who work with partners feel they get much more work done that way. One comedy team we spoke with feels they get *four times* the amount of work done as they would if they were on their own. That kind of potential output can certainly offset the fact that you're splitting the money—you're still making twice as much as you would on your own!

Bill Bickley, whose interview appears after Chapter Nine, expressed the feeling that he and his partner are able to produce high-quality work in a much shorter amount of time. In other words, on their own they could each write just as well, but they just couldn't do it as quickly. That's important, because speed counts for a lot in television.

It's been said that a freelancer must devote 50 percent of his time to marketing, particularly in the pre-agent stage. By "marketing," we're including anything that isn't sitting down and writing: pitch sessions, story meetings, agent meetings, get-acquainted meetings, phone calls to set up meetings or to postpone meetings or to cancel meetings, finding an agent or firing an agent or finding a new agent. In short, all of those things that no writer in his right mind wants to have anything to do with, but are a mainstay of the business world, with show business being no exception. Here's where a partner can come in very handy.

With a partner you can either split the work or, in a sense, double it. It becomes possible to schedule two meetings at the same time, with one partner covering each. Lists of phone calls that need to be made can be done in half the time. Finding work, finding an agent, attending seminars—all can be facilitated by a teamwork approach.

That's a key word: teamwork. The biggest advantage to having a writing partner is that the quality level of work produced is that much better because it was done by two people combining their own unique strengths and weaknesses to create one "perfect writer." This is why you'll find that many writing teams are made up of two people whose personalities are quite different—one might be quite gregarious, while the other a bit introverted. But they each bring something special, something invaluable, to the team. One might be very facile with witty dialogue, while the other has a sharp story sense. One might be a strong first draft writer, able to fill a blank page quickly, while the other is relied on for her rewrite capabilities. Whatever the arrangement, it has to function as a symbiotic give-and-take that works toward the same final result: a better script than either one could have done on his or her own. That's teamwork.

What teamwork *isn't* is one person who comes up with ideas, and one person who writes them. The trade papers are full of people who want to "collaborate" on an idea they have that would "make a great movie." Their proposal is that they'll fill you in on the idea, you'll write it, and they'll be happy to split the money. That's not symbiotic. It's parasitic. Successful writing teams invariably are made up of two *writers* who began on their own and teamed up when it seemed advantageous and desirable.

• WORKING METHODS FOR A SUCCESSFUL COLLABORATION

As you can see, the advantages of working with a partner can easily outweigh the disadvantages, if a working structure is set up right from the start that keeps the business end of the relationship clear.

First, draw up a basic working contract. It doesn't have to be a maze of legal mumbo-jumbo, just a clear agreement in plain language that outlines the responsibilities of each partner. It might be in the form of a chart, or a calendar, or a simple accounting sheet. However you want to handle it, it's best to put things like this in writing, no matter how long you and your partner have been the closest of chums. After all, even *marriages* are being kicked off these days with pre-nuptial agreements, and legal partnerships always have been. Think of a writing partnership as both a marriage and a legal partnership, combining many of the rewards and hardships of each, and it's easy to see why things need to be written down from the start.

This working agreement should cover the points raised when we discussed the disadvantages of collaboration. First, agree to split all money, no matter who finds the job for the team, who actually sold the script at a pitch meeting, or whatever. (The exception would be work done completely on your own, without the help of your partner—more on that later.)

Next, agree to share all expenses. Each member should keep a small diary of expenses, with reimbursements made at the end of each week, or each month, or whatever you agree on. This is a much neater and more efficient way to split expenses, as opposed to pitching in together every time one person has to run down to the post office or out for lunch. Don't forget to include phone calls, messenger services, and even computer paper. It all adds up, and if one person feels he's always stuck with the bill, resentment is sure to foul up the working relationship.

In sharing all expenses, it's necessary to agree on what merits expenditures. So, no money is to be spent without the consent of both members. Obviously, this will require a pretty liberal interpretation—after all, if you need to return a long-distance phone call and your partner is unavailable, you don't hold off on the call. But you don't run out and buy a new computer monitor "for the team," just because you saw one on sale and you think your partner won't mind.

Decide on regular working hours or at least a regular, predictable way of sharing the workload. This can vary greatly, depending upon the division of writing labor peculiar to your team. For example, some collaborators work a regular, eight-hour day together, sharing an office, breaking for lunch, just like—perish the thought—a normal job. Others work at home, communicating via computer. The writing team of Jim Cash and Jack Epps, Jr. (*Top Gun, Secret of My Success*) is separated by roughly 2500 *miles*. Cash works from his home in Michigan, while his partner maintains an office at Universal. A writing team currently with "Golden Girls" works on the "alternate scene" method (a method favored by many as a way of getting out a fast first draft). Each does a scene, they trade scenes, rewrite each other's scene, and then they move on to the next two scenes. Whatever your arrangement, make it clear from the start by writing it down. You can always change it later if you come across a better method, but it's a start.

Reach an agreement on how the secretarial chores will be handled. If you're fortunate enough to be able to afford a secretary part-time or full-time, then it's merely a question of paying the salary. If, as it is for most people starting out, a secretary is a luxury you can't afford, then you have to agree on a fair way to share the necessary typing, photocopying, mailing, filing, phone calls, etc. Some teams do this by taking alternating shifts on the typewriter. Others agree that one person will run the word processor, while the other answers mail, stamps envelopes, or whatever. One of us (Cox) pitched a "Love Boat" episode some time back to a writer/producer team in which one man took down elaborate story notes on the word processor, while the other smoked a cigar and shot out ideas that became discussion points for each of them. So spontaneous and natural was their interplay, after half an hour Kerry remembers getting the uneasy feeling they'd completely forgotten he was in the room. (Interesting note: As a way of showing how much interpersonal give and take a writing team requires, the man at the word processor had a huge fan set up to blow away the fumes from his partner's cigar. Compromise is an important part of collaboration.)

Your agreement should also include a line or two about rewrite rules. One highly successful writing team, particularly prolific in the theater, has an arrangement whereby one person cannot change another's line unless he can come up with something they *both* agree is better. This would seem to be a pretty good rule to use as a model, since its sole function is to make the script better, rather than protect each other's ego. Rewrites are a fact of scriptwriting life, and if your own partner can't tell you something stinks, someone else can and will. Better to hear it from a friend and get it fixed right at the start.

This brings up a very important point about your working methods: Attitude. It must be understood from the start that everything you both say and write is for the good of the project. Any comments you make or changes you suggest to each other are not to be taken as personal attacks, but as honest opinions and recommendations. The moment one member of the team becomes defensive about his or her work, the partnership is on its way downhill. If comments are withheld for fear of hurting the other's feelings or bringing on some sort of argument, then the main reason for having a writing partner in the first place has been destroyed.

The other important point about having a teamwork attitude involves ego suspension. The completed work is "ours." Not "his," not "hers." Ours. This is actually the easy part, because when you write for television or movies the final product usually is so far removed from anything you wrote, you sometimes wonder if either of you had anything to do with it at all!

Finally, it should be noted that either partner is certainly free to do work on their own, as long as it doesn't interfere with work assigned to the team. Most collaborators like to have little side projects of their own. These projects may be a bit less commercial and more artistic, works the writer can truly call his own, whether or not it sells.

• HOW DO I FIND A WRITING PARTNER?

When two people get married they're making a commitment based on what they've learned about each other through a relationship that began casually and gradually increased in intensity. The commitment made by two writing partners is not quite on the same level, but since their careers and futures are being gambled, at least for a short time, on the effectiveness of their relationship, it's certainly important to make the right choice. So, approach it as you would a marriage, and begin with casual dating.

Let's say you have a feature project in mind, a comedy. A writer friend of yours has had some success in the sitcom market, but has been itching to move into features. You feel his comedic flair could be just what the doctor ordered for your script. At that point, you bring up the idea of partnership on a one-time basis: "Hey, how about us working together on this project?" Then, if things work out, you may find that continued collaboration is the way to go.

Finding a collaborator when you have no contacts in the business and no friends who are writers is tougher, but certainly not impossible. Start by joining a writer's club. There are plenty of clubs in just about any city—drama clubs, mystery clubs, local theater groups, etc. Subscribe to the growing number of writer's publications that feature ads for collaborators (see Resource List at the end of this book). In other words, get out there and circulate a little. You'd be surprised at the number of people who are also looking for another writer to team up with, if only to facilitate the painful and frustrating process of getting that first big break.

And remember: it doesn't have to last forever. If the team is not working out, be honest with each other and dissolve the partnership.

On the other hand, many of the writing teams we've interviewed for *The Hollywood Scriptwriter* or come into contact with through pitch meetings, had been together long before they each met their future wife or husband, and long after they each obtained their divorce. It appears that the old Hollywood saying is true: Marriages come and go—but a good writing partner is forever.

VIDA SPEARS AND SARA FINNEY

Vida Spears and Sara Finney are proud of the fact that they are, to their knowledge, the first and only black female writing team in television. Getting their start for a company they began with as secretaries, they were put under a great deal of pressure to prove themselves, and their ensuing credits speak for their ability to meet the test. They have been staff writers on "The Jeffersons," "227," and "The Facts of Life," and have written on a freelance basis for "Mama's Family," "Silver Spoons," "Busting Loose," "What's Happening Now?" and several other sitcoms.

Can you give us an idea of what you were doing individually in terms of writing, before you decided to team up?

S: I was already doing some writing on my own. I had been working at Embassy as a secretary to the producers, after starting as a courier. But I did all those jobs with the intention of eventually breaking into writing.

I began by selling a freelance episode to "The Jeffersons." I'd also written a couple of spec scripts, and was in the process of getting a "solid" agent. I was set for a pitching appointment at "Silver Spoons," and Vida told me she was going to pitch, and I said, "Why don't we do it together?" So, that's when we hooked up. We sold an episode in that session, by the way.

Apparently you knew each other prior to this point.

Right, we had worked together as secretaries. She was on "Silver Spoons," and I was on "The Jeffersons." We'd known each other for a while.

Vida?

V: I was a secretary also. I began at Embassy as a receptionist, and during that time met Sara. To tell the truth, I was thinking about heading in a different direction, and going into management. But I was working for the producers of "Silver Spoons," seeing the scripts every day, and I thought to myself, "I can do this." I've always considered myself a very creative person, and Sara had asked me once before about writing, and at the time I declined. But she asked once again, and I thought, well, why not, why not try it?

So as a team, your very first effort resulted in a sale?

V: Yes.

That's pretty unusual.

Which made us think that maybe we had something going here.

S: We actually had our first writing experience together when we put on a little in-house Embassy show, one of those fun little things where the employees are the stars. It was a variety show, which we put together with two other secretaries, a couple of guys who are now Executive Story Editors at "Webster." They teamed up together right about the same time as Vida and myself.

There's going to be a big run on secretarial jobs at Embassy once this interview is published!

V: Actually, it's very unusual for things to happen the way they did.

Was the collaboration a difficult process for you initially?

S: It was fun at first! Then things started to get more and more serious. No, I don't think it was hard at first. Actually, the longer you're in the business the more you tend to believe strongly in your own ideas, which can make the art of compromise a little more difficult at times.

V: Because at first you're not sure of yourself, you really *need* somebody. You want their opinion more frequently. As time goes by, you're more at ease, more likely to rely on your own judgment.

What about the psychological benefits of partnership? Certainly it must help during that crucial breaking-in period to have the moral support of a partner.

V: During our first staff job, I think that if we didn't have each other we would have gone crazy.

It was a bad experience?

S: It was rough. There was a lot of pressure.

But you feel that working as a team has become more difficult now?

S: No, I don't feel that it's difficult. I just think that we're each more confident in our own judgment. I know what I want, Vida knows what she wants—and we both know what the other wants. In the beginning you don't know any of that. So I wouldn't say it's difficult, it's just a process of growing together and getting to know each other.

I think that most partners think along the same general lines. If they didn't, *then* I think things could become very difficult.

V: You simply have to learn how to compromise. There are times when you don't want to, and the more we work together, the more those occasions arise. But ultimately, if a project is going to get done you have to work things out.

Let's say you have an assignment, and it's time to get to work. What's the process involved?

V: We've changed a little bit, and it's much better now. Sara and I used to do everything together, line by line. Some people we know still do that.

S: First of all, we go over the story together. Say the producer has given us a story, and we've turned in the outline. We'd go over those notes together before going to first draft—every beat of every scene—then we divide it up by scenes.

So Vida would get the first scene, Sara the second, and then what? You swap them?

V: In a manner of speaking. We look them over together, make comments or changes on each other's scenes.

Once the script is finished, is there an additional step involved in which you both do some more editing, or is that pretty much an ongoing process?

S: No one person goes over the script. We go over it together. By the time it's done, we've both been over it so many times . . .

You figure it's done.

V: Right.

What do you see as the advantages of working as a team?

S: You get a chance to bounce ideas off each other, and that can be so important, especially in comedy. Sometimes, what you think is funny is not at all funny to somebody else, and you kind of need to hear that. You *really* need to hear that, as a matter of fact!

V: Sometimes you'd like to take a chance on something, and you may feel it's a little far out. But if you can get someone else's opinion, you can either go ahead with the idea with a bit more confidence, or you can decide the idea won't work and you don't try it at all.

S: Then again, sometimes both of us think something's great and the producers look at it and say, "I don't get this!" [laughter] And you say to yourself, "Well, we took a chance, but at least we went in together."

V: The best thing is to get another person's fresh approach to something. You might be working on a scene, and trying and trying and trying, and you've just run out of creative steam. That's when a partner can offer another way to approach the problem, and sometimes that's all you need.

What do you see as the advantage of having a partner when it comes time for a pitch appointment?

S: Basically, it's the strength of having two people excited over the same idea. If I start to stumble a little over an idea that may originally have been Vida's, then she's right there and can jump in to pump new life into the pitch. That of course works the other way, too. We always pitch together.

V: Working as a team is also very helpful when it comes to the process of coming up with ideas. Before we get together Sara will come up with some ideas, and I'll come up with some ideas. Then we meet, and we have a pretty good number of ideas to sift through.

What special qualities do you feel each of you bring to the team?

S: We're a lot alike, but I think Vida is more logical. I tend to go too far sometimes, and she'll be there to say, "Pull back," and sometimes I need that. But I think back to when we first started, and what was true then is true now: she's a very good story person. She puts things together very well, structures a story so it makes sense. I love dialogue, I just love to talk! But of course you have to have both.

Vida, do you concur?

V: I feel stronger in story and structure. Sara's great at dialogue, and also at coming up with some really unique ideas.

What do you find to be the disadvantages of working with a partner?

V: The only disadvantage or difficulty occurs when you feel very strongly about something.

S: You can't be married to your work.

V: You'll never get anything done if you are.

S: But that's true with any kind of writing, I think. I write plays on my own, and I really value the "reading" process, where I'm given feedback from other people. Some playwrights get very hurt by criticism, feeling their work is their baby—and it is, because a writer's words are sacrosanct in theater—but they have to accept criticism. Television gets you *very* accustomed to criticism! Rewrites and compromise are a way of life.

V: And I think that compromise usually leads to better work. If I come up with something Sara's not pleased with, or she writes something I'm not crazy about, we have to find another way. And sometimes that middle ground, that fresh approach, results in something much better.

Do you have a general rule regarding changes made in each other's work?

S: It's pretty simple, really. We just try to come up with something better. If we don't, fine, that's the way it goes. Usually we do.

Do you find more conflicts now in terms of your writing, as opposed to when you first teamed up?

V: I think our writing gets better and better with each script that we do. We know each other a little bit more each time, and it almost reaches the point where we start thinking alike.

Also, we'll write little notes to each other in the margins of our scenes, asking, "What do you think about this?" Or we'll give each other a couple alternative lines, and ask them which one they think is best.

Now, while you work as a team most of the time, do you still do some writing on an individual basis?

S: My first love is the theater, so I write plays. I think we both need to sit down and write a screenplay, and we've had people express an interest in having us do a screenplay, but I personally love writing plays.

V: I haven't written anything on my own as yet, but it's certainly something I think about and plan on doing.

What's the status of writing teams in the sitcom field? Is there a larger concentration there, as opposed to other types of shows?

S: I don't think drama writers feel that *need* that comedy writers do to bounce ideas and jokes off each other.

What advice do you have for someone who is looking for a writing partner?

V: Take the time to really get to know the person before making any commitment. I've seen teams involved in pitched battles, and . . .

S: Of course, we've seen teams do that and they are still best friends . . .

V: But I would take some time, maybe just try a script or two on a trial basis, see how well it goes. The most important thing is that each member be willing to compromise. If they can't do that, the partnership just won't work.

Do you ever hit times where you feel that one member of the team might be slowing things down, perhaps not pitching in enough?

V: I think it all evens out. There might be a time when I'm having a real hard time, slowing down the process, and there might be times when Sara's having a rough time. It all balances out, and the other person simply pitches in a little more and helps out.

S: Or one of us might go out of town, and the other has to finish the outline. It's no big deal, it's just part of being a team. You have to trust each other.

CHAPTER 15

How to Protect Your Work

IT'S EVERY WRITER'S NIGHTMARE: you work hard on a project that you believe in, you ship it around town to be seen by producers and studios, it's rejected . . . and then, a year or two later, a very similar project appears on the screen. You've been ripped off. Well, maybe you have and maybe you haven't. It does happen, but not nearly as often as new writers think.

• WHY IDEAS ARE DUPLICATED

If you stop to think about the nature of Hollywood, you will see that it is almost inevitable that there will be many duplications of ideas. There are thousands of writers employed in the film and television industry, some of them regularly, some of them sporadically. Their sole product is ideas (and the execution of those ideas in script form). With all of them sitting around trying to come up with the next hot new series or next blockbuster screenplay, all of them aware of the general conventions of the form, it is inevitable that there will be a great deal of overlap.

We have discovered this phenomenon in painful ways. Recently one of us (Wolff) developed, with a partner, an idea for a sitcom: a young widow with a small boy moves to the Midwest and, because of her background as a zoologist, gets a job as an administrator at a city zoo. Not long after he began pitching it, he discovered that CBS had commissioned a pilot called "Zoovet" and that a production company had sold to the Fox Network a series identical to his, but for the fact that the woman's child was a girl. No theft, just coincidence. Wolff also pitched to a major production company an idea for a Movie-of-the-Week. The executive there pitched the idea to her boss, who told her it was a terrific project—so terrific that a week before he had optioned something exactly like it. Again, a coincidence. This has happened at least half a dozen times over the past six or seven years.

The point is not that thievery never happens, but that it is wise to be slow to jump to the conclusion that it has happened to you. You have to know (and be able to prove) that those who came up with the similar idea had access to yours, and began their efforts after you began yours. In any court case regarding alleged plagiarism the timing associated with a project is a crucial piece of evidence and that is where you must make sure you protect yourself.

Registering Your Work

Some writers use the services of the Copyright Office, but we recommend using the Writers Guild Registration Service. In the words of the Guild, "The Guild's Registration Service has been set up to assist members and nonmembers in establishing the completion date and the identity of their literary property written for the fields of theatrical motion pictures, television and radio." Notice that you do not need to be a member of the Guild in order to take advantage of this service.

You can register scripts intended for radio, television and theatrical motion pictures, series formats, step outlines, and storylines.

You cannot register book manuscripts, stage plays, music, lyrics, photos, drawings, or articles of public record (such as the transcripts of an actual courtroom trial). Titles cannot be protected by registration with the Guild (nor, for that matter, by registration with the Copyright Office—more about that a bit later).

The fees as of this writing are $10 for nonmembers, $5 for members. You must submit each property separately (except that three episodes, skits, or sketches for an existing series may be registered as a single entity).

Your submission must be on standard size paper (8½ × 11) and unbound (no brads or staples). The title page should include your full legal name.

You may mail or take the material to the Guild Registration Office at 8955 Beverly Blvd., Los Angeles, CA 90048. If you go in person, make it between 10 A.M. and noon or 2 P.M. and 5 P.M., Monday through Friday. The fee must accompany the material.

The Guild will seal your property in a Guild Registration Envelope, note the time and date it arrived, and will mail you a receipt and a registration number. When you then send out that material to producers or anyone else, you can write on the title page or the page immediately following the title page, "Registered WGA No. ____" (the number will be on your receipt). Your registration will be valid for ten years. If you wish to renew it at the end of the ten years, you can do so for another ten years by paying the registration fee that is in force at the time. Otherwise the material will be destroyed when the registration period runs out.

What Can't Be Protected

You should be aware that there are limits to what can be protected. Basically, titles cannot be protected. However, this doesn't mean that you could film a little video movie in your backyard and release it under the title *Top Gun* or *E.T.—The Sequel.* In both instances you could be sued by the makers of the original films not because they can protect the titles per se, but because they can claim that you are seeking to hoodwink the public into believing that your product has some connection with a product already well established in the public mind. There is one exception to the rule of titles not being protected, and that is that producers have a mechanism for registering titles and more or less a gentlemen's agreement not to use any that have thus been registered. This service isn't available to writers, however. If you have a title in mind and somebody beats you to using it, don't worry too much. There is no title so great that it can't be replaced, and it is the final product that wins over the public, not the title. After all, on their own, titles such as *E.T.* or *Outrageous Fortune* don't have much zing.

Ideas also cannot be protected. If you tell someone you want to do a film about a group of nuns who clean up a crime-ridden neighborhood and then that person goes ahead and writes that story, you'll have a hard time collecting damages. But if you go beyond that to laying out the specifics: the background of the nuns, the criminals they battle, the techniques they use, and so forth, and then someone else steals all of those elements, you will have a case. What the court will consider is not just the idea, but the execution of that idea.

What Else You Can Do

Since everything hinges on proving that you were first with the project and that the people who allegedly stole it from you had access to your project, careful record-keeping is the key to protecting yourself.

Many people feel that a good way to establish a completion date is by mailing a copy of the material to themselves, and then leave the envelope unopened, the idea being that the postmark will serve as evidence of the date of completion. The problem with this method is that it is far too easy to fake. As the more sneaky of us (Cox) points out, all you'd have to do is mail yourself an unsealed envelope at any given point in time, and then seal your manuscript inside at some later date, thus making the postmark date predate the time of completion. This, obviously, is completely fraudulent.

The best method is to register the material before you show it to anyone else. In fact, don't wait to register it even if you're not going to market it extensively for a while. If it does come to a court battle, you won't impress a jury by saying that you finished the script on January 1 and in the meantime you did show it to a few people. The important date, the one they will believe, will be the date on your Writers Guild Registration Receipt.

When you send the material to anyone, whether it be an agent, a producer, a studio, a star, a director, or whomever, send along a dated cover letter and keep a photocopy of it for your files. Some people send such submissions via certified mail, with a return receipt requested, but others feel that this is overkill and may make the recipient think you are paranoid.

When you receive any kind of correspondence regarding the project, save it. It may be tempting to crumple up a rejection letter and throw it out, but don't do it. That letter may be your only proof that the parties in question had access to your material.

If you have any phone conversations regarding the material, make a note of the date, whom you talked to, and the gist of the conversation, and put it into the folder for that project. Better yet, send a follow-up note and keep a photocopy for your files. This can be a simple note: "Dear So and So: Thanks for your call. I'm glad you're going to be able to get my script, "A Great Movie," to Joe Superstar next week, and I look forward to hearing what he thinks of it."

In short, the better you can document when you wrote your material, and who saw it, and when they saw it, the better case you'll have if it turns out you have to take someone to court. However, let common sense rather than paranoia be your guide. Some new writers are so nervous about having their material stolen that they show it to as few people as possible. But if few people see it, the odds are small that it will be seen by someone who will fall in love with it and get it onto the screen. Get your material out there as much as possible, but take the sensible steps we've outlined in this chapter in order to safeguard it.

Release Forms

If ever there was a document guaranteed to raise the hackles of suspicion on any new scriptwriter, it is the release form. Ever mindful of the warnings of friends and the horror stories they've heard about unscrupulous producers, agents, stars, and everyone else in show business, the aspiring scriptwriter sees the release form as an obtusely worded license to steal, a litany of legal mumbo jumbo that leaves the writer completely defenseless. It is not.

The release form is designed to protect the recipient of your script from "nuisance" suits. However, if you, as a writer, feel you were ripped off, you can still sue in spite of having signed a release, and the other party will have to demonstrate in court that they indeed had "an independent legal right to use such material which is not derived from (you)." If you refuse to sign a release form, in most cases your work will simply be returned unopened, unread, and obviously, unsold.

A Sample Release Form

If you're unable to obtain a release form from the company you've targeted for your script, the following is a general form that can be used for just about any submission.

———————————, 19 ——

Title and/or Theme of Material
Submitted Hereunder:

———————————————————

———————————————————

———————————————————

Gentlemen:

I am today submitting to you certain program material, the title and/or theme of which is indicated above (which material is hereinafter referred to as the "program material"), upon the following express understanding and conditions:

    1. I acknowledge that I have requested permission to disclose to you and carry on certain discussions and negotiations with you in connection with such program material.

    2. I agree that I am voluntarily disclosing such program material to you at my request. I understand that you shall have no obligation to me in any respect whatsoever with regard to such material until each of us has executed a written agreement which, by its terms and provisions, will be the only contract between us.

    3. I agree that any discussions we may have with respect to such program material shall not constitute any agreement expressed or implied as to the purchase or use of any of such program material which I am hereby disclosing to you either orally or in writing.

    4. In the event that you have an independent legal right to use such material which is not derived from me, either because such material submitted hereunder is not new or novel, or was not originated by me, or has not been reduced to concrete form, or because other persons including your employees have submitted similar or identical material which you have the right to use, then I agree that you shall not be liable to me for your use of such material and you shall not be obligated in any respect whatsoever to compensate me for such use by you.

Yours very truly,

———————————————————

CHAPTER 16

How to Pitch Your Ideas

FOR MOST WRITERS, BEING GOOD at pitching requires some new skills. For the most part, these are the skills of the salesperson and, to some writers, they are quite foreign. But they are so crucial to success in writing for television or film that the wise writer will take whatever pains are necessary to learn them. The pages that follow are designed to make the learning process relatively easy and painless.

Having worked in instructional design and having read our share of how-to books, we came to realize the problem with most self-help materials is not that they tell too little, but that they tell you too much. Often you put the book down when you are finished with it and are aware that it contains a lot of good information, but you don't have a clear idea of exactly what to do now. All that you read sort of blends together, and because you can't do everything at once, you end up doing nothing.

The latest research into behavior changes reveals that in order to acquire a new set of behaviors, you must be *sufficiently motivated* (and must find ways of renewing that motivation frequently), and you must have a *realistic plan* for implementing the behaviors step by step.

We are assuming that your desire to succeed is strong and that you think about it frequently, so that we need not concern ourselves too much with your motivation. But what we have tried to do is give you a step-by-step breakdown of the process of successful pitching. We have broken it down into three phases: what you do *before* the pitch, what you do *during* the pitch, and what you do *after* the pitch. Each of the steps is small and reasonably easy to learn to do. When you put them all together, you have a powerful technique for presenting your ideas well.

A reminder: as with any new skill, the degree of success you attain will depend on how much you practice and how well you are able to learn from your mistakes. No one expects to be a concert pianist as soon as they've had a couple of lessons on the piano. Pitching becomes easier the more you do it, so the more often you practice the skills you are learning, the more quickly you will succeed.

• BEFORE THE PITCH

Know Your Objectives

Going into a meeting, know exactly what you want to get out of it. If you are going in to pitch an idea for a feature film, it may seem obvious that the objective is to have the person sign you up to develop that idea into a full script. Certainly that may be the overall objective, but you will have several others. These tend to be broader and to apply to your career, not only to this particular project.

Objective 1: To make a good impression on the person to whom you are pitching. You want to give this person the impression that you are the type of individual who would be good to work with, who is sane, who is flexible, who understands the nature of the business, and so on. A number of steps in this chapter relate to how to make a good impression.

Objective 2: To express your idea so clearly that the other person understands it completely. In many cases you'll be pitching to someone who, in turn, will have to pitch it to someone else if it is to get the green light. In order to do that well, the person to whom you pitch has to understand it in the first place. How well you pitch your idea and how well your back-up material supports your pitch will determine how well you achieve this objective.

Objective 3: To express your idea so enthusiastically and dramatically that the other person gets excited about it, too. This is partly a matter of how you structure your pitch, partly a matter of how you deliver it, and of course, partly a matter of how good the idea is to begin with.

Objective 4: To leave the meeting with a clear idea of what the other person is going to do next in regard to your project. Sometimes the next step is for him to pitch it to someone else in the company, or to present it at a staff meeting, or to think it over for another week. Be clear about this. If the idea didn't go over well, without being defensive try to get some reasons why; this will help you in future pitches there or elsewhere.

Objective 5: To have the other person agree to leave the door open for your return. If she didn't like this idea, tell her that you are working on something else and would like to present it to her when it is ready. Usually she will say yes.

Note that you can fail to sell your project and still achieve some of the above objectives. The point of clearly thinking through what you wish to achieve helps you to handle each pitch well not only in relation to the idea you're presenting, but in relation to your whole career. Building a network of contacts and having a number of places where your ideas are welcome are more important, in the longer run, than selling any one idea.

Find Out About the Person You're Pitching To

The more you know about the person you're pitching to, the better equipped you will be to pitch well. Knowing something about the individual's personal life can help in the ice-breaking phase of the pitch meeting. This could include the person's hobbies, family life, education, favorite travel destinations, and so forth. Knowing about their professional background will also give you some clues as to their general outlook and may help you slant your presentation accordingly.

Where do you get this type of information? Well, if an agent has set up the meeting, he or she may know some of these things. If that agent doesn't, maybe somebody else at the agency does. Alternatively, other writers you know may have pitched to that person before and will be able to give you some pointers. You should also start a reference file made up of articles from *Daily Variety, The Hollywood Reporter, The Hollywood Scriptwriter,* the *Calendar* section of the *L.A. Times,* and other industry publications. For example, if your area is television, keep clippings regarding story editors, producers, and network people. You don't need to bother with the tiny filler articles; what we're talking about here are the frequent longer profiles these publications run.

If you can't get this type of information before your pitching appointment, play it by ear and use the tips offered in the section called "Break the Ice." Just remember that even though the focus of the meeting is you and your ideas, shifting a little attention to the other person will always help you make a good impression.

Prepare the Pitch (Part 1: Sitcoms)

When pitching for existing television shows, you are dealing with central characters who are already well established and settings that generally are the same from week to week; this cuts down on the amount of time it takes you to tell the story. The producer or story editor expects to hear you briefly present from three to eight story lines. For a half-hour story, the pitch might take from two to six minutes. Initially, the listener is interested in the basic story—the beginning, middle, and end. He doesn't want to hear all the nuances, or all the funny lines, or all the details.

Producers and story editors vary in terms of how they like to have things pitched. Some like extremely short pitches to begin with. Let's take an example from a script one of us (Wolff) wrote for "The Ted Knight Show."

"Henry's writing a tribute to a leading citizen who apparently died of a heart attack at the wheel of his car. Henry finds some discrepancies that suggest maybe it was murder. He turns detective and eventually uncovers the fact that this family man actually died in the arms of his secretary, at her apartment. He and Mrs. Stinson have the dilemma of whether or not to print the story of one indiscretion that will overshadow all the good this man did in his lifetime."

If the producer is intrigued by this story he will ask you to pitch it in more detail if you are prepared to. That pitch might go like this:

"We open in the newspaper office, with Henry and Monroe working. Mrs. Stinson comes in, looking very glum. Monroe notices and asks jokingly, "Who died?" Well, unfortunately, someone really did die . . . Herbert J. Maxwell. He was an old friend of hers, and also the leading man in the community—this is a guy who was active in charities, he held public office and did wonderful things for people, just a perfect, well-loved family man. Mrs. Stinson asks Henry to do some research and to come up with a front page tribute to Maxwell.

"In the next scene we're at home. Henry has gotten a huge pile of stuff on Maxwell and is telling Muriel about what a saint this guy was.

He's been to talk to Maxwell's secretary, who'd been helping him with his memoirs. She told him that poor Maxwell left the office around seven, looking tired but otherwise OK. A while later, somebody called the cops and reported that Maxwell was slumped over the steering wheel of his car, the victim of a heart attack. But then Monroe comes in, and he's got the coroner's report, and it says that the approximate time of death was six o'clock—an hour before the secretary said he left the office. Suddenly there's a mystery. Henry decides they should investigate. Monroe says, 'Great, we'll be like Simon and Simon.' 'More like Simon and Simple Simon,' Henry says. But he says that their next step will be to talk to the man who phoned in the report about Maxwell's body.

"The third scene is at the *Bugler* office, with Henry and Monroe interviewing this man, who's sort of a Percy Kilbride type who keeps getting off track. But the important thing is he heard a car door slam just before he went outside and found the body. When he went outside, nobody else was there. At the end of Act I, Henry is convinced they have a murder on their hands.

"When we come back, we're at home, and Muriel is telling Henry that he's been watching too many murder mysteries on TV. But Henry thinks maybe there's something in Maxwell's memoirs that somebody wanted hidden and that he was murdered in a way that looks like a heart attack. He decides to go talk to Maxwell's secretary to see if she knows of any enemies he might have had. Monroe begs to go along, but Henry forbids it.

"The next scene is outside the secretary's apartment, and of course Monroe is waiting there for Henry. Henry is pissed off, but when she opens the door there is not too much he can do, and both of them go in. Henry's asking her some questions and she's getting very nervous. Monroe uses the bathroom and when he comes out he tells Henry that there's a bunch of men's toiletries in there, and when he peeked into her bedroom he saw a picture of Maxwell on the dresser. Henry puts two and two together and the secretary admits that Maxwell died at her place—in her arms. She carried the body out and put it in his car so there wouldn't be a scandal.

"The final scene is at the *Bugler* office. Henry has given Mrs. Stinson the file on Maxwell and she's shocked. She realizes that although they have a duty to report the facts, if they report the circumstances of Maxwell's death, it'll overshadow all the good things he'd done.

Henry gives her the draft story he's written—it doesn't refer to the nature of Maxwell's death, because Ted also felt that one indiscretion shouldn't ruin a dead man's reputation."

This is a pretty detailed pitch, necessarily so because the story is a mystery and you have to understand the major beats. Even so, it doesn't take long to tell. It may sound a bit heavier than most sitcoms, but in this case the producers were interested in having stories with more depth and with some serious moments. Also, Wolff had written for them before, so they knew he was capable of finding humor in a basically serious subject. But if you pitch a story that sounds somewhat serious, be prepared to talk about where the comedy will come in.

Prepare the Pitch (Part 2: One-Hour Shows)

Pitching for one-hour shows is very similar to pitching for sitcoms, the primary difference being simply that it will take a little longer, and that you tell the story without worrying about act breaks. Your format should follow that of the show. For instance, if the series in question opens with a murder every week, you'll describe that and then go into how the central character gets involved. You'll want to get across the primary plot points—the twists and the turns of the plot that move it along toward its resolution. Be sure that you have put the plot points in order of escalating importance, so that each one is more exciting than the one before it. Keep it simple, and don't leave out important points—there's nothing more destructive to a pitch than to have to say, "Oh, yeah, I should have mentioned that all this takes place in a cave and that the bad guy is wanted by the police." If the show has a major action sequence every week (for example, a chase) be sure to point out where this comes in, and try to describe it in a way that makes it sound at least a little different from the 500 other chases they've done.

Prepare the Pitch (Part 3: Movies)

A pitch for a movie or Movie-of-the-Week will naturally take longer to tell in detail than the pitch for a sitcom or a one-hour show. Most feature films last from an hour and a half to two hours, and most MOWs last 94 minutes (two hours minus time for commercials). Furthermore, you are introducing the listener to a whole new group of characters, not using the familiar characters in a TV series. The person to whom you are presenting your idea may still ask you to begin with a very brief pitch, and then follow up with a longer pitch if the basic idea intrigues him.

In your script, the first act takes about 30 minutes, the second act takes about an hour, and the third act takes about 30 minutes. (Here we are referring to dramatic acts, corresponding to beginning, middle, and end.) But in a pitch you'll spend almost as much time discussing the first act as the second, because at the beginning you have to set the mood, describe the characters, and give enough details to get the listener picturing the people and action in his or her mind.

It's a good idea to start by telling the listener the type of story he's about to hear: comedy, drama, sci-fi, etc. One thing we've discovered is that it's very useful to preface the story with some type of "teaser" opening that sets the scene and arouses the listener's interest. Some time ago Wolff was pitching a Movie-of-the-Week called "Mrs. President." It's about Woodrow Wilson's second wife, who took over running the country while the President was gravely ill. The first few times it was pitched, the opening was something like, "This story opens in the White House in 1915. Woodrow Wilson is in office, and his wife has just died . . ." Around this time people's eyes would glaze over and sometimes they would stifle a yawn. The story had some wonderful dramatic elements, but the problem was getting people not to turn off before those elements came along.

A much better opening was, "These days, people are talking about the notion of having a woman President, and the question is no longer whether, but when. Well, we've already had a de facto woman President. This woman made appointments to the Cabinet. When the Queen of England visited the United States, this woman caused an international scandal by refusing to curtsy because she felt she was of equal stature. She took on Congress for several months—and won. She was Woodrow Wilson's second wife, and this is her story." Invariably this opening created enough interest that the listeners didn't mind going back to 1915.

Be creative in coming up with this type of opening for your pitch. If your story has an interesting "What if?" hook, use that. For example, "What if a young man who'd given up hope of ever finding the right woman finally finds her—but she turns out to be a mermaid?" = Splash. If your story is more of a character study, give some information about what attracted you to write about this type of person.

To the greatest degree possible, simplify the story. If your listener gets lost somewhere in the middle, the second half of the pitch is wasted. Pare the story down until it's easy to follow. For example, see the movie outline following the section called "Prepare your back-up material." A verbal version of this outline is what you'd use for a pitch of a movie or MOW.

Prepare Your Notes

There is no stigma attached to using notes during your pitch. Most writers feel more comfortable if they have notes handy, even if only to fall back upon. Naturally, the complexity of the idea and the number of times you've pitched it previously will have an effect on the degree to which you actually need to use the notes. But the main point here is not to think that you are being unprofessional if you use notes.

The form that your notes take is up to you. It could be a simple indented outline (sample 1); a set of index cards (sample 2); or a graphic diagram because it gives you an overview of the entire story on one page—it's easy to jump quickly to any part of the story, and it eliminates the danger of dropping and mixing up a set of index cards. The one thing to avoid is just reading a prose outline (if you've ever had a professor who came in every day and just read his lecture to you, you'll know how deadly this is).

SAMPLE 1: INDENTED OUTLINE
"Ted Knight Show" — Believing is Seeing
ACT I.
   I. Scene one—Eye doctor's office—Day
      A. Mrs. Stinson is having eyes checked
      B. Dr. tells her she has cataracts
         1. Explains how easy it is to fix
           a. in-office procedure
           b. almost always successful
      C. Mrs. S. expresses concern
         1. "Almost" always isn't good enough
      D. Dr. convinces her to make appointment for the operation
         1. She still seems worried

SAMPLE 2: INDEX CARD OUTLINE
Knight: "Believing is Seeing"
ACT I—Scene one
   Eye Dr.'s office — Day
   Mrs. Stinson having eye exam

Dr. tells her she has cataracts
　—says, Easy to fix; in office procedure; almost always
　successful.

I/1/card 2

Mrs. S. alarmed
　"almost always" successful not good enough
Doc convinces her to make appointment for operation
　She's still worried.

SAMPLE 3: GRAPHIC OUTLINE

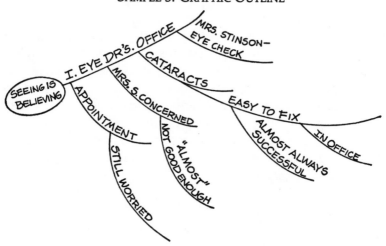

Anticipate Questions and Objections

Be as objective as you can about your idea in order to formulate a list of possible questions and objections that might come up during the pitch. Naturally you can't tell everything you know about your story and your characters in a brief pitch, but you should know a lot about the background of your characters, the details of plot sequences, settings, and so forth. The more readily you can come up with this type of information in response to questions, the more impressed the person to whom you are pitching will be. Sometimes he will come up with really off-the-wall questions, in which case you can be honest and say you really hadn't thought about that particular point.

The types of objections that come up frequently are: "It's too similar to what's been done already." "It's too different from anything that's ever been done." "I don't think it would attract a star." "It sounds too expensive." "It doesn't sound big enough for a feature film." "I don't quite see where the humor comes in." "It's too down-beat." "It doesn't sound like the main character is very likable," and so on. Play devil's advocate with your idea and see how many objections you can come up with—and then see whether you can come up with an appropriate response. For example, if your idea involves a conflict on another planet and you get the objection that it sounds too expensive, you can say that the type of terrain you had in mind is sand dunes like the ones in Baja California. Naturally, not all objections can be easily defused. If your film absolutely has to be shot in ten cities around the world and you are pitching to someone who wants to do a film for under a million dollars, then maybe you're pitching this idea to the wrong person. But in many cases a bit of thinking about possible objections suggests alternate ways of pitching the idea—ways that will co-opt the objections.

In addition to coming up with your own objections, try pitching the idea to friends and colleagues and see what kinds of negative comments they come up with. Don't be defensive or argumentative at this point—your goal is not to change their minds, only to detect the types of objections you may encounter later on in a professional pitching session.

Write the Appropriate Back-Up Material

What should you leave behind after a pitch? It depends on what you're pitching and the preference of the person to whom you're pitching. Here are some guidelines:

Sitcoms. After they have read a sample of your work, the producers or story editors will call you in to pitch four to eight stories for their series. Sometimes you're pitching to someone who can't give you a definite yes because he, in turn, has to pitch your ideas to his boss or to the network. Under Writers Guild regulations, they're not allowed to ask you to write anything up without paying you, but if you volunteer to leave behind a three to five line summary of each story, some of them will appreciate it. (See Sample 1.) The alternative is for them to depend on their own (often hurried) notes, taken as they listen to your pitch. If you have good summaries to leave behind, tell them so at the beginning, so that they have the option of not taking notes.

One Hour Dramas. The same as sitcoms, but your summaries will probably need to be a bit longer. (See Sample 2.)

TV Movies. Prepare an outline or treatment written in the present tense ("George walks across the room. He listens to the door," etc.). This can be anything from a one-page overview to a ten-page outline to a thirty-page treatment. We favor an outline that is ten to fifteen pages in length. Make sure that the tone of the outline matches the tone of the script you intend to write—if it's a comedy script, the outline should be funny. You can use some sample dialogue to give an indication of how your people talk, but of course there's not enough room in an outline for extensive exchanges. It's helpful but not mandatory to break the story down into seven acts at this point. Chapter 7 includes an outline of a Movie-of-the-Week.

Feature Films. Same as television movies, except that the seven-act structure does not apply. Chapter 5 includes a treatment of a feature film.

Series Proposals. Include a one-page overview of the series, a paragraph of character description for each major character, and four to ten sample storylines (each one taking perhaps five to six lines to tell). Optional but helpful is an outline for one episode, broken down into acts. Chapter 13 includes a series proposal.

If you already have credits or experiences that relate in some way to what you are pitching, it's also a good idea to leave behind a resume.

Whatever you leave behind, be sure it has your name and phone number on it, preferably on the first page. You may also want to include your agent's name and phone number.

• SAMPLE 1: SITCOM SUMMARY

"Too Close for Comfort"
When Jackie and her fiancé Brad have an argument about whether or not she should work after they're married, it sparks Henry's, Muriel's, and Iris's memories of a similar argument that split Henry and Muriel when they were engaged (theirs was about whether or not she should go on the road with her musical act). In flashback sequences we see each one's version of how he or she saved the day. In the end, Jackie realizes that she must solve her own problem, and when Brad refuses to consider her viewpoint she breaks up with him.

• SAMPLE 2: ONE-HOUR DRAMA SUMMARY

"Magnum, P.I."

Magnum gets a frantic call from a man saying that he's been receiving death threats and needs help. Magnum agrees to see him, but when he gets to the man's house, the man has been murdered by a car bomb. Magnum's investigation leads to the revelation that the man had been involved with the Mafia and had cheated them out of money, that he's been cheating on his wife (who had in public threatened to kill him), and that he'd embezzled money from a group of investors, any one of which would have a motive for the murder. Magnum discovers that the man had taken out a large life insurance policy payable to his brother. After talking to the brother, Magnum figures out that the brother is actually the supposed murder victim. In order to get away from all the people after him, the man had killed his brother and made it look like *he* was the one who had died. When Magnum exposes him, the man makes a run for it—and ends up driving off a cliff to his death.

Practice Your Pitch

The best practice session is the one that most closely approximates the conditions of the event you are practicing. In the case of pitching, this means that in your practice session you will pitch to another person, that the other person will give you feedback and raise questions or objections, that you will have a limited period of time to do your pitch, that you don't get to start over if you feel you goofed up, and so forth. Thus, the final practice session should be done with a friend or colleague, preferably someone for whom you can also provide the same service, and therefore someone who understands the nature and purpose of pitching.

Other types of practice sessions can lead up to this. To start with, just become comfortable pitching the idea by yourself, using your notes. Then do it again in front of the mirror, and watch your body language. Then record yourself on an audiotape and analyze your tone of voice, fluency, loudness of voice, etc. If you have a videotape recorder and camera, set it in a fixed position that takes in your entire body, and record yourself doing the pitch. Watch it as objectively as possible and see what type of impression you make. Then go over it again and pinpoint specific changes you can make in order to improve both the content and style of your pitch. Then you'll be ready for the practice pitch to a colleague.

Hardly anyone practices his pitch too often. However, the one thing to guard against is becoming stale—doing the pitch so often that you are merely reciting it by rote. If that begins to happen, vary your wording to make the pitch seem fresh again.

Dress Appropriately

The motion picture industry is more casual in many ways than almost any other large business. Top writers and producers often favor blue jeans over dress slacks, and old tennis shoes over wing tips. Since the writer is sometimes considered an eccentric type anyway, creativity in his or her wardrobe is not necessarily penalized. Having said that, we still advise people to dress up a bit when they go on a pitch. We think it's better for people to remember your idea than the funny hat you wore.

For men we suggest a sports shirt, sports jacket, and slacks with loafers. If you go too far in the direction of dressiness, e.g., a three-piece suit, you'll stick out just as much as if you show up in shorts and a t-shirt. For women, we suggest a skirt and blouse, a simple dress, or a blouse and slacks. Again, dressing as though you are heading for the opera is going to be just as distracting as dressing too casually.

If you don't know the people with whom you'll be meeting, the above guidelines are safe. If you do know them, take into account the way that they dress. One of the key factors of our decision as to whether or not we like someone we are meeting for the first time is how similar to ourselves we perceive him to be. So if we always go into the office wearing blue jeans with holes and wouldn't be caught dead in a tie, someone in an expensive suit is going to make us think he's not our type of folks (obviously the reverse would be true if we were dressy types). Some studios and production companies have reputations for being more dressy or less dressy than the norm. The networks are somewhat formal. Universal Studios is considered dressy, although that's not necessarily true of all the companies on the lot. If in doubt, ask your agent or friends, or even call up the secretary or receptionist and throw yourself on her mercy. Just explain that you're coming in to pitch something and are trying to decide what to wear, and ask how dressy the folks you're meeting with tend to be. If you are confident that you are dressed appropriately, that's one less thing to worry about during your pitch.

Relax

If at all possible, set aside 10 or 15 minutes prior to leaving for the pitch to sit down and relax. Sit in a comfortable chair, put your feet flat on the floor, and have your arms loosely at your sides or rest your hands in your lap. Take three or four deep, slow breaths. As you exhale each one, say to yourself, "relax." Then, without interruptions and without any sense of rushing, follow these steps:

Remind yourself of your objectives for this meeting.

Visualize yourself in the meeting, being relaxed, articulate, charming, and persuasive. Picture it as a pleasant experience in which there is an easy flow of communication between you and the person to whom you are pitching. Visualize her asking some of the questions that you have anticipated, and see yourself answering them. Visualize a phone call or a visitor interrupting the meeting, and then see yourself quickly getting the meeting back on track. See yourself responding enthusiastically to a favorable reaction and see yourself responding in a calm, friendly, and constructive manner to a rejection. In the latter case, see yourself exploring what follow-up opportunities may be present even in face of a rejection.

Remind yourself of your own abilities as a writer and of the good qualities of the material you are about to present. When you have created a sense of confidence, tell yourself that this sense of confidence will come back into your mind as soon as you shake the hand of the person to whom you are pitching. (All of the foregoing steps can be intensified if you are able to use them while under self-hypnosis.)

Get There Early

If you get to your appointment on time, there's at least a fifty-fifty chance you'll be kept waiting. That's fine. It gives you a chance to relax after your drive and to chat with the secretary or receptionist (we'll discuss the importance of this in a moment). But if you get there late you will definitely irritate the person you are to meet, and you may throw his or her schedule off. This double standard is part of the philosophy that the customer is always right. In this case, the person you are meeting with is the customer.

Murphy's Law (that everything that can go wrong, will) applies as much to scheduling your appointments as to anything else. Among the things that have delayed us are getting into traffic jams, getting lost on the freeway, finding out the studio parking lot was full and we'd have to park a mile away, finding out that the promised drive-on pass had not been arranged, getting lost on foot on the studio lot, finding that the elevator didn't work or was being used to haul freight, and patiently waiting in an empty office for the secretary to return and then realizing we were supposed to be next door. Now we try to leave an extra 10 or 15 minutes to spare for the next catastrophe. If you are more than 15 minutes early, you may prefer to sit in your car or in the cafeteria rather than making the secretary nervous. Being 5 or 10 minutes early is about right.

Chat With the Receptionist or Secretary

This person is the gatekeeper, the one who decides whether or not your call is important enough to go right through. Often he is a trusted associate of the boss, someone whose judgment is valued. If they discuss you, obviously it will help if the receptionist or secretary has a good impression of you. Usually he will tell you his name, or it will be on a nameplate on the desk. If not, ask. If you have a bad memory for names, jot it down as soon as you can.

What to talk about? The usual small talk is OK—the weather, the news, the nice plants in the office, the traffic, whatever. Even better is something more personal, and for that take your cue from what kinds of personal items (photos, pictures, posters, etc.) you see on the desk or the bulletin board or the walls. If there is a bumper sticker reading "I'd rather be skiing" plastered on the bulletin board, you have a good conversation opener. Do more listening than talking. This will be a novelty for most receptionists and secretaries.

Obviously you have to take into account the degree to which this person is busy. If the phones are ringing off the hook, that's not the time to get into a discussion of the finer points of the newest ski boots.

When you leave the pitch meeting, make a point of saying good-bye not only to the person you met with, but also the secretary or receptionist, and use his or her name.

• DURING THE PITCH

Choose Your Seat Carefully

This may seem trivial, but where you sit when you pitch is actually important. Frequently you are offered your choice of a couch or a chair. The chair usually is the better choice. Couches in producers' offices often are soft and bottomless, so that you feel like you're going down in marshmallow quicksand.

Position the chair so that you directly face the person to whom you are pitching. If you're pitching to a group, be sure that your position isn't excluding any of them. If you're pitching to someone who's sitting behind a large desk, pull the chair close to the desk. The more physical distance between you, the more emotional distance between you as well.

Pitch With Enthusiasm!

The single most important ingredient of the style of your pitch is enthusiasm. The people to whom you present ideas hear lots of pitches—sometimes dozens per day. If you don't sound excited about your own story, how can you expect them to be excited about it? Enthusiasm is infectious, just as the cliché says. Furthermore, your enthusiasm for your material inspires confidence in you. The listener feels you are genuinely interested in this story, you'd love to write it and see it produced. In other words, you're not just a hack who's tossing out ideas in hopes someone will find them commercial. Producers usually sneer at the notion that films are art (typically they feel, pretty accurately, that films are craft blended with commerce), but they do like to feel that they are dealing with a writer who is committed to what he or she writes.

Enthusiasm doesn't take the same form for everyone. Some people jump up and down and are manic. Others stay very calm but have a quiet intensity. Start with your normal personality and adjust it as needed. If you normally get hysterical, tone it down a bit to avoid frightening people (they don't mind hiring someone who's mildly eccentric, but they don't want someone who is likely to be institutionalized halfway through the project). On the other hand, if you normally speak in a whispery voice and avoid agitation at all costs, liven up a bit. In other words, adjust your basic personality somewhat, but don't go overboard. If you try to be something you are not, you'll feel uncomfortable and it will show.

Use Your Voice Effectively

Your voice is an important part of your presentation. First, it must be loud enough to be heard. If this is a problem for you, rehearse speaking more loudly, and in interviews pull your chair up close to the desk.

The deadliest pitch is one that's recited in a monotone; there's something restful and sleep-inducing about a voice that never varies. When practicing your pitch, pretend you are telling a story to a child. This is not an unkind implication about the IQ of producers, it's just that when we tell stories to kids we let ourselves get caught up in them. When we get to an exciting part we speed up and change our inflection upward, when we get to a scary part we slow down a little and use a lower voice. We also pay attention to how the child is reacting and do whatever's necessary to keep his or her attention. Naturally in a pitch you have to do this subtly, otherwise the listener will think you consider him or her an imbecile.

It's difficult to assess your own pitch while you are in the middle of it. The best way to get an evaluation is to use a tape recorder during rehearsals. Put the tape aside for a while and then listen to it as though it were someone else talking. What would you think of this person's enthusiasm level, clarity, speed of speech, and inflection? When you know what needs to be improved, do the pitch over and over again until it's as close to perfect as you can get. However, don't let it become mechanical. Change the wording a bit each time so it stays fresh and somewhat spontaneous.

Use Body Language Effectively

You may already be aware of the nature of your spoken language, but it's not likely you're as aware of your body language. Body language is the term some social scientists use for the nonverbal communication transmitted by the way we hold our arms and legs, whether or not we nod our heads, and so forth. Study after study shows that body language does make an important contribution to the impression people have of us. Probably at one time or another you've met someone to whom you took an instant dislike, yet you couldn't put your finger on why. It's likely that what turned you off was the other person's body language. Insincere people give themselves away when their mouths say one thing and their bodies say another, like the person who says, "Yes, I'm open to hearing your opinion," at the same time he crosses his arms and legs. We perceive this contradiction subconsciously even if we aren't consciously aware of it. Therefore, you want to make sure your body language fits what you are saying. The message you want to get across is, "This is a great idea about which I'm very enthusiastic." Here are five elements of body language that will support this message.

1. *Leaning forward.* We associate leaning back with lack of interest. If a friend says, "I'm going to tell you something very interesting, but you have to swear to keep it a secret," most likely at that point you lean forward. You know that something juicy is coming up and you don't want to miss a word. Similarly, when you lean forward a little when you pitch, the listener will subconsciously feel you are engaging his attention more strongly than if you lean back.

2. *Maintaining eye contact.* When people don't look us in the eye, we tend to think they're shifty or, at best, very shy. When they do look us in the eye they come off as straightforward and interested in us. Naturally this can be overdone; an unremitting stare makes the other person begin to wonder whether there's a piece of spinach jammed between his front teeth and eventually provokes hostility.

3. *Using animated facial expressions.* Just as a monotone suggests a lack of enthusiasm, so does a face with a blank expression. You should use both your voice and your expressions to back up the content of the pitch. If you're getting to a particularly suspenseful part of the story, or a shocking moment, let your face slightly reflect these emotions. This leads the listeners and makes them aware of how they should be reacting. Usually it gets a response from them. If you smile when you get to a funny part of your story, for example, it's almost an automatic response for the listener to smile a little, too, which is exactly what you want.

4. *Using hand gestures.* Using appropriate hand gestures makes for a more animated and interesting pitch. If this is difficult for you, watch some of your more animated friends and see how they use gestures to punctuate what they say. Watch TV with the sound off and see how good actors use body language so that you can tell what they're feeling even when you can't hear what they're saying. Then try it yourself until you feel natural doing it—and again, don't go overboard. Stay with what is basically comfortable for you.

5. *Keeping an open posture.* Crossed arms and legs make a person seem defensive. Sometimes writers keep an open posture while they're pitching, and then cross their arms and legs when hearing the reactions of the listener. The nonverbal message is, "Let's see you criticize that, you S.O.B.!" Be comfortable, but stay alert and receptive. Look as interested in the other people's reactions as you wanted them to look while you were pitching.

Respond to the Other Person's Body Language

Not only do you send body language messages, you also receive them. Normally producers won't interrupt your pitch to tell you what they think of your pitch as it's going on, but you can get clues to their reactions by paying attention to their body language as they listen. At first it's difficult to do this at the same time that you're trying to make your pitch as dynamic as possible, but once you know the pitch well you'll have enough concentration to do both.

Here are some clues to watch for and use to alter the pitch as you go along:

If the listener is yawning, checking his watch, or looking yearningly at the phone, you're losing your audience. If you see signs of boredom, move quickly to recapture the lost attention. Speed things up, change your tone of voice, change your body position—anything that will refocus the person's attention on what you're saying.

You may also see signs of confusion on the other person's face—a wrinkled brow, a puzzled frown, a raised eyebrow. Some people barrel ahead as quickly as possible to get past the point of confusion, but a major unresolved question may distract the listener for the rest of your pitch. It's better to allow a natural pause so the listener can ask a question. Or, if you have an idea of what was confusing, clarify it right then before you go on.

Deal Effectively with Interruptions

The ideal pitch sessions are ones in which the listeners give you their complete attention. However, sometimes there are interruptions: a call from the network or a star or a spouse, or a secretary breaking in with something that needs to be signed right away. Some producers (bless them) give their secretaries a "no interruptions" instruction at the beginning of the meeting, but don't count on it.

If there is an interruption, take it gracefully. Use the moment to evaluate for yourself how the pitch is going and what you can do to make it go even better. When you start again, don't pick up the story exactly where you left off. Do a brief recap of what was going on when you were interrupted. For example, "As I was saying, Parker finds out that his wife has had an affair with his best friend, and he hires a private eye to get the evidence to prove it. Now . . ." Usually a sentence or two to recap is enough to get your listener's mind off the phone call (or whatever) and back on your story.

Be Flexible

How you respond to the other person's reactions to your pitch is very important. People like to work with writers who are flexible and open to suggestions. If a producer has heard your pitch and immediately starts making suggestions or exploring ways it might be improved, you should be happy. It shows that he or she likes the pitch enough to devote some thought to it. People like to feel they can make a contribution to an idea, and when they add their own little touches they are psychologically buying into it. They're beginning to see it not as "your project" but "our project," which increases the odds that they'll go to bat for it with their boss or the network.

Problems arise when their contributions screw up the basic idea. Probably you've heard horror stories about a writer who goes in with a romantic comedy set in Tahiti and, by the time everyone has had their say, it has turned into a science fiction thriller set on Mars. There are two viewpoints on the issue of people who demand stupid changes. One is, "Never give in." The other is, "Never give in . . . unless the offer gets into six figures." The fact is that once you've sold your story or script, the buyers can do anything they want with it (it's only in playwriting that the writer's words are sacrosanct). But to what degree should you be open to suggested changes at the pitching stage, when no money has changed hands and no commitment has been made?

The first criterion is whether or not the suggested change makes the story better. Be open-minded enough to realize that producers and others who make their living dealing with scripts often do have good ideas. So if the change improves your project, embrace it.

Some ideas neither improve the project or harm it, they just make it different. Writer-producer Stirling Silliphant says that in a pilot he did for an eventual series he cast a British woman as a secretary. One of the people in power decided that the American viewing public doesn't like foreign actors and demanded that the Briton be replaced with an American. This rather irrational view peeved Silliphant, but he realized that it didn't make the project any worse and wasn't worth fighting about if it put the whole deal at risk. In situations like this, it's usually best to give in.

The final case is dealing with a suggestion that does damage to your idea. First, find out why the other person feels the change is needed. His solution may be lousy, but if the problem really exists then you may be able to come up with a better way of solving it. But if the only problem is that the person you are dealing with is a moron, stick to your guns. Don't be offensive about it and take time to explain why you feel your way works better or why you should both continue to look for alternatives, but be firm. After all, usually at this point you're dealing with someone who can't give you a definite go-ahead with your project anyway. If you incorporate his bad idea now, the project can still be rejected up the ladder—and maybe precisely because of his changes. Of course by rejecting his idea you take the risk that he won't present the project to his bosses, but that's better than seeing your project trashed.

• AFTER THE PITCH

Evaluate the Pitch

Within twenty-four hours of the pitch, sit down and evaluate how it went. Replay it in your mind and see what went right and what could have gone better. Take the time to pat yourself on the back for the things you did well and thereby reinforce them. Don't get down on yourself for the things that went wrong, but do consider how you can handle them differently the next time. In your imagination, replay the pitch, this time seeing yourself handling everything exactly the way you wish you had. If you feel that you learned any important lessons from the experience of this pitch, jot them down.

If you're dealing with a pitch that you'll be repeating elsewhere, consider how you might want to change the content. If you went on too long, take a look at exactly where and how you need to cut the presentation, and then rewrite your notes to reflect these changes. If the person you pitched to had a valid objection to some aspect of the story, think about how you might change it so that the same objection won't apply next time. Above all, if the pitch didn't go as well as you would have liked, realize that by learning from it you can make it a growth experience rather than a failure.

Send a Follow-up Note

Regardless of the outcome of the pitch, you should follow it up with a note thanking the person for taking the time to see you, telling them how much you enjoyed meeting with them, and restating the outcome of the meeting. For example, the outcome might be that they will pitch the idea to their superiors within the next week, that they will think about your idea some more and get back to you soon, or that although they did not think your idea was right for them, you are invited to return when you have completed work on another idea.

Sending this type of note will help the recipient to remember who you are, will demonstrate that you have unusually good manners, and will help document what actually happened during the meeting. For this latter purpose, you should also make a copy of your letter and file it. A sample follow-up letter follows.

Sample Follow-up Letter

19 October 19_____

Gary Prober
Vice President of Development
The Acme Company
1233 N. Western Ave.
Hollywood, CA 90028

Dear Gary,

It was a pleasure meeting you last week, and I appreciate the time you took to hear my ideas for "The Colonel and Me," and "What the Heck!" Naturally I was disappointed to hear that Acme is already developing a series along the lines of "Colonel," but quite happy to find that you may be interested in developing "What the Heck!"

As I understand it, your next step will be to discuss this project with the President of Acme, and I look forward to hearing his reactions.

By the way, I especially appreciate the way that you and Carol made me feel at ease—this was one of my first pitches and you really made it a pleasure!

Cordially,

Tina Brandt

A Note to Out-of-Towners

"All this advice about pitching is just great, but I live out here in Vacuum, Wyoming! Can't my agent pitch my projects for me?" The answer to that, in most cases, is no.

There are exceptions, however. If you are a feature writer, and your agent is trying to either sell your script or get you an appointment to pitch your script, she might shoot a thumbnail sketch of the project past the producer just to ascertain interest. It might go even further than that, and the agent may pitch the whole script for you, saving you the time, trouble, and in many cases, the airfare. In fact, established feature writers are scattered all over the country and don't find it necessary to spend a lot of time in Hollywood. For example, Jim Cash (*Top Gun, Secret of My Success*) never leaves his Michigan home at all! He collaborates via computer with a writer on the Universal lot and thereby avoids pitch meetings entirely.

If you're planning on breaking into episodic writing, though, get your Frequent Flyer card ready, because you're going to have to pitch in person. There are, by the way, a number of writers who don't live in L.A., yet make their living in episodics. They simply have their agent schedule all their appointments at once, and occasionally stay in town for a couple of days or so.

Interviews

Now we'd like to turn you over to two gentlemen who know a great deal about pitching. David Madden's interview concerns pitching features, while Larry Forrester's focuses on pitching for TV. What they have to say about the subject is very relevant because they are two of the people who determine whether your work is bought and produced.

DAVID MADDEN

David Madden started as a writer, both of screenplays and a musical play that was produced at the Kennedy Center. He worked as a story analyst at MGM and then at 20th Century Fox, then (at the time of this interview) served as Vice President of Production at Fox. Currently he is a Vice President of Production at Paramount.

You've read hundreds of scripts and heard hundreds of pitches. Most of them are rejected. What are the weaknesses you see most often?

It's actually unique to find something that has strengths. There are a lot of scripts that have no strengths at all. The things we look for, not necessarily in any order, are:

Characters that feel like real people—that are not just pawns moving through a plot, but rather have some dimension to them. They should be people that we care about, that get some emotional response from us.

Dialogue that isn't full of clichés. It should have some spontaneity and wit, but still sound natural.

A plot that has something in it that hasn't been seen before. It doesn't have to be the most unique thing in the world, however. For example, *Alien* wasn't a tremendously original plot. In a sense it was grafting *Jaws* to *Close Encounters* or *Star Wars*, but it had a twist to it that makes it work. Especially if you're an unknown writer you have to present something new.

It should be a story that isn't being seen on television. So many times we get things that are just so small-scale, so much like TV movies, that we reject them on that basis—unless they are extraordinarily well written.

It should have visual elements that make it appropriate for the big screen.

And, generally speaking, I look for a sense of professional craftsmanship—a sense of structure, of tying the threads together, of telling the story engagingly.

If you receive a script you can't use, but that reveals a strong writing talent, do you ever contact that writer?

That's almost always how an unknown writer gets an entree. It's very rare that an unknown writer hands in a script that we buy— generally because the unknown writer may lack experience, may not yet be fully aware of what works on the screen, versus what works on the page.

Even so, that script can be a door-opener?

Yes. What the new writer must do, and this is fairly obvious, is to write a "selling" script. Even if it's in a genre that doesn't work— for example, if it's a western, which are very hard to get off the ground these days—if it's well done it can make an executive say, "I don't want to buy this script, but let me hear your other ideas." That's usually how a new writer gets a first development deal.

And when you call the writer in, he or she then presents storylines for possible scripts?

Right. Obviously if a writer gives me a script that is a thriller there's no point in then pitching a comedy or a farce. The sample has to have something to do with the pitched idea. You'd be surprised how many times people come in and pitch things that are totally opposite to what they've given me to read.

Let's talk about the pitching process. How do you like to have ideas presented so that you can decide whether or not they interest you?

First of all I think that at least at major studios it's good to have a treatment to go along with the pitch. This is simply because I may want to present the idea to somebody else here, and my pitch may not be as strong as the writer's would be. The easiest pitches are those for genres that depend largely on plot—horror, thrillers, science fiction, fantasy, farce to a certain extent. With these, the concept and storyline do the work for you; either they are unique and engaging or they aren't. The genres that depend mostly on characterization and dialogue—romantic comedies, for example—are much harder to pitch.

What's a comfortable time period for pitching an idea?

I'd say 15 or 20 minutes.

Do you like to have the writer start with a brief summary of the idea before launching into the full pitch?

I'd like to know the genre we're talking about, but I don't think there's any need to give a precis beforehand. Obviously, in your pitch you want to capture as much of the mood of the movie as possible, especially if an element of suspense is involved. You don't want to give it away beforehand.

How much does the style of the presentation affect your response?

It's got to be told in a way that does not waste time, that doesn't spend a lot of time on exposition and backstory that really isn't important. It's got to be told with enthusiasm and energy, to suggest that the writer really believes in the story. A writer has to be a lot more than a literary craftsman; he almost has to be a salesman. A lot of it is delivery and personal impression. We go so much by instinct that even the initial stages of the talk, before we get to the pitch, almost precondition an executive to his or her response to the material.

What you've just said suggests that the writer would do well to rehearse the pitch, just as an actor or actress rehearses a part.

Most writers I know *do* practice their pitch, whether it's to their agents or to their friends. Because if you start losing the executive's attention you may never get it back, or at least not with the same enthusiasm.

It's a terrible moment when you realize that that's happening. Once I saw a producer's eyes glaze over right in front of me.

It happens to everyone sometime; but you can guard against it by making sure there's something in the first couple of minutes that grabs the listener, that makes the listener wonder why it happened and what'll happen next. And then you have to tell the rest of the story without getting off onto tangents and without losing the drive of the narrative.

What other mistakes do writers make in how they present themselves and their work?

The writer can't come in arrogantly, which sometimes happens. The author shouldn't come in and say, "I've got the next *Star Wars*!" or "I've got the next epic!" If you build up such high expectations, they can't be met.

You mention that you like to have the writer bring in an outline or treatment to leave with you. Roughly what length should it be?

I've found the longer the treatment, the greater its chance of success. The elements that you can get in a longer treatment—for example, characterization and structure—are the elements that often will make the difference between what seems to be an everyday, ordinary submission and something that seems to have an extra quality. A longer treatment gives the author more chance to show his or her writing, which is especially important if you don't have many credits. A five to ten page outline will usually establish the bare bones of the plot, and that's it.

So we're talking about twenty to forty pages, rather than five to ten?

Yes, and most treatments we get as first steps in project deals tend to be long treatments, because it gives the execs as clear an idea of the screenplay as possible, and that's really what they want. Any studio, any producer, anybody with money to invest, wants to gamble as little as possible, and the more there is to the treatment, the smaller the gamble.

Do you like to see sample dialogue in the treatment?

If it's a comedy, yes. It's not really necessary in other forms. Even in comedy it's not necessary if you have a writing sample that's similar enough to the pitch.

Earlier we talked about common weaknesses in scripts and pitches. Are there also common weaknesses in treatments?

The most frequent weakness I see—and this relates to why I favor long treatments—is that characters tend to be ignored in favor of telling a story. Thus you have characters that seem so run-of-the-mill that you have no real enthusiasm for the project. So much of a film consists of creating people that you care about and that will get the audience emotionally involved.

We should also get a good sense of the structure of the piece. From the treatment we should know that this scene will take about five pages, this scene will take only a page—we should get an idea that the author knows what will constitute his or her 120 pages. It should give the feeling that this has been very carefully thought out, that it's not just a rough idea but that the author almost has the whole screenplay in his or her head. And you can detect that from the treatment. If there's padding or a blur over the narrative line then that becomes very obvious.

Do you prefer to see the characters revealed in the course of the treatment, rather than described on a separate page that lists the characters?

Yes. Often you get a paragraph which says, "Irving is charming, witty, bright, engaging," and then you see nothing of that in the treatment. Those things are very easy to say, but not easy to accomplish.

From what you've said it's clear that the writer has to have done a lot of work before pitching the idea. He or she has to have defined the characters, carefully worked out the plot, and put this all into a polished, impressive twenty to forty pages. This differs from the notion that some writers have, that pitching merely consists of tossing out a few ideas to see whether anyone likes one of them.

Neil Simon could do that, Mel Brooks could do that. But writers whose work we do not know have to do as much of the foundation as possible. We need it as evidence that they can pull off the assignment.

I've heard it said that it's harder to sell an original screenplay than to sell the movie rights to a novel. What's your view of this?

Obviously if it's a novel that's done well there's always interest because there's a certain amount of pre-sale value. If a book sold well, we know it will attract a certain amount of audience just because the book was circulated widely. But the negative factor is you have to gamble that the screenplay will come out right. With an original screenplay the executive can see right then and there what the picture will look like. On that basis, the original screenplay is a better shot. Studios usually will be more likely to buy a book if a producer brings it in and wants to make it his or her project. In that case there is someone there whom the studio knows will oversee the project and make sure the material works cinematically.

When you look for someone other than the author to adapt a novel, do you restrict yourself to well-established writers?

For the most part, but not necessarily. Most novels are so expensive to acquire that the studios are reluctant to gamble on people who have not had experience. However, we have had a couple of novels in development by writers who have not sold anything yet. But usually those are cases where there's a well-established producer or director who very strongly believes in the writer. That person is kind of a guarantee to us—as much of a guarantee as there ever is—that the screenplay will look good.

You've made a couple of references to putting deals into development. About how many such deals are underway at any given time?
The average is about a hundred things in development.

How many of those will probably make it all the way to the screen?
Ten or twelve.

Actually that's good news for the writer, in the sense that initially there are opportunities for a hundred people— also money—not just for the ten or twelve who do the films that are produced each year.
Sure, and there are a lot of writers who live very comfortably from development deals and don't have any pictures made for years. As well as the money, it gives you the prestige of being able to say, "I'm working on something for such-and-such a studio." That immediately gives you an enormous amount of credibility compared to the person who has not done anything. The name-dropping helps.

There are definite trends as to the kinds of pictures that are produced at a given time. Do you think the writer should try to respond to them?
Major studios tend to have a long time-lapse between the time a picture is put into development and the time it actually appears in the theatres. Let's say low-budget horror films are doing well. If we put a glut of them into production now, by the time they got out the genre would probably be well exhausted. What a studio has to try to do is produce something that will work in and of itself. There was

no science fiction trend when *Star Wars* appeared, it just happened to fill a gap in the film market. So you should try to go into a market that is *not* being utilized, and hope that therefore you will be seen to be new and unique.

In other words, trying to outguess the market is a waste of time?

I think it's usually the scripts that writers genuinely feel and believe in, rather than the ones they try to contrive for commerciality's sake, that work and that impress people. The executives at Paramount and elsewhere are not solely marketing experts looking for the perfect gimmick; they're people, too. They really respond to the human qualities in a screenplay, to things that have some humane and emotional power to them.

We've talked about your direct contact with writers. Where do agents fit into the picture?

Most studios have a policy that scripts have to come in through an agent, so my first contact is with the agent. In some cases the writer may specifically ask the agent to submit the script to me. I also get scripts directly from agents who have a screenplay that they think will fit my tastes. If the material the agent sends is impressive, then we will contact the writer. A writer has to depend heavily on the agent. He has to be on the agent's back to make sure the material is being sent out—and sent out to the right places. There are certain properties that are perfectly suited for smaller companies but are not suited to a major studio, and vice versa, and not all agents recognize the difference.

It's very difficult, isn't it, for the writer to know whether or not the agent is on top of that?

Yes it is; I was on the other side of the fence as a writer with several agents. Getting a good agent is partly a matter of luck and partly a matter of paying attention to the business. I'd suggest that a writer read the trade papers and learn everything possible about the business and what's being made. That'll pay off in a number of ways. For example, often we'll have a writer who'll come in and say, "I have such-and-such an idea," and not realize that a movie with the same plotline is already being made. That damages the writer's credibility. This is such a competitive business that the successful writer is the one who is professional. That professionalism should be reflected in the meeting, the treatment, and ultimately in the scripts he or she writes.

Any additional advice for the writer wanting to sell a feature?

Frankly, it's usually easier to break in with a producer or with an independent production company—maybe with a low-budget feature—and then make the transition up to a major studio. Writers will certainly be welcomed at major studios if they have something special to offer, but they should be aware that being turned down by the majors is not the end of the road; there are alternatives.

LARRY FORRESTER ON PITCHING AND SELLING TO TV

Larry Forrester is a novelist, a TV writer/producer, a feature writer, and a story editor. Past credits include "Vegas," "Tora, Tora, Tora," "Baretta," "Switch," and "Fantasy Island." More recently he has worked on "Hardcastle and McCormick," "Call to Glory," and "Star Trek, The Next Generation."

How does a story editor select freelance writers?

It varies from show to show. On some series your supervising producer will have a general discussion with you on the type of shows he wants to do. He may say, "We want a Christmas story, we want a Valentine's Day story, we need a love story here, a horror story there." Then he may say, "Oh, old Bill Jones is real good on horror; he did a beauty for me a few years ago on 'Harry O.' See if he's around." If your supervising producer says that to you, he will want an explanation from you if you use some other writer. So you're obliged to hunt down Mr. Jones. Now Mr. Jones may be dead, drunk, in Mexico, or working on a feature or book and unavailable, in which case you can consider alternatives.

What's the source of the alternatives?

Every story editor has a list of trusted writers. Also he will have a secondary list. That list, in my experience, is built up from several sources. One, colleagues will call you and say, "Listen, my show is full up, but I've got a terrific young writer who did one very good script for me. Maybe you could use her; will you see her?" Another way is through contacts at the networks. And your own agent or another agent with whom you've dealt in the past may call to suggest a "new terrific writer."

Do you ever find a writer through the "slush pile"? That is, through an unsolicited script written on speculation?

Yes, it will happen sometimes that you get scripts out of the blue. First I will find out whether the script was submitted through an agent. If not, I will not read a word until they have signed a release form which I will send them. Then I'll read that script. If it's good—which is rare, I must tell you, quite rare—then I'll put them on the secondary list.

I know that on many shows it takes months before such a script is read . . .

Normally you only have time for the job, and any poor, flailing remnants of a sex life or a family life in the time left over. You really don't have a hell of a lot of time to read outside material or nurse people. We tend to do more and more in-house. It's the safest way to do it because you find time and time again you have to rewrite it anyway, so you might as well do it in the first place. In television now, production staffs are nearly always made up of writers. You have a supervising producer, two producers, an executive story consultant, and at least one story editor—five, maybe six people working on a weekly series. If they do four scripts each, there go twenty-four scripts—there's a season. Why use an outsider?

The insiders were once outsiders. How did they get in?

Every one of these people is chosen because he has contributed to the show in the past as a freelancer, in spite of the fact that an outsider is at a disadvantage. He doesn't know a rule maybe passed last week—for example, we may decide we have enough stories that go back in history. And next week I get three scripts or outlines with that kind of premise from the outside, and they're useless.

When you need a new staff writer, do you still draw upon the freelance pool?

Unfortunately, the best of the experienced freelance writers are now behind desks, doing the kind of job I am, or they're already on staff, or they're on multiple deals—they're not available out there. The ones that are out there, very largely, are the left-overs, the tired-out, burned-out. The freelance brigade, at the moment, is sorely depleted and battle-scarred.

Even so, the talented but unknown writer, the new writer, still has enormous difficulty getting any freelance work. Why is that?

It's very hard for a producer to risk money on an unknown writer. If it turns out they can't do it, you can guess who's going to sit up nights and rewrite the whole damn thing—unpaid. And then, if the rewritten script is good and it is shown time and time again, *they* pick up the residuals, not the producer.

You've been frank about the obstacles—but some people are either too determined or too crazy to let obstacles stop them. Let's say they manage to get on your secondary list in one of the ways you've mentioned—then what?

Let's assume I see one of these people from the secondary list. I stress it will be a totally unofficial meeting—it is not what the Guild calls a "first writer's meeting." It's just to "get to know you" meeting. We'll talk, I'll find out about their background—but I won't let them pitch specific story ideas.

Like many others in your position, you sound cautious.

It's full of traps and unfortunately it's when you try to help people that you are most vulnerable. You listen to an idea, and a year later you do something that is even *vaguely* similar and you are sued. I've been burned a couple of times. I do try to find some time to help writers, for the simple reason that I feel very fortunate: it took me a long time to get here, and people helped me. People like Carl Foreman, Lord Ted Willis in London, Leigh Vance, and Aaron Spelling. Therefore I feel I ought to help someone, too. The question is, *how?* It's really difficult, the way the industry works at the moment.

Well, if you do have that initial meeting and the person makes a favorable impression, what is the next step?

They may want to leave me something they have written—a book, a script, a play, something that's more or less the credential they bring. I will read that when I have the time to read it at one sitting. I always make notes. I will either send it back to the writer with these notes, or on rare occasions I'll ask the writer to come in again, for an official meeting.

What takes place at the official meeting?

I will explain to them, "Look, I don't have any openings on the show at the moment, but something that's in the works now may fall down. I will listen to your ideas and I will keep them. If something falls down and your ideas are any good, I'll put them up to my supervising producer to see if he likes any of them." I'll listen to the writer's stories, make notes, and afterwards I'll draw up a document which we call a "notion." It is a one- or one-and-a-half page document which simply outlines the basic theme of the idea.

What do you do with it?

If I like it well enough and there is an opening, I will circulate it to my supervising producer, and to the Line Producer. They'll read it and at our weekly story conference they'll give me a pass or a go. If they give it a go, they'll ask me, "Who is the writer?" Then it's my job to sell them on the writer.

Is there a particular time of the year when you see new writers?

At the beginning of a new season there's a better chance. Because you say, "Well, here we are in February and the network has given us a commitment for twenty-two one-hour episodes and two 90-minute episodes for sure, and we'll probably overcommit to thirty episodes, to have some in the bank as replacements. Now then, where are those people I saw last season? Secretary, get me out my secondary list." Now you say to those people, "We're renewed, I want you in here as soon as you can make it, with five ideas for this show. I'll send that newcomer sample scripts and a bible revised for the new season. When they come in, that's when the pitching starts—and they'd better have some terrific ideas!

What do you do if you like one of the ideas?

If that writer comes in here like Woody Allen and is brilliant and we all love him, or if it's a girl who charms us and pitches a very good, professional, original story with verve and emotion, we say, "great, go to a story outline." And it comes in and you may say, "Yuchh, it's rotten." Well, then not so much is lost because you haven't started shooting—you don't start shooting until May, and here you are in February. But you can only try so many at the beginning of a season.

It sounds very important to be able to pitch well.

In episodic television it's a critical skill. It is essential to be able to pitch and to respond. Unfortunately we've gotten into the habit of judging a man for his performance as a pitcher—as a salesman—rather than for what he puts down on paper, at least in the first instance. Mistakes are made that way. A very personable man who gets excited and tells the story with a lot of verve is more likely to get an assignment than a shy fellow whose responses are somewhat slower and whose reflexes may not be too sharp. That's no way to be judging writing, but it's the only game in town.

Pitching is done in person—let me digress slightly to ask whether therefore someone not living in the L.A. area should forget about writing for series produced here.

I occasionally get calls from Chicago, Montreal, all over—that's pretty hopeless. If by some miracle we are going to use one of these people, if they sent us the greatest spec script ever written, I'd have to have them down here. I must have the physical presence of the writer—I can't work by remote control or telephone. That's not the way the industry is geared.

For those that are here, can you tell us a bit more about the best style of pitching?

People pitch in different ways. One may come in, very poised, and say, "Yes, I know what you mean. I did a show like that years ago on 'Have Gun Will Travel,' and in that case . . ." and they will talk in a very cool but tremendously experienced way so you get a sense of authority and experience. These people name-drop with such aplomb that it doesn't in any way irritate you. In fact, if you are a wee Glasgow boy like me, who's impressed when the cop at the gate nods at him, you're somewhat enthralled by this. Others come in and literally pace the floor, jump about, act out the George Raft death scene, and the whole bit. I'm a bit like that myself, I'm rather volatile, I get rather excited about it. That's passionate, and it's good, too. You have to judge the person and the kind of story you want from them. If you want a story about international intrigue, you want a person with a diplomatic gloss about them. If you want a terrific love story that will tear your heart out, that's another kind of pitching. And comedy writers—well, God save us from comedy writers; hide the breakables when they come in here! Of course there are exceptions to all these types.

What kind of interaction takes place during a pitching session?

Some story editors throw a spanner into the middle of a story, while it's being told. I try not to interrupt, but it's awfully hard to sit through a 20-minute pitch when you know you've done the story before. So if a writer is getting a bit long-winded, I will occasionally say, "I'm sorry, I'm going to stop you right there, because A, B, or C. Will you go on to the next one?" Alternatively, I will say, "Hey, I'm going to stop you right there, because now you're getting close to a story. But supposing the girl was a guy, and supposing it wasn't an airplane but a boat, would that work for you? I like that because we've got a lagoon here, and a lovely boat." Suddenly that writer has to quickly, on his feet, adapt. If he adapts very well, you're impressed immediately. That's not entirely fair, because it has nothing to do with his writing ability.

But one thing it may show is whether the writer is unduly ego-involved with his or her idea. The new writer has to be pretty flexible, right?

Absolutely. You cannot write for a series and at the same time demand that your work not be changed. If you want to write work that will not be changed, go to a mountaintop and write poetry that no one will change—but no one will read. If you want to reach 30 million people—and at the end of a year, with repeats and foreign sales, 100 million people—and you have one sentence in your little episodic show that you believe in, that is your statement, your view, then you're going to communicate. And it's going to rub off. That's why I'm here; that's what I believe in.

The person who wants to be a Writer, with a capital "W," should stay away from TV?

We are not really, in a full sense, artistic writers. What we are is terrific technicians. But we are employed as Tonic and Toyota salesmen. We stand outside and say, "Roll up! Roll up! Come see the show and buy!" If you want to go and write works of art, that's marvelous, but it's a different line of work.

To wind up the subject of pitching, are there any other approaches that are used?

There's also high-level pitching in a group. Often we will come up with a story idea. If we can't do it in-house, we'll call in a writer who we know to be good, and I'll get together with him. We'll spend a morning or an afternoon—two hours, three hours or more if it takes it. And we will, step-by-step, go through that story, including some of the lines of dialogue. He will either have a tape recorder or a notebook and will get it all down. From there you give the writer the go-ahead to the outline stage. There are more conferences, and he goes on to the script stage, a draft and a final. Putting together an episode like that in a group, in concert—with lots of smoke in the room, lots of coffee—is very exciting . . . and it's Hollywood.

For the new writer who's set his or her sights on getting in on the excitement eventually—any more advice?

Anybody who is determined to write speculatively because they've decided it's the only way they're going to break in should call the show in question, early in the season, and ask the story editor or the story editor's secretary if they could provide a list of the subjects already commissioned for the year. And, if possible, could a sample script and show bible also be sent, along with anything else that might help. It would obviously be much better if the writer could have the agent do the calling, but one way or another the writer has to do some research to try to cut down the number of unknowns he's up against.

CHAPTER 17

How to Find an Agent

• WHAT AN AGENT DOES

THE GOOD ONES? WORK LIKE A DOG, mostly. Breakfast meetings, morning phone calls and deals, lunch meetings, afternoon client calls and deal-making, dinner meetings, and finally homeward to wearily read through a couple scripts before sacking out. Add to this a smattering of family life or something passing for a social life, and you have a pretty good idea of an agent's job.

And yet, there are those who absolutely thrive on it. They enjoy the negotiations, they love the excitement of discovering and nurturing new talent, they revel in playing such a pivotal role in their clients' careers.

All for the standard 10 percent. Off the *top*, by the way—but in most cases, it's a bargain. A good agent functions as a negotiator, troubleshooter, shoulder-to-cry-on, critic, mouthpiece, advisor, fan, advocate, and representative. However the most important job an agent can do for you is to make contacts, get you in the door. Once there, you're on your own, and how well you do depends on a combination of your talent and ability to perform under pressure, along with a certain degree of luck that comes in handy in any business.

315

An agent cultivates connections: planting an introductory seed, caring for and nourishing the contact through phone calls and lunches, and finally harvesting when the time is right. Each contact they make is, or may lead to, a potential employer for their clients, so connections are handled with care. By developing a reputation for sending quality writers and quality materials, an agent can find herself in the enviable position of having employers call *her*, rather than the other way around. Conversely, an agent who indiscriminately shotguns any and all material to everyone she can think of will soon find herself shut out and shut off. A good agent is quite selective about the material and writers she'll send out, since her name and reputation is on the line with each script and every pitch.

• WHAT YOU WANT FROM AN AGENT

Someone who will do all of the above . . . and more.

You're looking for someone who really believes in you. Someone who knows you're going to make it, in spite of the fact that your first couple—or couple dozen—pitch sessions resulted in a No Sale. Someone who swears to you they won't give up as long as you don't.

You want someone who will be honest with you. Someone who will tell you when a feature idea misses the mark, or a spec sitcom simply isn't funny. They're not only protecting *their* reputation, but *yours*.

You want an agent who tends to be a bit aggressive. Not obnoxious, necessarily—but definitely willing to draw a line and defend it. Aggressiveness is important not only when it comes to hammering out the best deal for a client, but in dealing with the bulletproof secretarial barriers set up by besieged producers. A good agent breaks through those barriers, without alienating himself in the process.

As a writer, you're no doubt familiar with rejection. It's an unhappy but inevitable part of the territory. An agent, however, must deal with that kind of rejection on a daily basis, on behalf of at least a couple dozen clients or so. They get rejected more in one day than you probably do all year! So, the ideal agent is one who will persevere, and not become discouraged in the face of rejection . . . after rejection . . . etc.

You want an agent who keeps the lines of communication open. He doesn't always wait for you to call him—every so often, he checks in with you, if only to see how you're doing. And he *always* returns your calls, even if it takes a couple days or so.

If you're able to find all of these qualities, you've surmounted one of the biggest hurdles in this business—gaining an ally who can help you build a successful career.

• WHAT AGENTS ARE LOOKING FOR

While most agents will tell you they have plenty to do just keeping their current stable of clients busy, they are also nearly unanimous in their agreement that they will always find room for one more writer. All that writer needs to be is *exceptional*—head and shoulders above the rest.

The agent's search for that kind of talent usually begins with a recommendation. One of their clients will come across a new writer who seems to have what it takes; a colleague will call, saying they've run across a gifted comedy writer, but they're up to their wazoo in comedy writers right now, and maybe he'd be worth a look? Friends, producers, lawyers—anyone with whom the agent has daily dealings are in a position to recommend a new writer. The percentage of recommended writers the agent will eventually accept may be small, but it's much larger than the percentage of those found by way of the huge amount of mail the agent receives every day.

However, not everyone is fortunate enough to be in the position to obtain a recommendation, in which case they're forced to make a frontal assault. This would begin with a query letter to the agent, detailing a bit about the writer's experience and current project (more on query letters later). The agent looks through each of these letters (or perhaps has a secretary do the initial screening) and weeds out the ones that are obviously hopeless. These get tossed, unless they come with SASE. Then, the rest of the mail is read more carefully, and returned in their SASE's, with or without comment as deemed appropriate. The agent is looking for that *one letter* that jumps out of the pile and hollers for attention, with a professional look and a topnotch idea communicated clearly and succinctly in a polished writing style. Most agents will tell you they feel fortunate indeed if they get one such letter every month or two.

Assuming this letter is yours (and why not?) the agent will either call or write back, requesting a look at your sample script. Once that arrives, a month or so passes until it gets its turn on the reading stack, and the agent will be looking to see if your writing ability lives up to the potential she sensed from your letter. If not, it's returned with or without a short note, depending upon the agent and how busy she is.

If the sample script is a good one, the agent will then want to assure herself that you're not a "One-Script Wonder" who got lucky the first time out, but lacks the consistency to make scriptwriting a career. She'll either call or write, asking if you've done anything else. This is a very crucial stage of the developing relationship. We'll give you an example.

One of us (Cox) wrote a spec comedy a long time ago, an extremely off-the-wall, slapstick kind of piece that basically sacrificed any kind of believable plot for 110 pages of machine-gun physical gags and vaudevillian one-liners. Now, Kerry was lucky enough to have had a spec "M*A*S*H" script he'd written sometime before catch the attention of a television producer who trained in the same karate dojo, and that producer had written a letter to Dan Wilcox, then the story editor on "M*A*S*H," who called once, said he liked the script, but they don't use anybody so thanks a lot and goodbye (with us so far?). However, Kerry had a copy of the very complimentary letter the producer had written, and he enclosed it with the script when he sent it out to prospective agents. Lo and behold, Kerry gets a call at one of his various part-time jobs from an extremely excited MAJOR AGENT, who raves about the terrific comedic energy of the script, and says he never reads spec scripts but he just happens to be Dan Wilcox's agent and the letter caught his eye so he figured he'd read a few pages, and he ended up reading the whole thing and DO YOU HAVE ANYTHING ELSE? To which a barely functioning swim teacher-slash-neophyte writer managed to croak, "Sure, lots of stuff." "Send it right away!" the agent shouted, and hung up.

Needless to say, there was nothing very good to send. Kerry had already been sending out his best script, as you would expect. But, too impatient to simply write another script and send *it*, he chose to ship off one of his earlier efforts instead. Three days later, back came the script with a form letter signed by the agent's secretary. Kerry was revealed for what he was at the time: A One-Script Wonder.

So our hypothetical agent wants to be sure this writer, who will take up a lot of time and effort, particularly if his credits are few, has the kind of staying power a career in scriptwriting demands.

This second script will probably be read a bit more promptly than the first, given that the agent's interest has already been piqued. If it lives up to the promise of the first, you've probably got yourself an agent. If not, you'll get it back.

The next thing an agent will look for is a client he can confidently send to meetings: someone who handles criticism, who deals on a mature and professional level with people, and who can verbally hold his own. Also, someone who will not embarrass the agent by storming out of a story session, or forget appointments, or flake out on deadlines. In short, someone easy to work with.

Finally, the agent wants to know that you will continue to produce top quality work, maybe not every time but with a degree of dependability the agent can rely on. She wants to know she'll be well supplied with material to sell, and that you'll be willing to upgrade or update samples if they seem to be going stale.

Combine what you're looking for in an agent, and what an agent is looking for in you, and you have a perfect business relationship. Either that, or a perfect marriage!

• PLANNING YOUR AGENT HUNT

When you set out to find an agent, you're undertaking a quest. And, as with any quest, you need to prepare yourself with the proper equipment, arm yourself with weaponry effective enough to meet and overcome any obstacles in the path to your final goal. Here's what you'll need:

1. A spec script. Not just a good one. A *great* one.
2. Another spec script. One so good that you're never sure whether to send this one or the first one.
3. A query letter.
4. The Writers Guild list of signatory agencies (available through the mail for one dollar, or for free if you stop by; see Chapter 20 for the address).
5. Any information on these agencies you can gather (e.g., *The Hollywood Scriptwriter* does an annual agency review; *Writer's Digest* Magazine occasionally spotlights certain agencies).
6. A telephone.
7. Plenty of manila envelopes and postage.
8. Patience. Lots and lots of it.

For starters, take your agency list and notice that it designates which agencies are willing to review unsolicited materials. If you have no agency connections at all, these are the ones you should probably begin with. Usually they are small agencies, one or two people, who are just starting out and need to build a respectable client list. Like you, they're hungry, fighting for a toehold in a highly competitive industry, and it could be that the two of you will be just the team that can do it.

Call the agency and verify with the secretary (or the agent, if they answer) that this agency is still willing to accept materials, and that their name and address is current and correct. Misspelling the agent's name is a sure way to get off to a bad start, and the agency list occasionally is inaccurate.

If the agent does happen to answer the phone, be prepared! You may be put on the spot right then and there, and be asked to describe your credentials or give a thumbnail sketch of your script. If you stammer incoherently, forget it. But, if you deliver a brief, polished summary, you'll probably be asked to send in the sample script, thus eliminating the need for a query letter.

Let's assume, however, that you have not yet been asked to submit a script. In verifying the address of the agency, you've also asked to whom your script should be submitted, because sometimes agencies have associates or readers do the initial screening. Your sample scripts are done, neatly copied and bound. Time to get that all-important query letter into the mail.

So crucial is a query letter to your success that we'll take a moment and break one down into its essential elements.

The Query Letter

This simple little letter has to work wonders. It has to jump out of a formidable stack of mail and grab an agent's attention and interest, it has to summarize your experience and expertise, it has to get that agent to pick up the phone and give you a call. How do you write a letter like that?

First of all, put yourself in the agent's place. An agent gets a ton of phone calls on a daily basis from people asking for representation. And frankly there are a lot of people out there who envision themselves as wonderful writers, but who possess none of the skill, talent, perseverance, and everything else it takes to actually succeed. So the agencies set up a very effective screening system to keep those people out. Unfortunately, it also keeps out those that *do* have the talent, dedication, etc.

So the first thing you have to do is make your letter look very professional. You're not a flake, you're someone who's dedicated to this craft, and you have something to offer. Begin by getting yourself some decent letterhead. It doesn't have to be showy; in fact, avoid anything too fancy. All you need is some nice, conservative letterhead, with your name, address, and phone number on top. We think it looks more professional *not* to put "Writer" or "Screenwriter" below your name.

Next, address your letter to a specific agent within the agency. Call the target agency, preferably at a less busy time (from four o'clock on) and see if there's anybody who has the time to chat for a moment. This may be a receptionist, a secretary, or sometimes after five o'clock the agents will answer the phones themselves. Explain your situation very succinctly: "I'm writing a letter of inquiry to your agency; is there one agent in particular who deals with new writers?" They may say no, or they may be able to help you. Sometimes there are junior agents just out of the mailroom who are in the process of being trained. They don't have a full roster of established writers yet, so they will occasionally look at new material.

Try to keep your letter to one page. Use two if necessary, but one is better. If you have background that is relevant to the project, mention it. For instance, if you've written a murder mystery that's set in the Navy on a destroyer and you happen to have spent twenty years in the Navy, then that's something that would interest the agent because he knows the story will be authentic.

If you've done a great deal of research on a project, such as you would when writing a historical drama, mention that. If what you've written is based on a true story, that should be in your letter. Even if the script is a departure from what really happened, but is close to your experience, that's worth mentioning. It is *not* relevant to say, "I've always really liked movies, and I've always wanted to be famous and rich," and so on.

Also, avoid apologizing for yourself. We've seen letters where people have started out by saying, "Well, I've never written anything before, and I don't know that you'd want to buy something from me, but I have this script." Try to establish a positive attitude, without doing what we've also seen: "I've got this script that will make *Star Wars* look like *Heaven's Gate*." That turns people off immediately.

Now, the hardest part of the letter is the next part, in which you try to give an exciting, curiosity-arousing, yet succinct summary of the script that you want them to read. It's got to tell them what this script is about, who's the central character, what's the nature of the conflict or quest or battle or goal that the central character goes through or pursues, who or what are the interested forces opposing this person or these people, and how it comes out.

Immediately you're asking, "You give away the ending?" Well, you don't have to give away all the details, but you have to tell the story. Most people don't want to give away the ending, but the fact is that one of the major things that an agent or producer wants to know is what is the tone of the piece. If you say, "This is a man who bravely battles against cancer for fourteen years," an agent would want to know if the poor guy dies in the end or not. It's going to change the tone of the piece if he comes through it and runs for the Senate and is happy forever after, or if he dies along the way. Both are interesting stories, but an agent can't judge the tone of the piece and decide who might be interested in it if he doesn't know how it ends.

Also, the first part of this section of the letter should of course give the title of the script and establish whether it's a comedy or drama. A note about this: if your script is a comedy, try to make the description of it humorous as well. However, don't force the entire letter into a jokey, comedic sort of tone, unless you're very good at that style of letter writing.

The best way to approach this difficult part of the letter is to imagine someone who's just seen your movie and is trying to tell a friend about it very briefly. The response you want from this friend is, "Gee, I gotta go see that!"

In wrapping this letter up, rather than saying, "I'll be calling you soon," we suggest you enclose a self-addressed, stamped postcard. Write on it, "Yes, please send me (the name of your script)." Another option on the card should be, "Sorry, too busy right now. Please try again in sixty days." And the last one is, "Other." Don't put, "No, go home, don't call me again." By putting, "Other," you've made them actually write something down, and rather than write, "No," they'll occasionally opt for the sixty-day option you've presented. Then, after sixty days, you call up and say, "As you requested, I'm re-contacting you. . . ."

By doing all this you're showing an agent you're considerate of their situation. Too many writers approach an agent saying, "What can you do for me, I need an agent, I need to sell this script, my house payment's due, what can you do?" But here, simply by enclosing this little postcard, you're showing an agent you realize they're very busy and you understand. And that makes a good impression.

How long do you wait for a response? If the agent doesn't return that postcard, or they say, "No," we wouldn't bother calling them at all. Ordinarily, it will take anywhere from two weeks to two months before you'll be getting any responses.

• A SAMPLE QUERY LETTER

Ben Maple
Terrific Writer's Agency
1111 Beverly Blvd.
Los Angeles, CA 90048

Dear Mr. Maple:

I'm aware that the trend today is toward action-adventure films, but I'd like to send you a script that gives the trend a unique twist: it's an action-adventure film of the mind.

The script is called "Mindquest." Its young hero volunteers to be the subject of sleep/dream experiments, and an untried drug suddenly traps him in a world created by his own mind: a world in which his deepest fears become fantastic beings he must conquer. It becomes a race against time, and he must reach his goal before the medical team brings him back to consciousness. If he doesn't, he'll be trapped in his nightmare forever.

Please use the enclosed stamped postcard to let me know whether I may send you "Mindquest" (along with an SASE, of course). I understand that you normally don't consider work from writers without a recommendation, but I believe that if you take the time to read the first ten pages, "Mindquest" will capture your imagination and be its own strongest recommendation.

Thanks for your time, and I look forward to hearing from you.

Sincerely,

A. Writer

If approached in this way—methodically, professionally, and with all due courtesy and common sense—the search for an agent needn't be a frustrating, overwhelming task. The following interview with Marcie Wright highlights and reinforces many of the points we've discussed, while also giving us a more personal look at the agent-client relationship.

MARCIE WRIGHT

An agent since 1982, Marcie Wright began as an associate in a small commercial agency as the head of the literary department. She is a former writer who became frustrated with her agent, and decided, "There must be a better way." For her, the better way was to become an agent herself, and she now operates her own agency, The Wright Concept.

Without necessarily naming names, can you give us an idea of the types of writers you're currently handling?

This past season I had the story editor on "Family Ties," a story editor on "Sanchez of Bel Air," two story editors on "Facts of Life," two staff writers on "Me and Mrs. C," and I presently have a staff writer on "Punky Brewster," another on "Out of This World," and the Executive Story Editor on "We Got It Made," a remake of the old NBC series now being done in syndication.

Obviously you're very strong in the television end of the business. Do you also have writers doing features?

Yes. One of my writers is currently writing *Police Academy V* for Warner Brothers. I also have two other writers working on independent features, and one writer with a CBS Movie-of-the-Week that went into production yesterday.

What do you see as your function in the agent-client relationship?

I referred to myself earlier today when I was asked that question as a "Yenta" for writers. My job is to introduce writers to producers and hope that they'll build a business relationship. So, I then find a job for my writers and negotiate the deals for them.

So of equal importance to negotiation expertise is simply the ability to make initial contacts for a writer?

I believe so. I believe that that's very important. Once you make the initial contact for the writer, it's really up to that writer to cement that relationship with product and with personality.

So, summarizing your responsibilities to the writer?

To find them work, and get them the best deal possible once we've located that work.

And their responsibility to you?

To provide me with material that is a good sample of their writing, one that I can use to get them work. And to be available for meetings, and once at those meetings, to present themselves well.

Describe a typical day in the life of an agent.

I'm usually in the office by eight, if I don't have a breakfast meeting. I do most of my own work, so I spend those morning hours, roughly eight 'til ten, doing letters, getting scripts out, preparing my phone sheet for the day, and basically getting in gear. It's very difficult for me to just walk in at ten and start calling people—I like to take some time to plan the day.

Working out a strategy, so to speak.

Right. Who to call, when to call them, and how best to approach whatever subject I'm dealing with.

Then, I try to spend as much time on the phone as possible, getting my calls out. I usually start making my calls around nine or nine-thirty, even though producers aren't normally in until later than that. My theory is that I'm more likely to get a call returned if I'm early on the phone sheet.

I usually have a business lunch. I *do* enjoy going to lunch! I find I get more work done at lunch in terms of laying good foundations than I do by going to a producer's office. I feel that I'm at less of an advantage in their office than when I'm sitting across from them at lunch—we're on more equal ground.

Then, the afternoon is spent on the phone, returning calls, following up . . . and also taking meetings with clients, prospective clients, etc. I try to limit my office meetings to one a day, because I have a tendency to enjoy talking with people, and a half-hour meeting can sometimes run into an hour. That's a big chunk out of my day.

So, that covers the afternoon. Now, the question on everybody's mind might be, when do new scripts get read?

Well, some afternoons I'll leave the office a little early, say three o'clock or so if it's quiet around here, and I'll go home and read five scripts or so. Sometimes I'll get up early in the morning and read one or two before I come in to the office. I try to read three or four over the weekend. I'm not always good about that, but since I do the majority of my own reading, sooner or later it does get read. Sometimes it's slow, but I get to it.

And what kind of a backlog do you normally have? Do you get a lot of submissions per week?

It varies, but I'm really limiting the number of submissions I'm taking right now, specifically because I'm doing my own reading. I used to have a reader help me in the past, but I just have come to believe that it's not fair to anyone. I've had a couple readers give me negative reports on writers, and I've later seen those writers' names on television, and it gives me such a sinking feeling! So I like to do it all, but I'm sometimes six, eight, or ten weeks backlogged. However, I tell writers this: if I agree to read their script, they have permission to bug me every two weeks. That keeps me on my toes.

How do you like to be approached by a writer? And I speak not just of you, but of agents in general—what's the best approach?

The best way to approach an agent is through a current client. Or, through a producer, who contacts the agent and says, "I've read this person's material, and it's worth looking at." If you can come in with a recommendation, you're going to get a little faster treatment, and the door will be a little easier to open.

On the other hand, people who don't know the agent or anyone who can give them a recommendation should begin with a letter. They should pitch themselves and their project, but keep it down to a page, a page-and-a-half. There's nothing more frustrating than getting a ten-page letter from a writer telling you about their various skills.

So, you're saying that a letter should come before a phone call?

Well, yes, but phone calls can be effective too. I personally return as many phone calls as possible, although I don't know if that's necessarily true of everyone else. I don't mind phone calls as a first contact. I *do* resent people sending me three or four scripts out of the blue, with me not knowing where in the world they came from.

So, one way or another it's best to introduce yourself, and have a couple lines ready on your script before you send anything over.

Yes. And I would think that's a good general rule for approaching all agents, not just me.

I was getting so much mail that one of the things I did was ask the Writers Guild to take me off the agent's list they send out. I was forced to do that simply because of the sheer volume of mail.

What do you dislike most about the ways writers have tried to approach you?

I don't like scripts coming in without a self-addressed stamped envelope!

It's hard to believe people still do that!

Oh, 50 percent of the scripts I get come in that way. I try to respond by either sending back the coverage (a summary of the agent's reactions to the script) or a letter of some sort. Invariably, if I throw a script away, one out of five of the writers will send me a nasty letter, or worse yet, call me. It's so frustrating! I simply can't afford to send everyone's script back, but some people just don't understand that.

Even the larger operations can't afford to send scripts back with no SASE.

Absolutely not. It's the first sign of the rank amateur, for one thing. For that reason alone the new writer should remember that envelope.

Anything else you don't like?

I don't think you should say to an agent, "This is the best script that's ever been written." I have heard that five thousand times. Just tell me what the script's about, and let *me* decide.

Okay, so in this letter you'd like to see a couple lines on the writer's background, a paragraph or two on the script they'd like you to see, and of course an SASE. Should they follow up with a phone call?

After a reasonable amount of time, that's fine with me.

Here's a question that's probably being asked more and more by frustrated writers everywhere—why have an agent? Is it possible to do without one?

Yes, I think it is possible to do without one. But, it's much harder. A writer wants to write, and if you're having to be a salesman also, then you're detracting from the time you spend writing and therefore splitting your energy. I don't write anymore, I'm just an agent now. And I make fifty to a hundred phone calls a *day*! If you're doing the same thing, I don't know when you fit in your writing.

Also, when it comes to negotiations, it's very hard to function in your own behalf. It's easier for me because it's not my talent I'm talking about, so I can be much more positive and glowing in my praise of your abilities. Also, negotiations can get a little nasty on occasion. I've had producers tell me that both I and my attorney were full of various substances, and if they were saying this directly to the writer, it's going to be very hard for that writer and producer to proceed on a positive note once the negotiations are done. On the other hand, if I take the flak from the producer, then the writer and producer can sit down once it's all over and have no hard feelings toward each other. I do believe that part of the agent's job is to get yelled at by the producer, and let them vent their frustrations on me instead of my client.

It could be argued, though, that a writer wouldn't be making as many phone calls as you do, since he or she wouldn't

be representing two dozen writers like you do.

That's certainly true. I still think, however, that a writer's time is much more wisely spent writing, rather than making phone calls or chasing down deals.

No argument there. With regards to the size of your agency—are you considered a small agency, a mid-size . . .

The Writers Guild considers any agency with under twenty clients to be a small agency. Twenty to forty is a mid-size . . . I have twenty-three, so much to my amazement I'm a mid-sized agency. Big surprise to me, since I'm just this one person trying to make it work!

What size agency is best for a new writer to aim for?

Definitely a small agency. In the beginning you need personalized attention. If you're able to get that somewhere other than a small agency, great—but your chances are obviously better someplace where you won't get lost in the crowd.

I like to think that, even with twenty-three clients, I give each of my writers a measure of personal attention. I don't have any clients complain to me about not being able to get me on the phone, and part of that reason is because I used to complain about never being able to get *my* agent on the phone!

I recently began representing a young guy who'd been with a larger agency, and he told me that he was going to call and dissolve his relationship with them—only he couldn't get them on the phone. He finally had to write them a letter! I don't want that happening to any of *my* clients.

A little about the business end of agenting. It's fairly well known that an agent gets 10 percent of any deal he or she negotiates for the client. Does that include residuals?

Agents are, by contract with the Writers Guild, only eligible for a percentage of the residuals if the original deal was at least 10 percent above scale. Now, in episodic television everybody works for scale on a per episode basis, so the writer isn't required to give the agent a commission on residuals. I do, however, have a couple of clients who have elected to commission me anyway, and I tell them right up front that they don't have to do this—

But thank you very much!

Right! I *will* cash the check! If the agent does negotiate a deal at 10 percent above scale, then they are entitled to that portion, according to the Writers Guild.

Regarding the people you have on staff. You get 10 percent of their salaries?

Yes.

And if they're assigned four stories, five stories per year, you get 10 percent of those?

Exactly. If they are story editors or above in rank, they get a fee for the script in addition to their salary. Staff writers' scripts are guaranteed against their salary, and at the end of the season the accounting department adds up the number of scripts they've written, and tallies that in terms of price against their salaries. If they've written more scripts at scale than their salary would equal, then the production company must pay the difference. If they've written less, they luck out.

Are negotiations for features different than television deals?

It depends. There is a flat weekly rate for working on features, much the same as story editors get on TV shows. It's a lower weekly rate. But generally, if you go into a production company with an original idea that they buy, we work out an amount that they pay you to begin writing.

If it's *their* idea, and they're coming to you to do it, they have to pay you a minimum of 10 percent of your fee before you start.

And in negotiating the entire deal, including back end protection, up front fees, percentage of the gross—you're eligible for 10 percent of that as well?

That's right. Let me give you a sample of a deal, one I just worked out over at Warner Bros.

We worked out an amount that my writer will be paid for writing the script, including story, first draft, and one set of revisions. Then there's an option on an additional rewrite, and an option on a polish. Then, on the first day of principal photography he will get a bonus which is double the amount he's being paid to write the script. We were also able to negotiate a percentage of the profits, but since it's a percentage of the net, and this is the fifth in the saga, that may be an academic point. But they're paying him half to start, half on completion of the first draft. Then, on rewrite, it's half the re-write fee to start, half on completion.

And a heck of a bonus if they shoot it!

A heck of a bonus! And we're all praying that there *will* be a first day of principal photography!

Are you personally open to submissions right now?

Yes and no. I know that doesn't answer the question too well, but let me explain. I'm always looking for good writers. I really do have a full boat right now, but if someone really good comes along I can't see myself passing on them.

We've talked at some length about the duties of an agent, how to find an agent, etc. Let's move several months or years down the road, and discuss that moment of truth that has to be faced when an agent or a client feels the relationship is just not working out. Is this a decision the writer usually makes, or the agent?

It can work either way, or it can be a mutual decision. I have had a couple of writers come to me and say, "It just isn't working, and I'd like to move on." I have gone to writers and said, "I just feel like I'm at a dead end and don't know what else to do. What do *you* think we should do?" I have also sat down with writers and said, "I don't want you to go, but things are not happening as fast as I think they should, and I know you're frustrated, and I'm frustrated, and if you feel it's time to move on we'll always be friends." There are hundreds of thousands of writers out there trying to break in, so the odds are astronomical. Obviously it can be done, but it takes perseverance and good product. And I can't always make it happen no matter how good the writer is or how hard I try.

I also feel that my contacts on a show may not be the same as another agent's contacts, and you may move on to another agent who can waltz right onto the same show and make it happen. It's the difference in personalities and techniques.

So it's not always an acrimonious scene, with accusations flying . . .

Oh, no, in fact I've only had one blow-up with a writer, where he told me I wasn't doing enough for him and I asked him to move on. And now every time I see "Night Court" I cry!

Is there any advice you would give to writers looking for an agent?

They should have more than one script to show an agent. I have, in the past, taken on writers who had only one script, but from experience within the industry, I now will no longer take on a writer based on his or her first piece. I really feel that a writer interested in episodic comedy should approach an agent with at least three or four writing samples. If you want to work action-adventure, have three or four of those. If you're aiming for features or MOWs, have at least two scripts written, same genre of course.

Don't shotgun your efforts. Don't do one action-adventure, one episodic comedy, one feature—concentrate on an area and establish a stronghold. Once that's done, *then* you can branch out. In the beginning, though, you really have to almost have tunnel vision in deciding what you want and going after that with everything you've got. Again, once you're established it's much easier to maneuver into other areas.

As a new writer, say a comedy writer, would episodic comedy be easier to break into than features?

Most definitely. I think episodic comedy is easier, if only because of the sheer volume of material they need. There will be 300 feature films produced this year, and there will be 21,000 hours of television produced this year. Right now we're in a big comedy boom, so there's more comedy than anything else.

Thank goodness for Bill Cosby.

That's right.

Same story for an action-adventure writer?

I think so, even though one-hours are not as popular right now as they were. They seem to be more difficult to sell into syndication. But hey, that's going to change. Five years ago comedy was dead, and that's when the Cannells and the Bellasarios really boomed. The pendulum swings both ways.

And your advice for writers wanting to do Movies-of-the-Week?

I personally think MOWs are the hardest to break into, because the networks have what they call "acceptable" writers. Now, they don't necessarily have an "A" list and a "B" list, but every executive at the network has writers they've worked with in the past, and they prefer to use these people. So, breaking a new writer into this field is very, very difficult.

I would recommend that you write a feature script as a sample, rather than an MOW. Because of the unusual act breakdown of the MOW script, it doesn't make a good writing sample. Television producers *will* read a feature as a sample when looking for MOW writers.

Do agents handle soap opera writers?

Yes. I don't, but there are those who do. There are also agents who handle animation writers, and others who handle game shows and variety shows. And they're all franchised by the Writers Guild, of course—at least, the ones you'd want to work with are.

What does that mean?

It means that the state has given you a license, and that the Guild has done some investigation into your moral fiber, for lack of a better term. It's a stamp of credibility. If you're not franchised by the Writers Guild, generally you don't have a state license, and as a writer you don't want to work with an agent that isn't licensed.

Any last advice?

I really feel that perseverance is as important in this business as any other attribute. Keep at it.

CHAPTER 18

How to Be an Effective Businessperson

FROM THE MOMENT YOU BEGIN your efforts to establish yourself as a successful scriptwriter, you should consider yourself a businessperson as well as a creative person. The overall name for our field is "show business" and it's no coincidence that "business" is part of that title. From the outside it may all look very glamorous, but that's only the facade; behind it is a mechanism not that much different from the one required to manufacture cars, produce computer software, or sell shoes. Fortunately, you will have an agent who will, in exchange for 10 percent of your income, perform many of the business functions for you, but you still have to be thoroughly professional in your part of the job.

• PROJECTING A PROFESSIONAL IMAGE

Let's pretend that there are two banks side-by-side. One is the First National General Trust, and it's a solid granite building, staffed by conservatively dressed and well-groomed tellers. The hours are nine to five. Next to it is Al's Bank, a ramshackle building staffed by people who dress any old way and often look like they slept in their clothes. The hours are anytime that Al feels up to coming in. You might prefer working in Al's bank, but probably you'd prefer keeping your money at First National. Sometimes, appearances are deceiving—it could be that Al is a financial genius with complete integrity, while the manager of First National General Trust is siphoning off your money to his Swiss bank account. Nevertheless, people go a lot by appearances. The appearance you project as a writer has two components, your "paper image" and your personal image. Let's look at both.

Your Paper Image

A lot of your contact with people initially will be via letters and the material you send them. How these things look will determine your "paper image." It's not difficult to project a professional image on paper. Here are the basic components:

1. Attractive letterhead. As already discussed in the chapter on getting an agent, we recommend a conservative letterhead: black ink on white or light paper, with your name, address, and phone number only. Any quick-print kind of shop can make up this letterhead for you relatively inexpensively. If you can afford it, also get matching envelopes. If not, get return address labels from a company like Walter Drake and Company (see the Scriptwriter's Resource List for details).

2. Business cards. These can match your letterhead and also should be conservative. Naturally they will include your name, address and phone number, and if you want you can also have the word "writer" or "scriptwriter" in small print underneath. Don't go overboard; we've seen some that read, "TV, Film, and Radio Writer" and one (obviously ordered by a gentleman who believed in killing two birds with one stone) that read "Locksmith and Writer." Five hundred will be plenty; in fact you'll seldom need business cards, but on those occasions when you do, it's nice to have them.

3. Large manila envelopes. For these, get customized address labels that include your name and address and then a larger space for the name and address of the person to whom you are sending the material. Large white envelopes are also available, and these make an even better impression. Never re-use these envelopes by covering over the old label and the old postage—yes, we've seen it done.

4. Script covers. We recommend Acco covers which consist of a front sheet, a back sheet, and metal prongs that go through the three

holes from the back, fold over and are held in place on the inside front. The front and back sheets are made either of pressboard or plastic. Alternatively, you can use stiff paper (at least sixty pound) for the covers, and hold the script together with brads. Do not put scripts in a three-ring binder and do not send them loose or just secured with a large paper clip or prong. Your local stationery store should have a variety of covers, or you can order them by mail from a company like Quill Office Supplies (see the Scriptwriter's Resource List). As soon as the covers show any wear, as they will after a couple of readings, replace them. You want the reader to get the feeling that he or she is turning the pages of a virgin script.

5. The script itself. It should be typed in a clear, easy-to-read typeface. If the "g" on your typewriter lands a quarter of an inch above the other letters, get it fixed or borrow a better typewriter. If you are using a word processor, be aware that the older dot-matrix printers do not give you the kind of print-out quality you need for professional submissions (the newer ones that have twenty-four-pin printheads do). Use a fresh ribbon so that the text comes out nice and dark and will photocopy well. If the photocopy shop gives you back copies that are gray or have spots on them or are too light, have them do the job over again. You don't want the person reading your script to be distracted by these sorts of problems.

It should go without saying (but won't, since we've seen this ignored so often) that anything you put in writing should be neat, in the correct format, and correct in terms of grammar and spelling.

Your Personal Image

Research shows that people gain a first impression of you within the first thirty seconds of contact, and then solidify that impression in the first four minutes. Thereafter, it takes a great deal for them to revise that impression. Let's see what goes into that first impression:

1. Punctuality. Most executives in the film and television industry are on tight schedules. Often they have meetings scheduled every half hour or hour, so if you show up a half hour late it will disrupt their entire schedule. Getting to meetings on time, or five minutes early, is the best policy. Admittedly it's not unusual for producers or story editors to keep writers waiting (another example of the Show Biz Golden Rule: He Who Has the Gold Makes the Rules) but you can use that time to

your advantage by chatting with the secretary or receptionist (as described in the chapter on pitching your ideas) or reviewing your notes for the upcoming meeting.

2. Grooming and clothing. On the whole, grooming and clothing standards in this business are pretty casual. One of us (Wolff), after spending nine months encased in suit and tie working in public relations, burned all of his ties and vowed never to wear one again, and so far this doesn't seem to have hurt his career. There's no need for a Marine style haircut or a three-piece suit. On the other hand, purple spiky hair and jeans with holes are likely to detract from the substance of your meeting.

3. Demeanor. By this we mean enthusiasm, responsiveness, and flexibility. All of these have been comprehensively covered in the chapter on pitching, and are mentioned here just as a reminder.

4. Follow-through. If you have promised a certain script by a certain date, deliver it or let the person who is expecting it know it won't be there on time, why, and when it will be there. If you have had a good meeting with someone, follow it up with a thank-you letter. If someone has done you a good turn (perhaps referring you to an agent, for example), think of something nice you can do for them. Sending flowers or a fruit basket with a thank-you note is old-fashioned—but it still works.

• DEALING WITH THE I.R.S.

When you sell scripts you become a self-employed businessperson and are eligible for certain deductions at tax time. Within the last couple of years the tax code has undergone extensive changes and it looks like more are on the way, so we will not attempt to give you details of what is and what is not deductible. If you use the services of a tax preparer or an accountant, be sure you select someone who has experience with people who are self-employed. If you prepare your tax returns yourself, write to the I.R.S. for the latest tax guidelines for self-employed people.

The most important aspect of being able to figure out your deductions and being able to satisfy the I.R.S. if you are audited is good record-keeping. You must keep track of all expenses relating to your conduct of your business. We found that the expense forms available didn't fit our needs too well, so we designed our own, and it is shown here. We had these printed, and use one per day. The date is written following the "D:" and then expenses are noted by category. Let's take a quick look at each category:

1. Mileage and parking: note your gasoline and other automobile expenses (assuming you are using your car for business purposes), the mileage that applies to business trips, parking fees, etc.

2. Photocopying/Printing: usually this is a major expense for writers. Note the cost of making copies of your script, having letterhead made, etc.

3. Postage: normally you will not only have postage for your submissions, but also for stamped, self-addressed envelopes that you enclose for the return of the material. If you're not already doing so, get a receipt every time you buy stamps.

4. Office supplies: keep track of expenses for paper clips, staples, paper, and so on. Small office equipment, such as staplers, rulers, etc., can also be put into this category.

5. Office equipment: this is for larger-cost items, such as typewriters, computers, printers, file cabinets, and so forth.

6. Messengers: if you live in Los Angeles, you may prefer to have a messenger service deliver scripts and contracts that need to get there in a hurry, rather than driving all over town yourself. If you use them a lot, the service will open an account for you and bill you on a monthly basis. Either way, keep track of those costs in this section.

7. Meals and entertainment: keep track of the costs of lunches and dinners held for business purposes. Taking your girl friend or boyfriend out to lunch to complain about how your agent doesn't return your phone calls doesn't count. You should note with whom you had the meal and what project was discussed, as well as where you ate and how much it cost.

8. Travel: this category is for travel other than that which you do in your own car. In other words, this is where you'd record your air fare, train fare, taxi fees, and so forth, as well as hotel and other expenses if the trip lasted for more than a day.

9. Misc.: the catch-all for anything else, such as public relations expenses, advertising expenses, relevant books and publications, and so forth.

EXPENSES

MILEAGE/PARKING	PHOTOCOPYING/PRINTING	POSTAGE
OFFICE SUPPLIES	OFFICE EQUIPMENT	MESSENGERS
MEALS/ENTERTAINMENT	TRAVEL	MISCELLANEOUS

Naturally you will require receipts to document your expenses. Writing checks or using a credit card whenever possible makes such record-keeping easier. You can keep your receipts one of two ways: either staple them to the back of each day's expense sheet, or make up manila envelopes labeled by category and file the receipts in them. If you do the latter, jot down the date on the receipt if it isn't already on there or isn't legible.

Although no one likes going to an audit, if you have a day-by-day accurate account of your expenses, you can walk into an audit fearlessly.

• THE ATTITUDE YOU NEED

When you are just starting out, it's a bit difficult to consider yourself a professional—after all, you haven't sold anything yet. That doesn't matter. Your professionalism has to start now, not when you get your first check. Think of yourself as being in the start-up phase of what is going to be a very successful business.

Being an effective businessperson requires a certain amount of self-discipline. Naturally, since your product is your writing, you have to have an equal quantity of self-discipline in the creative part of your endeavors, and that's what we'll cover in the next chapter.

CHAPTER 19

How to Maintain the Craft and Discipline of Writing

WHAT SEPARATES THE PERSON who wants to be a writer and who perhaps dabbles in it from the person who *is* a writer? Mostly perseverance. The writer makes a commitment and sticks to it. He or she takes pains to learn the craft, by reading books like this and taking classes, writes a script and then . . . keeps on writing. Hollywood is full of one-script wonders: people who have written one script and are waiting for it to make them rich and famous. It usually doesn't happen that way. Once in a while a writer will come up with a winner the first time out, but most successful writers will tell you that now they cringe at the thought of their first script, and often at the thought of their second and third, too. Writing is a craft like any other, and it's no surprise that it takes some time to get it right. It may be a long while before your writing brings you any kind of reinforcement, much less any money. Our interviewee for this chapter, Stephen Cannell, the writer/producer behind such hit series as "The Rockford Files" and "The A-Team," reveals that for his first few years of writing the only one who read what he wrote was his wife. It's tough to keep yourself going in those early days, but we have some suggestions for how to do it.

• KEEP A WRITING SCHEDULE

Many writers advise you to write every day. If you also have a full-time job and family responsibilities, that may be too difficult. In any event, set up a writing schedule for yourself, whether it be an hour a day or four hours every weekend. Make it realistic; if it's too ambitious you won't be able to keep it up and you'll only be depressed when you fail. A writing schedule is similar to an exercise schedule, and we all know how many of us pledge to go to the gym three times a week. The first week we work out like crazy, convinced that we'll soon be muscular, but then we realize it's going to take time, and six weeks later we're back to our sedentary ways. Both in exercising and writing, the way to go is to set modest, attainable goals and then go after them. Even if you're only writing a few pages a week, it's progress. Eventually all 120 pages will be there.

Don't put your writing at the bottom of your priority list, otherwise it will be supplanted by "more important" things every time. If the house is on fire and there's nobody else to man the garden hose, or one of your kids breaks a leg and there's nobody else free to take him to the hospital, then give up your writing period that day. Otherwise, stick to it. The dishes can wait, the storm windows can wait, the visit to your mother-in-law can wait. If you have a family, you have to make them realize that your writing is not a little hobby, not something that can be interrupted at will. It's something you take seriously and that must be respected.

• FIND A SEPARATE PLACE TO WRITE

Ideally you'll have a den or office set up especially for your writing, perhaps with a word processor and printer, a photocopying machine, file cabinets, a reference library, and a small refrigerator. Realistically, you may have a little desk in the garage or in the spare room. If even that can't be arranged, you'll have to find a quiet coffee shop where you can spread out your pages and write at least three coffee cups worth of script. The important thing is that you have a space where you will not be interrupted. If you're writing at home, that means putting up a "do not disturb" sign (figuratively or, if that doesn't work, literally) so that your roommate or spouse or kids are aware that you have to be given the chance to work.

You should also be fairly confident that when you come home

you won't find the backs of your script pages covered with crayon drawings or a shopping list, so you need a secure space to store your materials. A file cabinet, a drawer in a desk, or just a cardboard box stored on a high shelf will do.

• DON'T STOP!

When you have finished a script, take off a week or two. Enjoy the feeling of satisfaction of having met your goal. Then, when your specified rest period is up, start writing again. If the script needs another rewrite (most writers do three or four drafts of their scripts before they feel they're ready to submit), then begin that process. If you've already rewritten that script, then start on the next one. At the same time that you are submitting one script, work on another. Getting involved with the new story usually results when you're waiting to hear how people will respond to your last script. As we said above, a writer is a person who writes . . . and writes, and writes.

• KEEP UP YOUR MOTIVATION

If you feel discouraged, take active steps to recharge your batteries. Here are some ways to do that:

1. Read about other writers and realize that most successful writers had a period of struggle before their work was appreciated. Ibsen was fifty-one before he wrote the play that first got him international acclaim, *A Doll's House*. Between the ages of twenty and twenty-nine, George Bernard Shaw wrote four novels. All of them were rejected by publishers. He didn't write his first successful play until he was thirty-eight. How about novelist and playwright John Galsworthy? Upon receiving the Nobel Prize for Literature he said, "For nine years, indeed for eleven years, I made not one penny out of what I, but practically no others, counted my profession." The point here is not to discourage you, but simply to point out that if you're having a tough time breaking in, that doesn't mean you're not going to make it. Realizing that you're not alone in this predicament can help.

2. Read great screenplays and great plays. Good writing will inspire you. Collections of outstanding plays are readily available in book form, and within the last ten years or so collections of screenplays have also been published. If you live near a university with a good cine-

ma department, they may also have a collection of scripts that you can read on the premises.

3. Go out and see movies. The good ones will inspire you because you want to do as well. The bad ones will inspire you because you know you can do better.

4. Meet other writers and spend an hour or two exchanging complaints. There are writers' groups in most major cities. If you're in an out-of-the-way area, maybe you can find a writer pen-pal. Your writing will be a mystery to your family and most of your friends; it's good to be able to talk (or write) to someone who understands.

• IF YOU HIT A WRITER'S BLOCK, FIGHT BACK

Most writers sooner or later hit a writer's block, a period when the writing just won't flow, when ideas suddenly dry up. Don't sit around waiting for it to pass. Be active rather than passive. Here are some ways to fight back:

1. If you haven't had a vacation in a while, take one. Anyone can burn out if he just keeps on plodding. A vacation doesn't have to be a month in Paris; it can be a week or a weekend in the nearby mountains, or at a hotel in the next city, or even just a weekend at home during which you do something different, like going to the zoo, taking a hike, going to as many movies as you want, or whatever appeals to you and is different from what you normally do.

2. Stick to your normal writing schedule. If your script won't flow, just write whatever comes to mind: a letter, a diary, poems, limericks, shopping lists, whatever. The point is that you're telling your brain that you're not going to give up, that you're going to keep on writing one way or another, so it might as well send along some creative thoughts and let you get back to your script.

3. Reread some of your past writing and don't hesitate to give yourself some pats on the back for it. You did it before and you'll do it again.

4. Relax. The block may be indicative of tension in the rest of your life. There are inexpensive tapes available that will help you learn med-

itation or self-hypnosis. Twenty minutes a day on one of these activities, during your lunch hour if necessary, will help enormously.

5. Get some exercise. It's another way to recharge your batteries. You don't need to join a gym or plan to run in a marathon; a twenty-minute walk a day is good enough.

6. Remind yourself that this block is temporary. Many writers have had this kind of experience, and they've all gotten past it and started writing again. Be patient, keep up your efforts, and you, too, will find yourself back on track.

• KEEP GROWING AS A WRITER

It's enormously satisfying to feel that you are continuing to improve as a writer. Recognition from others (in the form of critical acclaim and paychecks) is wonderful, but even more crucial at the deepest level is how you feel about your writing efforts. Making a conscious effort to learn more and more is well worth the time. One way to foster your growth is to take classes. Scriptwriting classes are available in profusion in the Los Angeles area and increasingly are also being offered at colleges and universities around the country. Check with your local educational institutions and see what is available. If you have a writers' group, you may be able to afford importing a scriptwriter to teach a class for you. There are a number of writers and others who regularly do a teaching tour. One is Danny Simon, brother of Neil Simon and a very talented comedy writer in his own right. Another is former development executive Michael Hague. Another is (here comes the plug) one of the authors of this book (Jurgen Wolff). For information on these teachers, see the Scriptwriter's Resource List following this chapter. The List also names a number of publications worth reading in order to foster your craft and stay abreast of the business side of TV and film.

If you think that much of what has been suggested in this chapter adds up to self-discipline, you're right. We finish the chapter with an interview with one of the most talented and disciplined writers in the business, Stephen Cannell. Although he is now one of the most important television producers in town, he has never forsaken his role as a writer and still finds time to pound the keyboard for several hours every day. In other words, he doesn't just preach self-discipline, he makes it part of his life. Such people are always worth listening to.

STEPHEN CANNELL

Stephen Cannell is the prolific writer and producer responsible for creating such series as "The Rockford Files," "Black Sheep Squadron," "Tenspeed and Brown Shoe," and "The A-Team." He's sold more than a hundred scripts, and he won an Emmy for producing "Rockford." He has won numerous writing honors, including the Writers Guild Award for the pilot of "Tenspeed."

I understand that your first job in show business was as a go-fer at a game show. Was that any help to you in breaking in?

Zero help. The show was canceled after I was there for eight or nine months, and I was back on the street. I majored in writing in college, but it wasn't until after I went into another job in another industry that I realized I was bored and ought to be writing. Then I got back to my typewriter and the more I wrote, the more I liked it. I picked television as the most viable market I could get into and succeed in.

I felt like every other writer that starts: I felt that I had no chance, that there was no way I'd ever make it. Yet my need to write that stuff made me get to the typewriter each day. I still work every day as a writer, and I still view myself totally as a writer.

During that period when you were unemployed, were you getting any feedback on your efforts?

Yeah, from my wife. Certainly not industry feedback, because they didn't want to read it. But I was reading other people's scripts that were being produced—I had a friend in the mail room at Universal and he'd steal scripts for me. Often I'd read a script and say, "Gee, this guy is a better writer than I am, I wish I could write this well." You have to be honest or you don't go anywhere, you don't improve. Other times I'd read scripts and I'd say, "This stinks. I'm already a better writer than this guy, and he's getting produced." That would give me encouragement.

I have to have my own set of standards for what I do, and sometimes I meet my standards and sometimes I don't. When I don't, I have to be smart enough and brave enough to rip it up and redo it. I have to like it first, and obviously I want the actors to like it and feel comfortable with it, and I certainly want the network to like it. I'm not in that school of thought that says, "I'm the Creative Artist and everyone else can go jump in a lake." Sometimes you get suggestions from network executives and while it's fun to take potshots at network executives, I've had some very good suggestions from them. I've also had some very bad ones. You have to keep an open mind.

And to keep writing without being too afraid of rejection?
Sure. As far as new writers are concerned, I've found that most of them tend to be more in love with the idea of being a writer than with writing. Somebody once said that they didn't enjoy writing, but they enjoyed having written. All of that tends to cause us to procrastinate as writers. Every time I sit down and write something, even if it's just an hour of television that I'm producing, I always run that risk that the networks won't like it, that the actors won't like it—I'm really putting myself on the line. I'm the creator of the show, I have a lot at stake, I have my ego—and all of a sudden I have to put all that aside and put the words on paper and let them be judged by a lot of people. If they say it's no good, I have to deal with that rejection. You never get away from that; no matter who you are or where you are in the business, you always have to deal with the possibility of a rejection.

Dealing with other people's standards is something that's forced on you, but I'm especially interested in what you've said about establishing your own standards—rewriting when you know it's just not good enough.
Let me give you an example—a Rockford I wrote once. The script had a terrific theory; it was called "Feeding Frenzy." A guy had ripped off a bank for half a million dollars at a time when his life was in total turmoil: he'd been fired from his executive job, his wife had left him and taken along their daughter, and so on. He took the half million and buried it, and he was going to wait for the statute of limitations to run out on his crime, at which point the money would be his, free and clear. He started selling bait on the pier near Rockford's trailer. Rockford has known the guy for seven years. During that time the guy's life had really improved: there was no job pressure, his daughter had come back to him and was living with him, and he

had a lot of friends. And all of a sudden he realized that his pursuit of the dollar had been what screwed him up. So he goes to Rockford and tells him about the robbery, and asks him to give the money back—he doesn't want it anymore, he doesn't want to change his life.

What happens is the insurance investigators who had investigated the crime had figured out who stole the money right away. The two cops who'd investigated—they had figured it out. Everyone who was on that case knew, and they were *all* waiting for the statute of limitations to run out. All of these elements from this poor guy's past descend on him and he ends up going crazy. The theme of the show is you have to pay for your mistakes, there is no quick way out.

I wrote this script before a vacation and when I came back we were preparing to shoot it . . . and deep down inside I knew it wasn't right. I hadn't gotten to the heart of that story, I had plotted it incorrectly, I had not gotten to the really valuable thematic things I wanted to do, and where I *had*, it was preachy. My own colleagues weren't going to tell me I'd written a bad one because we were all friends, Jim Garner didn't complain, the network hadn't bitched—but I knew it was terrible, and I sat down and totally rewrote that script from "Fade in." I made it better; I never really made it great, but I learned from that experience to be much more critical of myself. It's more important to me that it's the best work that I can do than that I ever get paid for it. The minute you start writing for money, you are automatically a hack—that's the definition of a hack: a man or woman who writes for the money.

You said you chose episodic television because it was the most promising gateway for you. What's your feeling about that now, for new writers?

I'd suggest to new writers that they go for the episodic market because it is a big market even though much of it is staff written now. Those of us in series television are always looking for good new writers—but I know that there are good writers out there who can't get past the phone minefield I've got set up here. Eventually the good ones will, but in order to do that they have to continue to work at it all the time; they have to never stop writing.

That's discipline, and there are several kinds. I believe in time discipline. I write every day for four or five hours at the same time—from 5 A.M. or 6 A.M. to 11 A.M.

Even if it's just an hour—you'd be surprised what you can achieve if you work for an hour every day. It doesn't even have to be at the typewriter; some of that time should be spent figuring out what your story's going to be and structuring it. Sometimes you'll spend two hours and come away having accomplished nothing, not having solved one problem in your story. But that's OK; you have to say to yourself, "I didn't make it today but I'll do it eventually." That all counts; it's still part of the writing discipline.

Unplug your phone, don't allow any interruptions. There are some writers, you call them up and say, "Am I calling at a bad time?" and they say, "No, no, I'm just writing; what's going on?" They just can't wait to be interrupted. With me, if anybody calls while I'm writing, I burn 'em. I've had writers set their alarms for 5 A.M. to call me because they know I'll be here, but I won't talk to them. I've gotten up early so I can have this time for my writing.

There's the discipline of writing whether you feel like it or not. That idea that "I'll write when I'm in a creative mood," that's horseshit. Yes, we all have those moods but they don't come often enough. You have to say, "I'm going to write even when I have the flu, or when I'm tired, or when I'd rather go to a movie—I'm going to write every day."

In terms of the writing process itself, are there any tricks or procedures you'd recommend?

We're all in the clean-plate club from birth in this country. Our parents tell us to finish everything on our plates and that tends to become part of our mind-set. So when we're writing we tend to finish the scene or finish the act. Well, there's a great deal of inertia created when you're trying to create the next scene. The next morning you come in and you face that blank page and now you have to write a whole scene that you know nothing about, except what the plot points are.

One of the things I learned early was always to go into that next scene, even though I'm tired—go half or three-quarters of a page in. The next morning you may not even like that half page, but then you can start out like a typist—just start copying it and pretty soon you'll be rewriting it. This is a good intermediary step for getting you going in the morning.

Any other tips or rules?

There's one other thing that I think is very important. When I made this rule for myself I made a quantum leap forward as a writer, and this was before I'd sold much of anything. I was turning out a lot of unfinished manuscripts. They are absolutely worthless—all of the time, all of the energy you've invested are wasted.

Why do we have them? The reason is that act one is traditionally the definition of the problem, and in act two you complicate the problem, and in act three you resolve it. Everybody can write act one. It's a snap, it's the springboard for the whole story. In "Feeding Frenzy," the example I mentioned earlier, act one is that there's a guy who stole money, he's waiting for the statute of limitations to run out, and when it does he hires Rockford to give back the money because he doesn't want it anymore. That's it. Act two becomes real tough—it's what the heavies are doing, what happens to Rockford, the kidnapping of the robber's daughter, all those things—plus how those reflect the theme you're trying to present.

What happens to us as writers is very often we get that idea and we get so excited by it that we say, "I gotta write this!" You get to the typewriter, you write act one, and it comes out great. Then you get to act two and you say, "Now wait a minute . . . what happens now?" And you end up in a quagmire or up a box canyon. And you quit. Then you've got an unfinished manuscript that's worthless in two ways. You can't sell it or use it to get an agent, and, because you didn't confront the story problems, you haven't learned anything from the experience.

I made a rule for myself twelve years ago, and it's the best rule I ever made, and it may be the reason I'm sitting in this office today. I said to myself, "I will never again start anything I don't finish—ever."

The next idea I came up with was a spec idea for "Mission Impossible," called "The World Bank Is Being Robbed." I thought, "Terrific! Who's ever seen the World Bank being ripped off?" Same thing happened. I was just writing a treatment at this stage; I wrote the first act, it was great. Then I got to act two and it fell apart. I suddenly realized that the title World Bank is great, but it's still just a bank, it's not as unique or picturesque or cinematic as I had thought. It was a dry subject. I started to junk it, but I decided I had to finish this sucker. By this time I was a full-time freelance writer. I'd sold one script, put the money in the bank, and was living off that script. I had eight months, then I'd be out of business. But I spent two full weeks of that time to finish "The World Bank Is Being Robbed." The end result was that it was a bag of shit, but it was a three-act, finished bag of shit. I read it. I realized I couldn't submit it to anybody because I didn't think it was any good, but I had done it.

That experience taught me two things. One is to choose my ideas more carefully, because I knew that if I chose badly like I had with the World Bank, I'd be stuck with that idea until it was finished. It was OK to make notes and "what-ifs," and write little paragraphs about concept and idea and all that. But the minute I started to turn it into a manuscript I was married to it until I finished it. This also got me to the point where I got further ahead in the story structuring process before writing. Now I never write anything until I have it structured all the way to "Fade out." Boy, that saves me a lot of time.

When you've worked out the characters and worked out a story in your mind—and it sounds like you do that pretty comprehensively—what's the next step?

I do work hard at knowing exactly what my story is, scene for scene with temp dialogue and everything. Then I'll call in Juanita Bartlett or someone else to tell them the story. I usually don't tell it to Grace, my secretary, because I find it's valuable to get her fresh reaction to the script when she's typing it. I ask her, "Did I telegraph that point, did you see it coming?" But I'll tell it to someone else and then put it on audio tape. Sometimes in the telling I'll realize a weakness and think of a way to fix it or to fine-tune the story. Only then do I sit down and write it, and it goes pretty quickly. If I think of better ideas, I'll take them, but the structure is pretty much set.

CHAPTER 20

Resources for the Scriptwriter

PUBLICATIONS

The Hollywood Scriptwriter. 1626 N. Wilcox, #385, Hollywood, CA 90028. (818) 991-3096. Published monthly. Contains informative interviews with top writers, producers, directors, and agents. Annual agency review. How-to articles. Inside tips from the pros on how to break in. Markets for your work. Sample issue and brochure $1.

Writer's Digest Magazine. 205 W. Center St., Marion, OH 43305. (614) 383-3141. Published monthly. General interest writer's magazine. Scriptwriting column, markets coverage occasionally includes scriptwriting opportunities.

Writers Guild of America, West Newsletter. 8955 Beverly Blvd., Los Angeles, CA 90048-2456. (213) 550-1000. Published monthly. Guild news and events, along with feature interviews and television show contact list. Free to Guild members. Non-members call or write for rates.

Writer's Market. F&W Publications, 1507 Dana Avenue, Cincinnati, OH 45207. Published annually. Comprehensive listing of all types of markets, including sections for scriptwriters, and a directory of literary agents. Available in most bookstores.

American Film Magazine. Subscription service, P.O. Box 966, Farmingdale, NY 11737-9866. "The magazine of film and TV arts." Free to members of the American Film Institute (see "Organizations"). Feature articles on major films, occasional articles on writing. Slanted more toward film buffs than writers.

Writers Guild Agency List. Writers Guild, West, 8955 Beverly Blvd., Los Angeles, CA 90048; Attn: Agent's List. (213) 550-1000. $1 through the mail, no charge if picked up in person.

Hollywood Creative Directory. 451 Kelton Ave., Los Angeles, CA 90024. (213) 208-1961. A comprehensive listing of all production companies, including independents. Updated quarterly. Listings include East Coast. Call or write for current price of yearly subscription or single-issue purchase.

Pacific Coast Studio Directory. 6313 Yucca St., Hollywood, CA 90028. (213) 467-2920. Published quarterly. Updated listings of ad agencies, agents, guilds, production houses, TV stations, studios, etc. Subscription or single-issue purchase.

Blu-Book. 6715 Sunset Blvd., Hollywood, CA 90028. "The one book that tells everything you need to know about Hollywood." Published annually by *The Hollywood Reporter.* Can be ordered over the phone with credit card, or send order through mail.

Los Angeles Times. Times Mirror Square, Los Angeles, CA 90053. Circulation office: (213) 626-2323. Daily "Calendar" section is mostly geared toward mainstream readers, but some good "inside" articles and features on articles. Follows the trade papers closely.

Reel West Digest. Reel West Productions, 310-811 Beach Ave., Vancouver, B.C. V6B 2Z5. (604) 669-4797. Published annually. Directory of Canadian production houses, agents, producers, studios, etc. Basically a phone book format.

TRADE PUBLICATIONS

Daily Variety. 1400 N. Cahuenga Blvd., Hollywood, CA 90028. (213) 469-1141. Daily, except Saturdays, Sundays, and holidays. Up-to-the-minute coverage of entertainment industry news. Financial news, weekly television ratings report, movies in production, television shows in production. Classifieds.

The Hollywood Reporter 6715 Sunset Blvd., Hollywood, CA 90028. (213) 464-7411. Daily, except for Saturdays, Sundays, and holidays. Entertainment industry news. Ratings, production charts, classifieds.

Dramalogue. P.O. Box 38771, Los Angeles, CA 90038. (213) 464-5079. Published weekly. Targeted toward performers, but contains a "Writers Wanted" listing in its classified section.

CLASSES AND CONSULTANTS

Jurgen Wolff. 249 N. Brand Blvd, #507, Glendale, CA 91203. Conducts seminars on pitching, "Guerrilla Warfare" for the writer trying to break in, writing features, finding an agent. Seminars announced in *The Hollywood Scriptwriter*, trade papers, and educational institutions. Video-supported, highly practical for both beginners and those experienced in the industry.

Michael Hague. "Screenwriting A to Z." Two-day seminar on the art, craft, and business of screenwriting. Travels the U.S. and abroad. Announcements in *The Hollywood Scriptwriter* and other writer's publications.

Truby's Story Structure. 739-A Tenth St., Santa Monica, CA 90402. (213) 393-2999. "In forty-eight hours, you'll write a great script." Intensive seminar on principles of story and structure. Tapes available.

Hollywood Scriptwriting Institute. 1300 Cahuenga Blvd., Dept. S, Hollywood, CA 90028 (213) 461-8333. Various classes in scriptwriting. Accredited educational institution. Guest instructors, practical workshops.

Linda Seger. 3920 Huron Ave., Suite 4, Culver City, CA 90230. (213) 838-2616. "The Script Doctor." Monthly column for *The Hollywood*

Scriptwriter, and *Women In Film* magazine. Highly refined script analysis method. Consultant service.

Danny Simon. 15233 Magnolia Blvd., #302, Sherman Oaks, CA 91403. Classes in comedy writing. Former writing partner of his brother, Neil Simon. Announcements in trades, newspapers.

EDUCATIONAL ORGANIZATIONS

American Film Institute. L.A. Campus, 2021 N. Western Ave., Los Angeles, CA 90027. (213) 856-7600. Enormous variety of programs, workshops, seminars. Two-year curriculum for student body. Their goal is to develop new talent, and further film-making as an art. The only national arts institution dedicated to film, television, and video. Grants given.

Women in Film. 6464 Sunset Blvd., Suite 660, Los Angeles, CA 90028 (213) 463-6040. Dedicated to recognizing and furthering the role of women in film-making. Conducts seminars, film festivals, and classes. Publishes a monthly magazine.

OFFICE SUPPLIES

Walter Drake. 3105 Drake Bldg., Colorado Springs, CO 80940. Inexpensive return address labels, personalized stationery.

Quill Corporation. 100 S. Schelter Rd., P.O. Box 4700, Lincolnshire, IL 60197. Mail order office supplies. Primarily a supplier to businesses, so indicate that you're a business.

BOOKSTORES

Samuel French. 7623 Sunset Blvd., Hollywood, CA 90046 (213) 876-0570. Specializes in publications for and about the entertainment industry. How-to, biographies, reference material, etc.

INDEX

Other Books of Interest

General Writing Books

Beginning Writer's Answer Book, edited by Kirk Polking (paper) $12.95
Beyond Style: Mastering the Finer Points of Writing, by Gary Provost $14.95
Getting the Words Right: How to Revise, Edit and Rewrite, by Theodore A. Rees Cheney $14.95
How to Become a Bestselling Author, by Stan Corwin $14.95
How to Get Started in Writing, by Peggy Teeters (paper) $9.95
How to Increase Your Word Power, by the editors of Reader's Digest $19.95
How to Write a Book Proposal, by Michael Larsen $9.95
How to Write While You Sleep, by Elizabeth Ross $14.95
If I Can Write, You Can Write, by Charlie Shedd $12.95
International Writers' & Artists' Yearbook (paper) $14.95
Just Open a Vein, edited by William Brohaugh $15.95
Knowing Where to Look: The Ultimate Guide to Research, by Lois Horowitz $18.95
Make Every Word Count, by Gary Provost (paper) $7.95
Pinckert's Practical Grammar, by Robert C. Pinckert $14.95
The 29 Most Common Writing Mistakes & How to Avoid Them, by Judy Delton $9.95
Writer's Block & How to Use It, by Victoria Nelson $14.95
The Writer's Digest Guide to Manuscript Formats, by Buchman & Groves $16.95
Writer's Encyclopedia, edited by Kirk Polking (paper) $16.95
Writer's Guide to Research, by Lois Horowitz $9.95
Writer's Market, edited by Glenda Neff $21.95
Writing for the Joy of It, by Leonard Knott $11.95

Nonfiction Writing

Basic Magazine Writing, by Barbara Kevles $16.95
How to Sell Every Magazine Article You Write, by Lisa Collier Cool $14.95
How to Write & Sell the 8 Easiest Article Types, by Helene Schellenberg Barnhart $14.95
Writing Creative Nonfiction, by Theodore A. Rees Cheney $15.95
Writing Nonfiction that Sells, by Samm Sinclair Baker $14.95

Fiction Writing

Creating Short Fiction, by Damon Knight (paper) $8.95
Dare to Be a Great Writer: 329 Keys to Powerful Fiction, by Leonard Bishop $15.95
Fiction is Folks: How to Create Unforgettable Characters, by Robert Newton Peck (paper) $8.95
Fiction Writer's Market, edited by Laurie Henry $19.95
Handbook of Short Story Writing: Vol. I, by Dickson and Smythe (paper) $8.95
Handbook of Short Story Writing: Vol. II, edited by Jean M. Fredette $15.95
How to Write & Sell Your First Novel, by Oscar Collier with Frances Spatz Leighton $15.95
How to Write Short Stories that Sell, by Louise Boggess (paper) $7.95
One Way to Write Your Novel, by Dick Perry (paper) $7.95
Storycrafting, by Paul Darcy Boles (paper) $9.95
Writing the Novel: From Plot to Print, by Lawrence Block (paper) $8.95

Special Interest Writing Books

The Children's Picture Book: How to Write It, How to Sell It, by Ellen E.M. Roberts (paper) $15.95
Comedy Writing Secrets, by Melvin Helitzer $16.95
The Complete Book of Scriptwriting, by J. Michael Straczynski (paper) $9.95
The Complete Guide to Writing Software User Manuals, by Brad M. McGehee (paper) $14.95
The Craft of Comedy Writing, by Sol Saks $14.95
The Craft of Lyric Writing, by Sheila Davis $18.95
Editing Your Newsletter, by Mark Beach (paper) $18.50
Guide to Greeting Card Writing, edited by Larry Sandman (paper) $8.95
How to Make Money Writing About Fitness & Health, by Celia & Thomas Scully $16.95

How to Sell & Re-Sell Your Writing, by Duane Newcomb $10.95
How to Write a Cookbook and Get It Published, by Sara Pitzer $15.95
How to Write a Play, by Raymond Hull (paper) $10.95
How to Write & Sell A Column, by Raskin & Males $10.95
How to Write and Sell Your Personal Experiences, by Lois Duncan (paper) $9.95
How to Write and Sell (Your Sense of) Humor, by Gene Perret (paper) $9.95
How to Write Tales of Horror, Fantasy & Science Fiction, edited by J.N. Williamson $15.95
How to Write the Story of Your Life, by Frank P. Thomas $14.95
How You Can Make $50,000 a Year as a Nature Photojournalist, by Bill Thomas (paper) $17.95
Mystery Writer's Handbook, by The Mystery Writers of America (paper) $9.95
Nonfiction for Children: How to Write It, How to Sell It, by Ellen E.M. Roberts $16.95
On Being a Poet, by Judson Jerome $14.95
The Poet's Handbook, by Judson Jerome (paper) $9.95
Poet's Market, by Judson Jerome $17.95
Successful Outdoor Writing, by Jack Samson $11.95
Travel Writer's Handbook, by Louise Zobel (paper) $11.95
TV Scriptwriter's Handbook, by Alfred Brenner (paper) $9.95
Writing After 50, by Leonard L. Knott $12.95
Writing for Children & Teenagers, by Lee Wyndham (paper) $9.95
Writing for the Soaps, by Jean Rouverol $14.95
Writing Short Stories for Young People, by George Edward Stanley $15.95
Writing the Modern Mystery, by Barbara Norville $15.95
Writing to Inspire, edited by William Gentz (paper) $14.95
Writing Young Adult Novels, by Hadley Irwin & Jeanette Eyerly $14.95

The Writing Business

A Beginner's Guide to Getting Published, edited by Kirk Polking $10.95
Complete Guide to Self-Publishing, by Tom & Marilyn Ross $19.95
Editing for Print, by Geoffrey Rogers $14.95
Freelance Jobs for Writers, edited by Kirk Polking (paper) $8.95
How to Bulletproof Your Manuscript, by Bruce Henderson $9.95
How to Get Your Book Published, by Herbert W. Bell $15.95
How to Understand and Negotiate a Book Contract or Magazine Agreement, by Richard Balkin $11.95
How to Write Irresistible Query Letters, by Lisa Collier Cool $10.95
How to Write with a Collaborator, by Hal Bennett with Michael Larsen $11.95
How You Can Make $25,000 a Year Writing (No Matter Where You Live), by Nancy Edmonds Hanson $15.95
Literary Agents: How to Get & Work with the Right One for You, by Michael Larsen $9.95
Professional Etiquette for Writers, by William Brohaugh $9.95
Time Management for Writers, by Ted Schwarz $10.95

To order directly from the publisher, include $2.50 postage and handling for 1 book and 50¢ for each additional book. Allow 30 days for delivery.

Writer's Digest Books
1507 Dana Avenue, Cincinnati, Ohio 45207
Credit card orders call TOLL-FREE
1-800-543-4644 (Outside Ohio)
1-800-551-0884 (Ohio only)
Prices subject to change without notice.

Write to this same address for information on *Writer's Digest* magazine, Writer's Digest Book Club, Writer's Digest School, and Writer's Digest Criticism Service.